Playing the Organ Works
of
César Franck

Portrait of César Franck by Jeanne Rongier, 1888

Playing the Organ Works of César Franck

by

Rollin Smith

THE COMPLETE ORGAN No. 1

PENDRAGON PRESS
STUYVESANT NY

Also By Rollin Smith

Toward An Authentic Interpretation of the Organ Works of
    César Franck

Saint-Saëns and the Organ

The Organist's Book of Days

The Reynolda House Aeolian Organ

The Aeolian Pipe Organ And Its Music

Library of Congress Cataloging-in-Publication

Smith, Rollin
    Playing the organ works of César Franck / by Rollin Smith. p. cm. — (The
    complete organ : no. 1)
    Includes bibliographic references and index.
    ISBN 0-945193-79-3
    1. Franck, César, 1822–1890. Organ music.2. Organ Music—Interpretation
    (Phrasing, dynamics, etc.) 3. Performance practice (Music)—19th century.
    I. Title. II. Series
ML410.F82S58 1996
786.5'092—dc20   96 – 43042
                                                                   CIP
                                                                    MN

for Anthony Baglivi

Inquire, I pray thee, of the former age, and prepare thyself
to the search of their fathers . . . Shall not they teach thee
and tell thee, and utter words out of their heart?

Job 8: 8, 10.

Contents

List of Illustrations

Plate credits: Bibliothèque Nationale, Paris (30, 32, 34, 35, 44, and 45); Phil and Pam Fluke (21); Allen Hobbs/Jean Langlais Collection, Duquesne University (49 and 50); Kurt Lueders (4, 9, 22, 23, and 24)

Preface

Toward An Authentic Interpretation of the Organ Works of César Franck, appeared thirteen years ago, and since then, during organ lessons, masterclasses, and workshops, it has been apparent that what the average and even the quite-above-average organist really needed was not so much a dissertation on historical performance tradition, but a manual that explained how to play some of the most beautiful music in our repertoire. The centenary of César Franck's death in 1990 provided the impetus for a series of articles in *The American Organist,* "Playing the Organ Works of Franck." The positive response to that series has prompted the present volume, revised and extended, with an additional introductory chapter, "César Franck and the Organ."

In addition to discussing each piece, its history, and its dedicatee, I have tried to elucidate the sometimes confusing registrational instructions (particularly confusing to those unacquainted with the French language), and to discuss technical problems encountered, not the least of which, in Franck's music, are the reaches required in the manual writing.

While in my earlier book I relied on primary sources and first-person testimony, I have here broadened the spectrum to include students of Franck's own pupils and contemporaries. This has served to strengthen the idea that a Franck style was not limited, as some would suggest, to Franck's successors at his church, Sainte-Clotilde.

I hope not only to have helped students to master some of the inherent technical problems in learning this great literature but also to have helped them to understand the era in which it was created.

Rollin Smith

CHAPTER I

César Franck and the Organ

César Franck's student and biographer, Vincent d'Indy, heralded his maître's greatness by noting the coincidence of Franck's birth in Liège, Belgium on December 10, 1822, with the very day that Beethoven completed his *Missa Solemnis*. The significance of these two occurrences being that Franck was destined to succeed the German master in the realm of sacred and symphonic music. D'Indy's opinion, far from being that of an overzealous disciple, has proven accurate, for Franck was one of the few Parisian composers during the Second Empire and Third Republic whose fame rests with his instrumental music.

Franck was a Parisian musician in that, from the age of sixteen, he lived in Paris. But, he was not a *French* musician and this has always been a source of annoyance to the natives. Franck's father, the son of a burgomaster, was from Völkerich and spoke in a Germanic dialect—"something between Low German and Netherlandish, but spiced with French words."[1] His wife, six years older than he, was the daughter of a cloth merchant whom he met while a student in Germany. So their son César, Belgium and France's most illustrious organ composer, was Austro-Netherlandish on his father's side and pure German on his mother's. César Franck spoke German with his mother and to the end of his life always said his prayers in German!

Nicolas-Joseph Franck held a menial bank position in Liège at the time of his son's birth. He was an arrogant, pretentious egotist and a harsh authoritarian who, as much to satisfy his sordid avarice as to live vicariously through his artistic children, insisted

---

[1]Léon Vallas, *La véritable histoire de César Franck* (Paris: Flammarion, 1950). Translated by Hubert Foss as *César Franck* (New York: Oxford University Press, 1951) 12.

on careers in music for César and a second son, Joseph, born three years later. To that end both boys were enrolled in the Liège Conservatoire. From the age of eight, César Franck studied solfège, harmony and piano. His solfège teacher at the Conservatoire was Dieudonné Duguet (1794–1849), organist of the Church of Saint-Denis and, although organ was not taught at the school, it is possible that Franck had his first organ lessons from him.[2] Franck's progress in all his subjects was so remarkable that by the age of eleven and a half, he was a student-teacher of solfège and piano.

In 1834 Franck's father arranged a short recital tour, that included a performance in Brussels before King Leopold I at the royal palace. César appeared in several Belgian cities as pianist and composer playing his own fantasies on popular airs. The next year his brother, Joseph, joined him in concert as a violinist.

Father Franck decided the time was ripe to conquer Paris and in the spring of 1836 moved his family to the French capital and secured two leading musicians as teachers: Pierre Zimmermann for piano and Anton Reicha for counterpoint. By November a debut recital was arranged for César, and, although well publicized, it went unnoticed by the press and did nothing to establish a virtuoso career. Franck made no public appearances for the next year. While he studied, his father waited to recoup his financial loss and applied for French citizenship so that his sons might be admitted to the Paris Conservatoire.

In the interim, César Franck published a sonata and a fantaisie for piano, two concertos for piano and orchestra, two trios and a symphony! In March, April, and May 1837, he was heard, as was the custom, at concerts in which several artists performed. On April 30, for instance, he appeared with Johann Pixis (a greatly esteemed pianist and teacher who, with Liszt, Chopin, Thalberg, Czerny, and Herz, had written the *Hexameron*), Charles-Valentin

---

[2]Certainly he would have been influenced by Duguet, who raised church music standards in Liège and introduced the music of "German masters and of the school of Cherubini . . . absolutely unknown in the rest of Belgium." (François-Joseph Fétis, *Biographie universelle des musiciens et bibliographie générale de la musique*, Supplement, Vol. 1, (edited by Arthur Pougin [Brussels: Leroux, 1878–80] 286). Cited by Orpha Ochse, *Organists and Organ Playing in Nineteenth-Century France and Belgium* (Bloomington & Indianapolis: Indiana University Press, 1994) 173.

Alkan (to whom he would later refer as "The Poet of the Piano" and to whom he would dedicate his *Grande Pièce symphonique*), and Franz Liszt. The press notices foretold a future as a major pianist and referred to his "ease . . . self-possession . . . intelligence . . . passionate energy . . . expressiveness and musical feeling."

By September the Franck family's naturalization papers had arrived and César was enrolled in the Paris Conservatoire, entering Pierre Zimmermann's piano class and Simon Leborne's counterpoint class. What would an already prodigious (if not yet famous) virtuoso expect to gain from studying at the Conservatoire? The prestige of winning a first prize from Europe's most esteemed musical institution. Even the great Franz Liszt had applied for admission a few years earlier but had been refused entry because of his Hungarian nationality.

In August 1838 Franck competed for the first prize in piano. Alkan was among the eight jurors. Franck played Hummel's *Concerto in B Minor* brilliantly and, in a brazen exhibition of skill and confidence, transposed the sight-reading piece down a minor third, a feat viewed as not being within the regulations. However, an amicable decision was reached that attests to how well Franck was regarded by the Conservatoire faculty. Having unanimously awarded him first prize, the jury decided that he stood "so incomparably far ahead of his fellow competitors that it is impossible to nominate another to share the prize with him." So to set him apart he was given, in addition, a Grand Prix d'Honneur.

After three years in the counterpoint class Franck won a first prize in July 1840. In the fall he entered François Benoist's organ class, undoubtedly to improve his improvisational and compositional skills, thereby enabling him to compete for the Prix de Rome. There were only two requirements to win a first prize: the improvisation of a four-part accompaniment to a piece of plainchant (referred to as a "chorale") and the improvisation of a fugue in four parts. Both themes were given by the jury. No composed music was required and the improvisation of a piece on a free theme was not added to the requirements until 1843.[3]

His achievement in the organ class was considerably less than the highly acknowledged work in piano and counterpoint. He

[3]Orpha Ochse, *Organists and Organ Playing...*, 149.

played two semi-annual examinations and we quote the juror's comments (the class taught by the juror follows his name in parenthesis). The examination of December 7, 1840:

> Luigi Cherubini (director): "Fugue played—not very well."
> Simon Leborne (counterpoint, fugue, composition): "Needs to work."

At the examination of May 26, 1841, all jurors but Henri Berton indicated that Franck be allowed into the July competition:

> Luigi Cherubini (director): "Chorale, neither good for bad. Fugue, rather good."
> Henri Berton (composition): "Poor [*Faible*]."
> Félix Le Couppey (piano and harmony): "Chorale in the bass: bad—better, the chorale in the upper voice. Much less, though, than the preceding (Henri Duvernoy) for fugue."
> Jean Schneitzhoeffer (singing): "The chorale with the theme in the bass was wrong. He did the theme in the upper voice better. He wandered a bit in the first part of the fugue. His improvisation was a little vague and monotonous."[4]

In July Franck entered the competition, winning a second prize. One of the jurors, Étienne-Jean Pastou, a professor of ensemble singing, noted of the eighteen-and-a-half year old Franck's performance: "Chorale—bass fair, upper parts excellent. Fugue—some good points at the beginning but often poor in the working-out."[5] The facts discredit Vincent d'Indy's apocryphal story of Franck's superimposing the subjects given for two separate improvisations—fugue and a piece in sonata form—and treating them simultaneously "to such unaccustomed lengths that the examiners, bewildered by such a technical feat, awarded nothing," (even though he quotes Franck as later saying that he was "very successful in combining the two subjects."[6]

Franck was enrolled in the composition class the following year, but in April he withdrew from the Conservatoire. No plausible explanation has been advanced for this sudden withdrawal in the middle of his fifth academic year and with the Prix

---

[4]"César Franck et ses Examinateurs," *L'Orgue* (April-June 1953) 62.
[5]Léon Vallas, *César Franck*, 32.
[6]Vincent d'Indy, *César Franck* (Paris: Alcan, 1906) 34.

de Rome unattained. The family returned to Belgium and, for about five months, visited relatives.

They returned to their apartment at 42, rue Lafitte in Paris, and by October the nineteen-year-old César Franck was announcing private classes in piano, harmony, counterpoint, and fugue. He had been giving these classes since the fall of 1838, soon after winning the first prize in piano at the Conservatoire, and they were organized according to the Conservatoire curriculum: three lessons a week of two hours each and limited to five pupils (if that many ever applied). Since this was the family's sole means of support it was necessary to supplement these lessons given at home by traveling about Paris teaching in various institutions: a pensionnat, or girl's boarding school, in the rue des Martyrs near his home; another at Auteuil; a public school, Collège Rollin (42, rue des Postes); the Augustinian College of the Assumption (234, rue Faubourg Saint-Honoré); and the Jesuit College of the Immaculate Conception, a school for advanced ecclesiastical studies, (26, rue de Vaugirard).

His life was miserable and if, as mentioned previously, Franck was Beethoven's musical successor, the two shared a further similarity: that of sons abused by a brutal, tyrannical father.

> It was a hard life for him . . . not made easier by the ill-tempered and vindictive behavior of his father, who, in his egotism, continually wielded a grim and sometimes brutal authoritarianism that indelibly scarred his children's memories . . . It was forced labor indeed; the last ounce of pianistic energy was squeezed out of him daily, and in the matter of out-of-pocket expenses he was treated like a common thief. His itinerary was settled before he started, and the journeys between two lessons timed in advance with exactitude. Outside his professional calls he had no acquaintances. His day ended as early as possible after sundown so as to avoid unnecessary expenditure on candles.[7]

To his teaching, composing, and concertizing, Franck added the responsibilities of a   professional organist: not as *organiste titulaire* but at the most menial of church music posts, as *organiste accompagnateur*, or choir accompanist, in the church at the end of the street where he lived, Notre-Dame-de-Lorette.

[7]Vallas, *César Franck*, 37–38.

Plate 1. The Nave, Notre-Dame-de-Lorette

335 PARIS. — *L'Eglise Notre-Dame de Lorette.* — LL.

Plate 2. Facade of Notre-Dame-de-Lorette

Built in the style of a Roman basilica (in imitation of Sancta Maria Maggiore in Rome), Notre-Dame-de-Lorette is the most elaborately decorated church in Paris, its painting and gilding giving it anything but a devotional character. It was then a new church, having been completed in 1836, and it soon became known as the Church of the Demimonde, or of the "Lorettes" (the mistresses of the bourgeoisie who were named after the immediate neighborhood) and for whom its marble, stucco, and gold would seem to have been intended. As the parish church of the Conservatoire, then in the rue Bergère, it was attended by many student and professional musicians. It also had the distinction of housing the first organ Aristide Cavaillé-Coll built in Paris, a forty-seven-rank, four-manual instrument inaugurated in 1838. While it is not unlikely that Franck would have played this instrument from time to time, substituting for Alphonse Gilbert, the titular organist, his own organ, behind the high altar, was an old two-manual Somer that had been brought from the former church, Saint-Jean-Porte-Latine. As choir accompanist Franck was subordinate to both Gilbert and Girac, the maître-de-chapelle, so he derived little esteem from the post, but, as

7

274. - PARIS. - Eglise St-Jean-St-François

Plate 3. Church of Saint-Jean-Saint-François

the church was attended by 48,000 parishoners, he received considerable income from funeral and, probably, wedding stipends. The music program was of the highest order, thanks to a sympathetic pastor, Abbé de Rollot, and to the famous musicians who had been in the choir and orchestra of Notre-Dame-de-Lorette early in their careers. Franck, in a not unpolitical gesture, dedicated an *Ave Maria* to the pastor in 1845, perhaps in the hope of one day obtaining the post of maître-de-chapelle.

As a composer Franck was industrious and produced a three-part oratorio, or biblical eclogue, for soli, chorus, and orchestra, entitled *Ruth*. Its first performance on January 4, 1846, caused little excitement, but the previous November, at a run-through of the work at Érard's salon, with Franck playing the orchestral parts on the piano, Spontini, Halévy, Meyerbeer, Adolphe Adam, Moscheles, Pixis, Stephen Heller, Alkan, and Liszt were to be seen in the invited audience. On October 27 he completed his first organ work, *Pièce en mi bémol*, an experimental, multisectional *Grand Chœur*, which remained unpublished until 1973.[8]

Among Franck's many pupils was a girl at the boarding school in the rue des Martyrs (the street that ran behind and north of Notre-Dame-de-Lorette). The daughter of actors at the Comédie-Française (her mother was a tragedienne of some reputation), Félicité Desmousseaux was two years younger than her piano teacher. The Desmousseaux household, to which Franck became a frequent visitor, provided a pleasant haven from his own tempestuous home life. In time, the teacher-pupil relationship deepened and the two were married at Notre-Dame-de-Lorette on February 22, 1848. Of their four children, two sons survived infancy. Georges became a history professor, and Germain, a senior clerk of the P.L.M. railroad.

One of the curates of Notre-Dame-de-Lorette, Abbé Dorcel (or Dancel), was appointed pastor of Saint-Jean-Saint-François (a small church in the Marais district) in 1851 and soon hired Franck as his organist. It has not been possible to discern the date when Franck actually assumed his duties; early writers (d'Indy, Emmanuel, and Tournemire) give no indication as to whether Franck

---

[8]It was edited by Norbert Dufourcq for Les Éditions Musicales de la Schola Cantorum et de la Procure Générale de Musique.

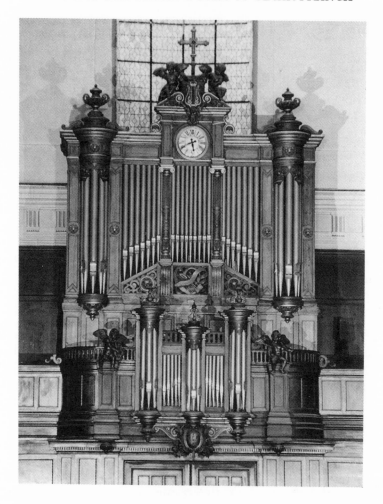

Plate 4. The Organ, Saint-Jean-Saint-François

went with him or followed some time after. Félix Raugel dates Franck's tenure from 1851.[9] The church (renamed Sainte-Croix-Saint-Jean and today serving an Armenian congregation) stands on the corner of rue Charlot and rue de Perche. It was built in 1623 as the chapel of a Capuchin monastery and dedicated to the Immaculate Conception. Madame de Sévigné, whose *hôtel* was nearby,

[9]*Les Grandes Orgues des Églises de Paris* (Paris: Librairie Fischbacher, 1927) 182.

frequently attended Mass there. The church's communion vessels, borrowed for use at the last Mass celebrated in the Temple for Louis XVI the morning of his execution, are on display in the sacristy. In 1790 the monastery was nationalized and the following year, with the constitutional schism, the order's chapel was made a parish church dedicated to St. Francis of Assisi. When the church was reopened after the Concordat its new pastor, who came from the recently-demolished church of Saint-Jean-en-Grève, brought many of its furnishings with him and added the appelation of Saint-Jean to that of Saint-François.

The first organ was destroyed during the Revolution. Jean Somer installed a two-manual, thirteen-stop organ in 1818 and Gervais-François Couperin was appointed organist, holding the post simultaneously with that of Saint-Gervais. On his death in 1826 he was succeeded by his unmarried daughter, Thérèse-Célestine, the last descendant of the illustrious family. She resigned the last day of 1829[10] and nothing is known of her successors until the appointment of César Franck.

A contract for a new organ was given to Dominique and Aristide Cavaillé-Coll in 1844. An eighteen-stop organ then on display at the Paris Exposition was later installed in the church and officially accepted on December 29, 1846. Franck was so enchanted with the fine tone of this modest two-manual instrument that, when asked about it, he exclaimed, "My new organ? It is an orchestra!"[11]

---

[10]Her resignation was not a surprise. Like her father she was simultaneously organist of Saint-Gervais and seems to have given preference to that parish and too frequently sent poorly-qualified substitutes to Saint-Jean-Saint-François. In a letter of November 17, 1829 the Conseil de Fabrique wrote that "due to so many complaints from the parishioners on the manner in which the organ is played on feast days, she is hereby notified that if she sends anyone else in her stead before January 1 her employment will be terminated." (Félix Raugel, *Les Grandes Orgues de Paris* [Paris: Librairie Fischbacher, 1927] 179–80.)

[11]He was, nevertheless, well aware of the difference between the symphony orchestra and Cavaillé-Coll's organs, and did not confuse the two. We have but to note that such magnificent orchestral works as *Chasseur Maudit* and the *Variations symphoniques* are impossible of being successfully transcribed for the organ.

Saint-Jean-Saint-François

Compass: Grand-Orgue, 54 notes: C^1-F^5

Récit, 37 notes: F^2-F^4

Pédale, 20 notes: C^1-G^2

Grand-Orgue		Récit expressif		Pédale	
8	Montre	8	Flûte harmonique	16	Flûte ouverte
8	Bourdon	8	Viole de gambe	16	Bombarde
8	Salicional	4	Flûte octaviante		
4	Prestant	2	Octavin		
2⅔	Nasard	8	Trompette		
2	Doublette	8	Cromorne		
III	Plein jeu	8	Cor anglais		
8	Trompette				
4	Clairon				

It was not until this time, when Franck was in his thirtieth year, that his life as an organist and his associations with colleagues, was documented. He was in the audience with Gounod, Boëly, Alkan, and his old teacher, Benoist, at Saint-Vincent-de-Paul in January 1852 when Jacques Lemmens, the Belgian virtuoso, inaugurated Cavaillé-Coll's new organ. He must have been well acquainted with the already-established organbuilder, for he and Mme Franck were among the dinner guests following Cavaillé-Coll's wedding in 1854. It is all the more remarkable, then, that his first recorded concert appearance as an organist should be on an instrument by a rival organbuilder, Pierre-Alexandre Ducroquet, at the church of Saint-Eustache. Franck was one of four organists who inaugurated this organ on May 24, 1854. He was heard in a "carefully composed and energetically performed fantaisie."[12]

His next two performances were not in church but at Cavaillé-Coll's organ factory. An organ built for Saint-Michel's Cathedral at Carcassonne had been set up in the erecting room and for a year was demonstrated at innumerable soirees by various noted organists. Franck was heard twice. During the last week of August 1856 he played the first version of his *Fantaisie in C* and what were described in the press as "brilliant improvisations." On Saturday, April 25, 1857, he shared a program with students

[12]*Revue et Gazette musicale de Paris* (May 26, 1854) 175.

from the École Niedermeyer, Franck "demonstrating the resources of the fine instrument." Balthasar Waitzennecker played a fugue on the "Laudate Dominum" by Lemmens and other students were heard in various pieces of sacred music. Undoubtedly, one of the

pieces Franck played on this occasion was the *Andantino* [in G Minor], published that year by Richault. The manuscript in the Bibliothèque Nationale[13] bears Franck's registration for this four-manual instrument.

In the fall of 1857 Franck was appointed organist of a new church still under construction in the fashionable Faubourg Saint-Germain. The Church of

Plate 5. Chapelle-de-Sainte-Valère

Sainte-Clotilde, the first neo-Gothic church in France, was built over the course of eleven years, from 1846 to 1857, under the direction of two successive architects. The contract for the new organ had been awarded to Cavaillé-Coll in 1854, but work did not begin for more than a year, being delayed by the architect's final plans for the case. Franck began his duties inauspiciously by directing the choir and playing a harmonium in the Chapel of Sainte-Valère.

By the end of September 1857 the case pipes were in place and the wind system installed but, while the action and console had been built, they still had not been delivered in time for the dedication of the church on November 30, 1857. The music for the dedication of Sainte-Clotilde was not conducted by Franck, but by Jules Pasdeloup who led a choir and orchestra of young Conservatoire students for the elaborate ceremony; the program included a March by Adolphe Adam, a Prelude by Bach, an *O salutaris* by François Auber, an *Ave verum* by Palestrina, a *Dominum salvum* with quartet, choir, and orchestra, and, finally, the "Laudate" from the Gloria of a Mass by Ambroise Thomas.

[13]No. 8564

Plate 6. Dedication Service, Church of Sainte-Clotilde,
November 30, 1857

14

Plate 7. Church of Sainte-Clotilde Under Construction, 1856

Sainte-Clotilde is unusual in that it has two rear galleries, one above the other. The lower is for the choir; the upper, much smaller, holds the organ console. For two years Franck, an organist without an organ, directed his choir from the lower gallery. By 1858 he had induced twenty-year-old Conservatoire student Théodore Dubois to give up his post as organist of the Chapelle des Invalides, just a few blocks away, to come to Sainte-Clotilde as his *organiste accompagnateur*. The only instrument for accompanying the choir was a harmonium that was used for thirty years until Joseph Merklin installed an electropneumatic orgue-de-chœur in the front of the church.

Franck took his church duties seriously. Knowing he would soon have a new organ, he obtained the most up-to-date practice instrument, a pédalier (or piano pedalboard) which, instead of merely coupling the piano keys to the pedals, was completely independent, having its own strings, hammers, and mechanism. A set of thinner 8' strings playing simultaneously with the 16' strings produced a remarkably full sound. Louis Niedermeyer wrote enthusiastically about the new instrument in *La Maîtrise* in December and Franck's was delivered on February 28, 1858. His initiative in improving himself is all the more remarkable because Félix Danjou, writing in May 1859, "could not name ten organists who had a pedal piano on which they could practice daily and familiarize themselves with the beautiful fugues and pedal parts of Bach, Mendelssohn, and Lemmens."

Franck's *Cinq Pièces pour Harmonium* date from this year, but the rest of his output was for voice and included a *Messe solennelle* for bass solo and organ; *Trois Motets*, Op. 4 (*O salutaris, Ave Maria,* and *Tantum ergo*); and a third setting of *O salutaris*, for soprano and tenor duet.

Among Franck's acquaintances at the Jesuit College of the Immaculate Conception where he taught piano was a priest, Louis Lambillotte. The good father, aptly described by Saint-Saëns as a "ridiculous composer" of "dreadful music," who left an indelible impression on the Catholic church with such hymns as "Come, Holy Ghost" and "On This Day, O Beautiful Mother," was also active in the movement to reintroduce Gregorian chant into the churches of France, and published chant collections, articles, and even a facsimile of the Saint-Gall manuscript. He died in 1855 and it was left to Franck to oversee the publication of their collaboration, a five-part *Chant Grégorien: restauré par R.P. Lambillotte; accompagnement d'orgue par César Franck*. The success of the three volumes was demonstrated by its republication in 1912.[14] The work, Franck's accompaniment of Lambillotte's modern notation transcriptions of plainsong, was issued in three parts, divided into five sections:

I. Ordinary of the Masses for the church year;
II. and III. Roman Hymnal with each hymn harmonized for organ in a comfortable key for the [unison men's] choir and in a higher key for three or four voices;

[14]By the Librairie de l'Art Catholique, 6, Place St. Sulpice, Paris.

IV. and V.

    1. Proses and Sequences

    2. Antiphons for the major feasts of the Blessed Virgin

    3. Various hymns for Benediction and

    4. Fauxbourdons.

The theory behind this note-for-note harmonization of Gregorian chant has long been retired and the practice of plainchant accompaniment has gone through several stages of theoretical development. The Preface to this *Chant Grégorien* is the only prose César Franck ever published and sufficient reason to include it here in its entirety.

PREFACE

It is generally agreed that it is difficult to accompany plainchant correctly. Most of the melodies used in church have such a special character, so far removed from present-day musical thought, that in order to harmonize them it is necessary to isolate them as much as possible from our leanings toward modern tonality. We must impart to Gregorian chant its own tonality and, consequently, preserve its character. This difficulty has been serious enough to cause many otherwise capable musicians to doubt their ability to accompany plainchant and despair of reconciling two seemingly noncomplementary elements. We admit that restoring the use of such pristine melodies was not intended to make the role of the organist easier and that, even momentarily giving up the sonority of unaccompanied chant, we must relinquish recently developed musical skills, including counterpoint. However, the organ is so universally used as an accompanying instrument today that there is a pressing need to provide written accompaniment for those who must accompany choirs in Gregorian chant, lest the organ become more hinderance than help in the hands of the less skilled.

However, it is necessary to guard against systematization and archaism. It is also necessary to have a clear idea of the musical resources of a parish, so as to provide solutions at the level of the least trained organists. We have tried to adhere to these two points, since there is not space in this short foreword to give a treatise on accompaniment, which will be the subject of another paper. Leaving the appreciation of this offering to the more knowledgeable, we are content to give some practical observations.

Plate 8. Two Examples of Plainchant Harmonized by César Franck:

1. *Agnus Dei*, Mass IV, In Festis Duplicibus

2. *Victimae paschali laudes*, Sequence for Easter

1. In three-part writing, it is easiest if only one voice is given to the left hand, so that the organist can play it in octaves in the same hand or double it in the pedal. This way of writing leaves the bottom line of the accompaniment—the contrabass or ophicleide part—perfectly clear, restoring instruments not playing in unison with the chant to their correct place, in accordance with the deplorable practice found almost everywhere.

2. Everyone agrees that having the text written above the accompaniment is a great help to the organist.

3. The vocal range chosen enables male voices to reach the notes of each piece. We strongly urge choir directors to adhere to the written key unless there is a particular difficulty. Everyone knows the practice of certain singers who do not want to go beyond A of the middle octave and thus produce a cavernous tone unsuitable for the ordinary bass part of even the most correctly written music.

18

4. As a general rule, the organ should not play passing notes or the small notes; however, a tasteful organist may sometimes accompany melismas.

5. We have written all chords individually, but when a note is common to several consecutive chords, it must be tied as long as it is part of the harmony. This is too basic for any organist to ignore.

Our project is to publish successively, in separate volumes, a complete organ book that will include all liturgical chants. We first offer organists this volume that contains the chants for the ordinary of the masses, as well as the *Benedicamus* and the *Te Deum*.

The second volume, now in preparation, will contain the *Hymnal*. In it will be found not only hymn accompaniments in the choir's range, but the same hymns written in three voices in a higher key, so that, where resources and abilities allow, they can be sung in parts at Vespers and at Benediction.

Subsequent volumes will contain the series of offices, beginning with the Common of Saints.

Reference sections and tables of contents will facilitate exhaustive research.

The numbering system at the top of the pieces refers to the Graduale. The first number is for the edition in modern (round) notation, the second, for the edition in Gregorian (square) notation.[15]

It was during his vacation in August and September 1859 that Franck began composing short organ pieces that were published after his death as the second volume of *L'Organiste*. The Franck family, now consisting of two sons and a daughter, spent their vacation with the family of Auguste Sanches, a wine merchant in Azille. Sanches was the amateur organist at the local church and asked Franck for some easy organ pieces he could play. From time to time Franck obliged.

This same year Louis Niedermeyer published *Trois Antiennes* in the music supplement of his journal, *La Maîtrise*. Brief pieces that could be played as versets, or interludes, by organists who could not

---

[15]"Avertissement," *Chant Grégorien, restauré par le R.P. Lambillotte; accompagnement d'orgue par César Franck* (Paris: Le Clére, 1858) iv.

improvise, the *Quasi lento, Allegretto,* and *Lent et trés soutenu,* appeared after Franck's death as numbers 10, 11, and 17 of *L'Organiste,* Vol. II.

On August 14, 1859 Franck completed his *Seven Words of Christ,* undoubtedly for performance at Sainte-Clotilde during Holy Week the next year.

The new organ at Sainte-Clotilde was finished and playing in August; Cavaillé-Coll sent his final statement to the architect on August 29, 1859, and the inauguration was set for December 5. It was decided that Lefébure-Wély would share the dedicatory recital with Franck who now set himself to arranging his part of the program. On September 13 he completed a *Pièce symphonique* (included as No. 26 in the second volume of *L'Organiste*) and may have considered playing it. He almost certainly composed his *Final* in B-flat at this time, or earlier, as it was mentioned in reviews of the recital and dedicated to Lefébure-Wély.

The first two performances on the organ of Sainte-Clotilde were not by the *titulaire* but by Lefébure-Wély. The first was a private demonstration for Empress Eugénie's sister, the Duchess of Alba, and other ladies of the imperial court; the second, on September 29, was a society wedding performed by the Bishop of Carcassonne.

Plans for the inauguration went according to schedule right up until December 2 when it was discovered that careless workmen, installing the cornice at the top of the organ case, had let sawdust and wood chips fall into the organ chamber, creating such a mess that the recital had to be postponed two weeks until it could be cleaned up.

The inauguration of what was to be one of Cavaillé-Coll's most significant organs, due not only to its being an acknowledged masterpiece but also to its connection with and influence upon the greatest organ composer of the nineteenth century, was held on Monday evening, December 12, 1859. A freezing temperature of six degrees and heavy fog did not prevent the Parisian public from filling the church and overflowing into the organ loft itself. Scheduled for 7:30 o'clock, the concert was delayed forty-five minutes, leaving many of those invited sitting in an unheated church until 8:15.

The program[16] of the inauguration was as follows:

Improvisation
            Lefébure-Wély
Mater amabilis   Mozart
            Choir of Sainte-Clotilde
Improvisation
            César Franck
Sancta Maria   Haydn
            Choir of Sainte-Clotilde
Improvisation
            Lefébure-Wély
Prelude and Fugue in E Minor   J.S. Bach
            César Franck
Symphonic Improvisation
            Lefébure-Wély
Improvisation-Final
            César Franck

The accounts state that Lefébure-Wély began the séance with a long improvisation—"a remarkable demonstration of the forty-six stops, going through them successively by means of a brilliant crescendo followed by an impressive diminuendo." The choir sang Mozart's *Mater amabilis* with good ensemble and precision. Franck then played a brilliant improvisation in which he spent too much time demonstrating "particular stops" with not enough time devoted to "the organ's true character." The choir's performance of the second motet was less successful than the first. They did not know their parts, hesitated at entrances, and had poor intonation. In his second improvisation Lefébure-Wély demonstrated the solo stops in an extremely remarkable way.

Two very different reports appeared in the musical journals describing Franck's performance of Bach's *Prelude and Fugue in E Minor*. Adrien de la Fage wrote that Franck succeeded in giving "color and character to express the soul of the music. He revealed a perseverance which gave him a place among organists of the first order."[17] However, an unsigned review in *La Maîtrise* gave a conflicting account::

[16]Marie Escudier, "Actualities," *La France musicale* (December 25, 1859) 566.
[17]Adrien de la Fage, "Inauguration de l'orgue de Sainte-Clotilde," *Revue et Gazette musicale de Paris* (January 1, 1860) 4.

Plate 9. The Organ of Sainte-Clotilde

I awaited the performance of S. Bach's *Fugue in E Minor* that was announced on the program but, in place of that fine piece, I heard only some detached musical phrases that sounded nothing like a fugue. Perhaps I was too distracted or was not paying attention just then. If that were so, I beg M. Franck's pardon and retract my assertion.[18]

In spite of the dissimilarity of these reviews, the latter seeming to describe the *Prelude* rather than the *Fugue*, there is no doubt that the Bach work in question was the "Cathedral" or "Nightwatchman" Fugue, BWV 533.

Lefébure-Wély then returned for a symphonic improvisation. Taking the hymn *Adeste fideles*, "he treated it with all the studied refinements of counterpoint" and produced "the sweetest sensation" by playing it on the Voix humaine. Continuing his scenic tableau of the birth of Jesus, he closed with *Il est né, le divin enfant* on the full organ.

The concert ran so late that many of the audience left before it was over and the pastor even cancelled Benediction, with which organ dedications traditionally ended. The evening concluded with what was probably a Sortie played by Franck. The Improvisation-Final was almost certainly the *Final*, Op. 22, in which "he showed himself at his best . . . in this Final the conception and execution of a true master was recognized."

Franck's *Mass in A Major*, Op. 12, for three voices (soprano, tenor, and bass), harp, cello, bass, and organ, was premiered at Sainte-Clotilde not on Sunday, but on Easter Tuesday, April 2, 1861. Two months later Théodore Dubois was awarded the Premier Grand Prix de Rome and left for Italy where he was to stay for the next five years.

With Dubois's departure Franck again assumed the responsibility of the choir at Sainte-Clotilde and his name appeared frequently in published lists of church musicians as "maître-de-chapelle et organiste de Sainte-Clotilde." Because of the unique arrangement in this church of having both the choir loft and organ loft in the rear of the church, Franck was the only organist

[18]"Inauguration de G.-O. de l'Église Sainte-Clotilde," *La Maîtrise* (December 1859/January 1860) 138–39.

Sainte-Clotilde

Plate 10. The Church of Sainte-Clotilde, 1863

of a major church who was able to go up and down between the two galleries and alternately conduct the choir and play the organ. The parish had little success in acquiring or retaining choir-masters. The former maître-de-chapelle of Saint-Pierre-de-Chaillot, Delort, was appointed to Sainte-Clotilde early in 1863 and conducted Loisel's *Seven Last Words* on March 27, 1863, but "some days later was forced to give his resignation!"[19]

Franck dispatched his duties as well as other choirmasters and his selections were no better nor worse than those of his colleagues. For instance, on All Saints' Day, 1862, he conducted a Mass by Dumont, a motet of his own at the Offertory, and an *O salutaris* by Haydn at the Elevation.[20]

On April 29, 1862, Franck, together with four other organists, took part in the inauguration of Cavaillé-Coll's largest instrument, that in the church of Saint-Sulpice. One critic dismissed Franck's playing as "severe without pedantry,"[21] and another mistook his

[19]*Le Plain Chant* (July 1861).
[20]*Revue de musique sacrée ancienne et moderne* (November 15, 1862) 34.
[21]Antoine Elwart, *Revue et Gazette musicale de Paris* (May 11, 1862) 155–56.

Plate 11. Church of Sainte-Sulpice

performance of his *Fantaisie in C* for an "improvisation which left the audience with the impression that he had played a well-worked-out piece!"[22] Had he but known that Franck had been "working it out" for the last six years! "Its opening had the fullness of those powerful harmonies reminiscent of *Fingal's Cave* and the foundation stops had as much poetry as could be given them. The improviser had only one shortcoming: he did not end soon enough." *L'Univers musical* completely ignored the inauguration of the organ but devoted an entire page to its "Deuxième audition," three days later, by the twenty-five-year-old Alexandre Guilmant and mentioned Franck among the artists in the audience.

Franck was probably instrumental in securing two contracts for a fellow Belgian imigré, the organbuilder Hippolyte Loret, who had just relocated his business in Paris. He built two organs for the Jesuits: one in 1860 for the Church at the Collège de Vaugirard, where Franck was on the faculty, and another in 1862 for a recently completed little thirteenth-century-style Gothic chapel at 35, rue de Sèvres. For the inauguration of the modest two-manual organ, Franck joined the chapel's organist, Monsieur

[22]Louis Roger, "Inauguration du Grand Orgue de Saint-Sulpice," *Revue de musique sacrée ancienne et moderne* (May 15, 1862) 231.

Scola, and his friend, Alexis Chauvet, then organist of Saint-Bernard-de-la-Chapelle. "These three artists pitted their talents against one another to demonstrate the qualities of the instrument."[23]

Franck's second published organ work, *Offertoire sur un Noël Breton*, appeared on October 15, 1867, in the first issue of a new monthly sacred music journal, *L'Athénée Musical*. Written on two staves, it has registration for both grand-orgue and harmonium.[24]

On October 10, 1867, Franck, Alexis Chauvet, Auguste Durand, and the organist of the church, P. Serrier, inaugurated Cavaillé-Coll's organ at Saint-Denis-du-Saint-Sacrament.

The year 1868 was significant for the French organ world: it saw the completion of the organ of Notre-Dame-de-Paris and the publication of César Franck's *Six Pièces*. Over its seven hundred year existence the great twelfth-century Gothic Cathedral of Paris had suffered a multitude of indignities, outside as well as within. With the Romantic movement sweeping over Europe, a new respect was growing for medieval architecture. Victor Hugo greatly influenced this neo-Gothic revival and in his book, *Notre-Dame-de-Paris*, enumerated the alterations to which the cathedral had been constantly subjected under the guise of changing taste and fashion: the brilliantly-colored stained glass was gone, the interior

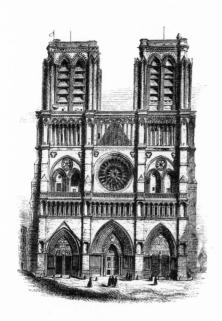

Plate 12. Cathedral of Notre-Dame de Paris

[23]L.-C. Laurent, *Revue de musique sacrée ancienne et moderne* (November 15, 1862) 20.
[24]Reprinted in facsimile in *The American Organist* (November 1990) 77–81.

had been whitewashed, its chapels over-decorated in contemporary fashion, the choir floor marbled, the sanctuary filled with academic statuary, the flèche removed, and the north portal mutilated. It was the young architect, Eugène-Emmanuel Viollet-le-Duc, who was entrusted with the restoration, and for twenty years, from 1845 to 1864, the Cathedral of Paris was repaired from its foundation to the tiling of the roof.

François Thierry's 1733 organ, which had been rebuilt by François-Henri Clicquot in 1784, was rebuilt and enlarged between 1863 and 1868 by Cavaillé-Coll. The organbuilder was responsible for assembling at the inauguration on Friday, March 6, 1868, the greatest organists in France: César Franck, Camille Saint-Saëns, Alexandre Guilmant, Charles-Marie Widor, Alexis Chauvet, Clément Loret, and Auguste Durand. Franck played his *Fantaisie in C*.

Franck played the organ three more times: on March 22 in a half-hour of organ music at the 1:30 o'clock Mass before a talk given by the famous Jesuit preacher, Father Félix; with Auguste Durand at a demonstration of the organ on April 24; and with Eugène Sergent, the *organiste titulaire*, on July 8 in a demonstration for the Société Scientifique.

Later that year Maeyens-Couvreur published Franck's *Six Pièces d'Orgue*. Over an hour and twenty minutes of music that has remained in the repertoire for more than 125 years, this was the first major contribution to French organ literature in over a century, and the most important organ music written since Mendelssohn's. Franck was the first to realize the potential of the symphonic organ and to have the talent, originality, and imagination to utilize it for his own ends. This collection, in the words of Félix Raugel, constitutes "a monument to the resurrection in France of the great art of the organ."[25]

---

[25]Félix Raugel, "La Musique religieuse française de l'époque révolutionnaire à la mort de César Franck," *La Musique religieuse française de ses origines à nos jours* (Paris: *La Revue Musicale*, Numéro Spécial, No. 222, 1953–54) 119.

Plate 13. Church of La Trinité

In November Théodore Dubois, who had resumed his post as *maître-de-chapelle* when he returned from Rome in 1866, left Sainte-Clotilde to take up a similar post at the Madeleine; Franck again assumed the double title of organist and choirmaster.

The new Church of La Trinité was designed by the same architect as Saint-Clotilde and its new Cavaillé-Coll organ was but one stop smaller. The organ was inaugurated on March 16, 1869 by Franck, Saint-Saëns, Durand, Widor, Henri Fissot, and the first organist of La Trinité, Alexis Chauvet. Franck, the first to be heard, "played a vigorous well-developed improvisation in which he sought to display the greatest possible number of sonorities."[26] Widor recalled long after that "the themes, their development, and execution, were equally admirable: he never wrote better."[27]

---

[26]*Revue et Gazette musicale de Paris* (March 18, 1868) 85.
[27]Félix Raugel, *Les Grandes Orgues des Églises de Paris*, 220.

Musical education in France came to a standstill during the Franco-Prussian War and the Commune; the Paris Conservatoire was closed for the 1870–71 school year. When it reopened in February 1872, François Benoist retired as professor of organ (he lived on until 1878 and served on the examination juries) and César Franck was appointed to succeed him.

Chroniclers have been unwilling to admit that Franck was the best man for the job and have insisted on surrounding his appointment with an air of mystery. Vincent d'Indy concluded that no one knew how he was appointed and that Franck, "a stranger to all intrigue, understood it less than the rest . . . the mystery has never been elucidated."[28] Several people advanced a solution to the mystery, however. Saint-Saëns twice stated that he had recommended Franck to the minister of education "so that . . . he would no longer be compelled to waste time in giving piano lessons that could more profitably be devoted to composition,"[29] and Cavaillé-Coll's biographers claimed his responsibility—repeating Widor's assertion that it was an attempt to appease Franck for Cavaillé-Coll's having recommended Widor instead of him as organist of Saint-Sulpice. The most credible source, however, is Théodore Dubois, who, as Franck's longtime confrère at Sainte-Clotilde, was in the best position to know what Franck could do at the organ and who, in 1904, in a speech at the unveiling of the Franck monument in the park in front of Sainte-Clotilde (a speech heard by Vincent d'Indy but ignored in his book published two years later), recounted that he had recommended Franck to the Conservatoire's director, Ambroise Thomas, saying, "There is at the moment only one man who is fit for the post, and that is César Franck." Thomas's reply, "You're right," is verified by history.[30] Franck was appointed.

In the thirty years since Franck had been a student, two further requirements had been added to the Conservatoire's curriculum: the improvisation on a free theme and the performance of a Bach fugue. The year of Franck's appointment the requirement of playing a Bach fugue was changed to playing a "classic"

[28]d'Indy, 46.
[29]Camille Saint-Saëns, *Les idées de Monsieur Vincent d'Indy* (Paris: Lafitte, 1918).
[30]Théodore Dubois, "Discours," *Souvenir du 22 octobre 1904. À César Franck, ses disciples, ses amis, ses admirateurs* (Paris: Cabasson, 1904) 4.

piece from memory. Indeed, Franck may have been responsible for the change.[31] Franck described the curriculum in a letter written in 1883 to an unnamed correspondent:

> A piece to be played from memory—which is but a sort of accessory to the examination; to accompany a piece of plainchant in strict counterpoint (first the chant is in the bass part, then in the upper part); to improvise a fugue; to improvise a piece the equivalent of the first movement of a sonata.

Three quarters of the course was devoted to improvisation. The class served not for the study of organ literature but to sharpen improvisational skills useful to stimulate a composer's creativity. Submitting to the strict rules for the end-of-term examinations, it is all the more surprising that Franck was able to cover as much repertoire as he did.

Three classes a week, on Tuesday, Thursday, and Saturday mornings from eight to ten o'clock, were taught on a dreadful organ assembled by Cavaillé-Coll from remnants of Pierre Érard's organ in the Tuileries chapel that had burned in May 1871 and from the old organ upon which Franck had played as a student. Its specification[32] was as follows:

Plate 14. The Square and Church of Sainte-Clotilde, 1869.

[31]Archives nationale AJ[37] 251. Cited by Ochse in, *Organists and Organ Playing*, 155.
[32]Norbert Dufourcq, *Autour des Orgues de Conservatoire National et de la Chapelle des Tuileries* (Paris: Floury, 1952) 26.

Compass: Manuals, 54 Notes: C^1 - F^5
Pedal, 25 notes: C^1 - C^3

Grand-Orgue		Récit		Pédale	
8	Dessus de montre	8	Flûte	16	Soubasse
8	Flûte	8	Gambe	8	Flûte
8	Bourdon	8	Voix céleste	4	Flûte
4	Prestant	4	Flûte	8	Basson
8	Trompette	8	Hautbois (free reed)		
		8	Trompette		

During Franck's first ten years of teaching at the Conservatoire five of his students won first prize in organ. The first, Paul Wachs (1851–1915) had won a second prize while in Benoist's class but had to wait until July of 1872 to compete for his first prize—which he won after only a few months' study with Franck. Wachs, organist of Saint-Merry from 1874–1896, was a composer of salon piano pieces, and the author of several educational works on harmony, counterpoint, and fugue.

Vincent d'Indy (1851–1931) was in the organ class for two years, but won only a first accessit, or honorable mention, in 1875. He was one of the more famous Franck students—as his biographer, in particular—a noted composer, and founder and director of the Schola Cantorum.

Samuel Rousseau (1853–1904) was in the class for over five years, finally winning a first prize in 1877. The same year he became maître-de-chapelle at Sainte-Clotilde. He taught harmony at the Conservatoire and, from 1892, was conductor of the Théâtre-Lyrique.

Henri Dallier (1849–1934) won first prize in 1878 and the next year succeeded Édouard Batiste as organist of Sainte-Eustache. He succeeded Gabriel Fauré as organist of the Madeleine in 1905.

Auguste Chapuis (1858–1933) won first prize in 1881 and was later inspector of music teaching in the Paris city schools, a harmony professor at the Conservatoire, and organist of Saint-Roch from 1888–1906.

Franck played infrequently in public after his Conservatoire appointment. At the third program of the Société des Concerts du Conservatoire, in January 1873, which featured the first perform-

Plate 15. The Church of Sainte-Clotilde, 1874.

ance in France of Schumann's *Manfred Overture*, and with the president of the Republic in attendance, Franck "was applauded for the severe beauties of a Bach *Prelude and Fugue in E Minor*."[33] In May he played the new organ set up in Cavaillé-Coll's erecting room destined for the Albert Hall, Sheffield, England. It was to be the largest organ he would ever build for Great Britain and his first with sixty-one-note manual compass.[34]

Two ensemble appearances followed in quick succession. Franck played the harmonium, and Vincent d'Indy the piano, in Franck's duo arrangement of the *Prélude, Fugue et Variation* at a Société Nationale concert in February 1874.[35] In March, at a Concert Danbé performance of Handel's *Alexander's Feast* with chorus and orchestra, Franck played the organ, Saint-Saëns the piano, and the two accompanists "vigorously supported the voices."[36]

In 1876 Guillaume Couture (1851–1915), a Canadian, was appointed maître-de-chapelle at Sainte-Clotilde and, for the first time in eight years, Franck had only the duties of the *organiste du grand orgue*. Couture remained there one year and was succeeded by Samuel Rousseau.[37] Then in 1878 a situation identical to that of Dubois's arose: Rousseau won the Premier Grand Prix de Rome and left for Italy for five years. What happened in the interim is unknown. Perhaps Franck again conducted the choir; perhaps the choir organist filled in—his nephew, Clotaire-Joseph Franck (son

[33]Ch. Bannelier, *Revue et Gazette musicale de Paris* (January 5, 1873) 5. A subsequent notice in the March 9 issue of the same journal (p. 78) mentions that on March 1, at the second of his "Petits Concerts" Alkan played a *Fugue in C Minor*, "the same that C. Franck played on the organ at the last Concert du Conservatoire."

[34]Oscar Comettant, writing in *Siècle* (May 19, 1873), quoted in *Le Grand Orgue de la Nouvelle Salle de Concert de Sheffield en Angleterre construit par Aristide Cavaillé-Coll à Paris* (Paris: Plon, 1874) 23.

[35]Maurice Emmanuel relates that after the *Prélude* a tumultuous ovation broke out and Franck, not bothered by delaying the *Fugue*, got up and said, "Thank you, but . . . not just now!" (*César Franck* [Paris: Henri Laurens, 1930] 16).

[36]*La Chronique musicale* (April–June 1874) 33.

[37]Couture returned to Canada, held positions as maître-de-chapelle in various churches until finally settling in 1893 at the Cathedral of Saint-Jacques in Montréal where he remained until his death. Among his pupils was Lynnwood Farnam. (Alix de Vaulchier, "Guillaume Couture," *Encyclopédie de la musique au Canada*, 814.) I am grateful to Simon Couture of Casavant Frères for bringing this article to my attention.

of his brother, Joseph), and a former student, Georges Verschneider (1854–95), both served as *organiste de l'orgue de chœur*.
Rousseau returned to Sainte-Clotilde in 1883 and served until his
death in 1904. So distinguished was his career that the charming
little park in front of Sainte-Clotilde was named Square Samuel
Rousseau. It is on the east side of this square that the sculptor Lenoir's famous monument depicting César Franck improvising at
the organ was dedicated in 1904.

The 1878 Universal Exposition held in Paris was the setting for
what was the most important organ recital of Franck's career. The
new building, which was to serve as the permanent headquarters for
the expositions then being held every eleven years, was the gigantic
Moorish-pseudo-Byzantine Palais du Trocadéro, named for a small
fort on the Bay of Cádiz captured by the French in 1823. Within the
palace was the Grande Salle des Fêtes, or Festival Hall, a five-thou-
sand-seat circular auditorium and, across the stage stood a sixty-six-
stop Cavaillé-Coll organ—the first large organ in a concert hall in
France. It was featured in a series of fifteen hour-long recitals played
by prominent organists. For two months these programs were presented twice a week at three o'clock in the afternoon on Wednesdays
and Saturdays. Admission was free and since this was the only time
the general public could get in to see the celebrated hall without
having to pay to attend a concert, the organ recitals drew larger
audiences than any other event at the Trocadéro. The sightseers
stayed for one or two pieces and then left, but an audience estimated
at between 1,500 and 2,000 persons stayed for each recital. During
these recitals Charles-Marie Widor premiered his *Sixth Symphony* and
Camille Saint-Saëns played the first performance outside Germany
of Liszt's *Fantasia on "Ad nos."*

César Franck, then fifty-five years old and, as professor at the
Paris Conservatoire, at the height of the organ profession in France,
played the thirteenth recital on October 1. For his program he composed three new organ works, completed within seven days, two
weeks before the recital. These were the *Trois Pièces* and they were
interspersed throughout the program:

Fantaisie
Grande Pièce symphonique
Cantabile
Improvisation
Pièce héroïque
Improvisation

Of the new *Trois Pièces*, the critic for the *Revue et Gazette musicale de Paris* found the *Fantaisie en la* a beautiful, very skillfully wrought piece, "but all the details were not well brought out: the soft stops lacking presence and distinctness in the hall. The *Cantabile in B Major*, an impressive melody of noble character, was more effective thanks to the telling Récit stop employed. The *Pièce héroïque*, although containing some excellent things, seemed less interesting than the other works. As for the *Grande Pièce symphonique in F-sharp Minor* it has long been known and justly

Plate 16. The Palais de Trocadéro

Plate 17. The Salle des Fêtes of the Palais du Trocadéro as seen
from one of the balconies.

appreciated. The *Andante*, as always, was warmly welcomed."[38] Perhaps because of the negative criticism, Franck never played the *Pièce héroïque* again.

Franck's first improvisation was based on themes by French masters: the first chorus of Félicien David's *Le Désert*, two themes from Hector Berlioz's *L'Enfance du Christ*, and two themes from Georges Bizet's *L'Arlésienne*. "He brought out charming details in his free-style treatment of these themes, expecially those of Berlioz." Franck concluded his recital with another lengthy improvisation on two popular Russian themes, first treated separately, and then superimposed upon Swedish, Hungarian, and English themes. "The themes were too numerous and it would not have been possible to take advantage of each one sufficiently without fatiguing the audience. With this slight reservation, we happily pay homage to the most elevated and complete talent known.

---

[38]"Nouvelles Musicales de l'Exposition," *Revue et Gazette musicale de Paris* (October 6, 1878) 321.

Once again we are to be congratulated that so peerless an artist is at the forefront of organ teachers in France."[39]

At the end of the month, on October 29, Franck, Gigout, and Paul Wachs, the *organiste titulaire,* "played some beautiful pages by Bach, Mendelssohn, and Boëly"[40] in a recital at Saint-Merry to inaugurate the organ just restored and renovated by Cavaillé-Coll. He had rebuilt the original Clicquot organ in 1857 when Saint-Saëns was organist and had made several tonal changes over the following twenty years. This was to be the organbuilder's last association with Saint-Merry, as it proved to be Franck's last professional association with Cavaillé-Coll.

For the inauguration of the tubular-pneumatic organ built by Fermis & Persil for the new church of Saint-François-Xavier, Franck again played his *Cantabile.* The other organists, Widor, Gigout, and Albert Renaud, the church's organist, each played their own works on the recital. The organ was unique: in addition to its "modern" action, it had a sixty-one-note manual compass; five of its pédales de combinaison were duplicated by pistons; couplers enabled the anches and fonds of the Positif and Récit to be operated independently; there was a sub-octave coupler for the Anches Pédale; a crescendo pedal controlled the full organ, and chimes (Cloches) were available on the Positif. Franck's solo took advantage of none of these state-of-the-art appliances, but they certainly could not have escaped his notice.

On March 21, 1879, the last convocation of important organists in which César Franck would be included was held for the inauguration of the new Merklin organ in Saint-Eustache. Franck's latest first-prize winner, Henri Dallier, had recently been appointed organist. Franck played at the inauguration of the former organ in 1854; it had been severely damaged by shells in a bombardment during the Franco-Prussian War of 1870–71 and remained in disrepair ever since. Franck was a member of the organ commission along with Guilmant, Dubois, and Gigout, and all four, with Dallier, played on the inaugural recital.

[39]Ibid.
[40]"Nouvelles diverses," *Revue et Gazette musicale de Paris* (November 10, 1878) 367.

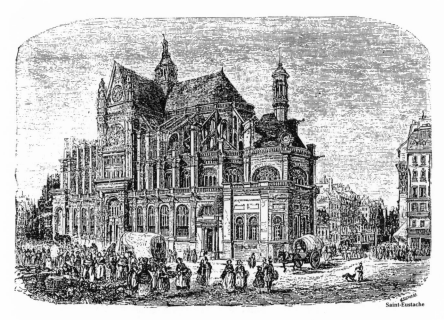

Plate 18. Church of Saint-Eustache

M. Franck, the senior artist, magesterially played his beautiful *Fantaisie en la*, in which inspiration and technic, like two estranged sisters, entwine and complement each other on billowing waves of rich harmony randomly rushing from modulation to modulation.[41]

The publisher Durand took over the rights to Franck's *Six Pièces* and, using Maeyens-Couvreur's original plates, brought out their own edition in 1880—in a very conservative printing of twenty-five copies! They were somewhat more optimistic with the *Trois Pièces*, which they published in 1883 in a run of 150 copies.

During the last decade of his life Franck's activities were divided primarily among teaching, composing, and playing the organ at Sainte-Clotilde. His income was derived almost exclusively from teaching, both at the Conservatoire and his private

---

[41]Abbé H.-J. Ply, *La facture moderne etudiée à l'orgue de Saint-Eustache* (Lyon: Perrin et Marinet, 1878) 275. The *Revue et Gazette musicale de Paris* (March 30, 1879, 101) mentioned that the *Fantaisie* was incorrectly designated *Cantabile* on the printed program; from these two reviews it is apparent that only the one piece was played.

organ and composition students. He maintained connections with several schools in Paris, notably the National Institute for Blind Youths where he was one of the examiners; several graduates entered his organ class at the Conservatoire and left with the first prize.

There was either an improvement in the talent of students who entered Franck's organ class, or Franck gradually came to understand just what was expected of them at the end-of-term juries, because throughout the 1880s more students than during the previous decade won first prize—at least one a year:

Gabriel Pierné (1863–1937) won first prize in 1882 and upon Franck's death in 1890 succeeded him as organist of Sainte-Clotilde—a position he held for eight years. He was an unsuccessful contender for the post at Notre-Dame-de-Paris in 1900, but a noted composer and conductor of the Orchestra Colonne from 1910 to 1932.

Anatole-Léon Grand-Jany (1862–91) competed successfully for the first prize in organ in 1883 and was, for a time, choir organist at Saint-Vincent-de-Paul.

Plate 19. Improvisation themes from Franck's notebook

Henri Kaiser (b. 1861) won first prize in 1884 and was appointed professor of solfège at the Paris Conservatoire in 1891.

François Pinot (b. 1865) won first prize in 1885. He was appointed *organiste d'accompagnateur* at Saint-Vincent-de-Paul in 1887.

Adolphe Marty (1865–1942) was Franck's first student from the Institute for Blind Youths to win first prize in organ at the Conservatoire (1886). He succeeded Louis Lebel in 1888 as professor of organ at the Institute and also taught composition, directed the choir, and conducted the orchestra. Among his students there were Louis Vierne, André Marchal, Jean Langlais, and Gaston Litaize. Marty was organist of Saint-François-Xavier for half a century until his death.

Plate 20. César Franck at the age of sixty in 1882.

Césare Galeotti (1872–1929) won first prize in 1887 at the age of fifteen! He became a noted composer of symphonic works and operas.

Joséphine Boulay (1869–1925) was blind and had the distinction of being the first woman to win a first prize in organ at the Paris Conservatoire (1888). She taught piano and organ at the National Institute for Blind Youths for thirty-seven years.

There were two first-prize winners in 1889: Georges-Paul Bondon (b. 1867), who later taught solfège at the Conservatoire and was organiste-de-chœur at Saint-Philippe-du-Roule, and Albert Mahaut (1867–1943). Franck described Mahaut as the "perfect student"; he played the *Prière* on his final examination. The first organist to play an all-Franck recital (at the Trocadéro on April 28, 1898), Mahaut was professor of harmony at the National Institute for Blind Youths from 1889 to 1924, concertized well into his seventies, and was an indefatigable spokesman for the cause of blind musicians.

Marie Prestat (b. 1862) was in Franck's class for three years. A brilliant student ("no lessons interest me more than yours," Franck wrote her), she was the first woman to win a first prize in counterpoint and fugue, and for many years was the only woman to have won five first prizes at the Paris Conservatoire. She taught piano at the Schola Cantorum from 1901 to 1922.

Franck's two most famous students, Charles Tournemire and Louis Vierne, did not win their first prizes until after his death.

The list of first-prize winners, augmented by all of those awarded lesser prizes and those who did not compete, gives an idea of the number of Franck students who were active in the early decades of the twentieth century.

In spite of Vincent d'Indy's morose picture of Franck's unappreciated and ignoble life, considerable recognition did come to him. It came slowly and late in his life, but it did come. As an organist and teacher, he could hardly have achieved more than to teach at the Conservatoire. His music was published and, at least the organ music, was performed by not just a handful of organists. He was awarded the Prix Chartier for chamber music by the Académie des Beaux-Arts in 1881, and the cross of the Légion d'Honneur in 1885. He was elected president of the Société Nationale in

1886—the music society he himself had been a founding member of in 1871. The aim of the society was "to favor the performance and publication of all serious works, published or not, of French composers." He attended a Franck festival organized by his students at the Cirque d'Hiver in 1887. He even had his portrait painted by Jeanne Rongier showing him seated at the console of the organ of Sainte-Clotilde, and saw its exhibition at the Palais des Champs-Élysées in May of 1888.

César Franck, the composer, came into his own only in the last ten years or so of his life. The list of works from this period is impressive not only because of the number of masterpieces that follow in succession, but because the composer was older than most other creative artists when he produced them: 1879, *Quintet* in F Minor, and the oratorio, *Les Béatitudes*; 1880, the biblical scene for solo voices, chorus and orchestra, *Rébecca*; 1882, the symphonic

Plate 21. Mustel Modèle K Harmonium

poems, *Le Chasseur maudit*; 1884, the symphonic poem, *Les Djinns*, and the *Prélude, Choral et Fugue* for piano solo; 1885, the opera, *Hulda*, and *Variations symphoniques* for piano and orchestra; 1886, the *Sonata for violin and piano* and the symphonic poem, *Psyché*; 1887, *Prélude, Aria et Final* for piano solo; 1888, *Symphonie* in D Minor; 1889, the opera, *Ghisélle* and the *String Quartet in D Major*. Organ works included a *Petit Offertoire*, which appeared in an 1885 collection, *L'Orgue de l'Église*, an arrangement for organ of ten excerpts from Charles-Valentin Alkan's *Préludes et Prières*, published in 1889, and, in the last summer of his life, *L'Organiste* (Volume I) and the immortal *Trois Chorals*.

César Franck, the organist, was never far from the teacher or the composer and in the midst of Conservatoire classes and juries, the composition of operas, sonatas, symphonic poems, and symphonies, there was always Sainte-Clotilde—and its duties. Around 1885 Franck recommended, and was instrumental in the parish's purchase of, a Mustel Modèle K Harmonium for choir accompaniment.[42] This was a nineteen-stop stock model that in addition to the standard four free-reed ranks, included an 8′ Voix céleste and an 8′ Harpe éolienne, as well as the special Mustel features: Métaphones, Prolongement, and Double-Expression. We do not know if this harmonium were used in the rear choir gallery or in the chancel. There was a movement afoot to relocate the choir to the front of the church, its traditional place in France, and an instrument in the chancel had been considered at different times, but the idea was always dismissed for lack of space.

Then, in 1887, Joseph Merklin was given the contract for an orgue-de-chœur to be installed in the sanctuary of Sainte-Clotilde. In a letter to the organbuilder dated August 8, Franck wrote:

[42]In 1994 there was still in one of the chapels of Sainte-Clotilde a Victor Mustel Modèl 39 one-manual harmonium in a rosewood case. This instrument was sold September 1, 1861 and may have been purchased new for use as the orgue-de-chœur or to provide music in one of the chapels. Its specifications is: Forte Expressif, Pianissimo [operates on the ④ Basson], ④ Basson 8′, Basse 8′,② Bourdon 16′, ① Cor Anglais 8′, Grand Jeu Tutti, Expression Pédales, ① Flûte 8′,②Clarinette 16′,④Hautbois 8′, Musette 16′, Voix Céleste [16′], Forte Expressif. There is no percussion, double expression, heel nor knee levers. (Information conveyed by Phil and Pam Fluke, curators of the Victorian Reed Organ and Harmonium Museum, Victoria Hall, Saltaire Village, West Yorkshire, England.)

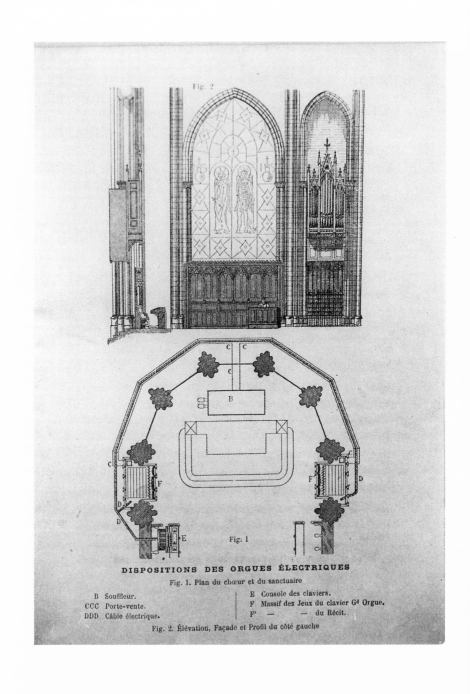

DISPOSITIONS DES ORGUES ÉLECTRIQUES

Fig. 1. Plan du chœur et du sanctuaire

B Souffleur.	E Console des claviers.
CCC Porte-vente.	F Massif des Jeux du clavier Gᵈ Orgue.
DDD Câble électrique.	F' — — du Récit.

Fig. 2. Élévation, Façade et Profil du côté gauche

Plate 22. Elevation, Profile, Facade and Disposition of the Merklin
orgue-de-choeur at Sainte-Clotilde

44

> I am pleased to learn from your good letter that all is now ready regarding the choir organ for Sainte-Clotilde. So we are finally going to have this organ so desired and so long awaited, thanks to your electropneumatic action which I find simply marvelous.

Such a testimonial from the professor of organ at the Paris Conservatoire was not long in finding its way into the firm's advertisements.

The installation of an organ in the front of the church had posed a physical problem in that, until the advent of electric action, there was no way an organ could be placed in the sanctuary without taking up too much room and covering up architectural detail. Merklin solved the problem by dividing the organ

> into two sections of equal size and placed in elevated positions, in the side arches of the apsidal sanctuary, in line with the steps of the high altar. [The Grand-Orgue on the left side with the console; the Récit, opposite, on the right.] The console is located at the end of the stalls on the left as one faces the altar...and the bellows are placed immediately behind the high altar.[43]

The organ was playing by March of 1888 and the commission that approved it consisted of a close Franckian circle: Théodore Dubois, the former maître-de-chapelle, now organist of the Madeleine, Samuel Rousseau, the maître-de-chapelle of Sainte-Clotilde, and Georges Verschneider, a Conservatoire student of Franck's who won first accessit in 1875 and was then *organiste de l'orgue-de-chœur*, and, of course, the *organiste titulaire*, César Franck.

Each manual division was separately enclosed and the three pedal stops were borrowed from the Grand-Orgue. In addition to the usual *pédales de combinaison* there were four *boutons électrique de combinaisons*—preset pistons that added stops: Pianissimo, Mezzo forte, Forte, Fortissimo.[44] This Merklin organ never worked very

[43]George Ashdown Audsley, *The Art of Organ Building*, Vol. I (New York: Dodd, Mead & Co., 1905) 95.
[44]*L'Orgue de chœur de Saint-Clotilde à Paris, construit après le Nouveau systeme electro-pneumatique.* Rapport de la commission, 1888 (Paris: Watelet, 1888).

Plate 23. The Organ, Saint-Jacques-du-Haut-Pas

well and in 1934 was replaced by a poor-quality, two-manual instrument built by the successors of Cavaillé-Coll and installed in the choir tribune.[45]

[45]Gustave Helbig, *Monographie des Orgues de France* (Bibliothèque Nationale, Rés. Vmc. ms. 13, Vol. 2) 413.

Orgue de Chœur of Sainte-Clotilde

Compass: Manuals, 56 notes: C^1 - G^5

Pedal, 30 notes: C^1 - F^2

Grand-Orgue	Récit	Pédale
16 Bourdon	8 Flûte harmonique	16 Soubass
8 Montre	8 Gambe	8 Bourdon
8 Bourdon	8 Voix Céleste	8 Violoncelle
8 Salicional	4 Flûte octaviante	
4 Prestant	8 Basson-hautbois	
8 Trompette	Trémolo	

On May 27, 1889, Franck inaugurated the new organ in the church of Saint-Jacques-du-Haut-Pas, an interestingly-designed rebuild by Merklin et Cie. A new four-manual console situated behind the high altar controlled the two existing orgues-de-chœur, that retained their original mechanical action, as well as the Grand-Orgue in the rear gallery, which was fitted with electropneumatic action. At the inauguration Franck played two improvisations

utilizing one after the other the resources of the new system with infinite artistry. All the stops were heard in pleasing solos and melodious dialogues. First the orgue-de-tribune accompanied the melody, then it was followed by the orgue-de-chœur and the finest chiseled phrases reached us from the uppermost vaults so that the whole church was filled with a new harmony coming simultaneously or alternately from opposite ends of the building. The demonstration was conclusive and very acceptable: the organ affords new means which can be put to the best use. Franck played a beautiful fantaisie of his own composition on the orgue-de-tribune division only, and demonstrated thereby that the action everywhere yielded to the same submissiveness and the same ease.[46]

Early in January 1890 Franck went to Lyon for a performance of his Mass at the Church of Saint-Bonaventure. The organ had been rebuilt and enlarged with partial electropneumatic action by Merklin three years before. Franck improvised an Offer-

---

[46]"L'Orgue de Saint-Jacques-du-Haut-Pas," *Le Monde Musical* (June 15, 1889) 8.

Vous êtes prié d'assister aux Convoi, Service et Enterrement de

Monsieur César FRANCK

Professeur au Conservatoire National de Musique
Organiste de Sainte-Clotilde
Chevalier de la Légion d'Honneur

décédé en son domicile, 95, boulevard Saint-Michel, le 8 Novembre 1890, dans sa 68ᵐᵉ année, muni des Sacrements de l'Eglise;

Qui se feront le Lundi 10 courant, à MIDI TRÈS PRÉCIS, en l'Eglise Sainte-Clotilde.

DE PROFUNDIS

On se réunira à la Maison Mortuaire.

De la part de Madame CÉSAR FRANCK, sa Veuve; de Monsieur GEORGES FRANCK, Professeur au Lycée Lakanal, et Madame GEORGES FRANCK, de Monsieur et Madame GERMAIN FRANCK, ses fils et belles-filles; de Monsieur ROBERT FRANCK, de Mademoiselle THÉRÈSE FRANCK, de Monsieur FRANCIS FRANCK, ses petits-enfants;

De Monsieur et Madame JOSEPH FRANCK et leurs enfants, de Monsieur et Madame PAUL DESMOUSSEAUX, ses frère, beau-frère, belles-sœurs, neveu et nièces;

Et des familles BOUTET DE MONVEL, FÉRÉOL, BRISSAUD, HALMAGRAND, CHOPY, LASSAILLY, SIMONET, CAYOL et PIERCEAU, ses cousins et cousines.

L'Inhumation aura lieu au Cimetière du Grand-Montrouge.

Plate 24. Announcement of César Franck's funeral procession, Requiem, and burial

48

toire and a Sortie that "confirmed the great reputation which he enjoys in Paris as virtuoso and composer."[47]

In early May, while on his way to a rehearsal at a student's home, the cab in which Franck was riding was hit in the right side by the carriage pole of a passing horse-drawn omnibus. William Ober, a New York pathologist, conjectured that "the chest injury was probably more severe than he first realized, and he *may* have cracked a rib and had a pleural reaction."[48]

Although Franck was forced to cancel numerous engagements, including the last concert and end-of-the-year banquet of the Société Nationale, and had to be excused from serving on the piano jury at the Conservatoire at the end of July, he, nevertheless, had been able to join four other organists on June 6 for a reception of the orgue-de-chœur at Notre-Dame Cathedral. Merklin had restored the 1863 organ and converted it to electropneumatic action; Franck played a Meditation and a Caprice to demonstrate the advantages of the new changes.[49]

Franck's health was improved enough for him to enjoy a leisurely and productive summer vacation: during August and September he composed his magnum opus the *Trois Chorals*. He was able to begin classes at the Conservatoire at the beginning of October,

> but on October 17 he developed a respiratory infection which turned into pneumonia. As was not uncommon in the pre-antibiotic era, the lung infection spread and Franck developed pleurisy and pericarditis. . . and died on November 8. Though he may have been in good health until the time of his accident in May, his terminal illness in October-November 1890 could not be considered an unusual pattern for pneumonia in a man in his seventh decade. Franck's case raises the question of proximate cause, and it is somewhat difficult to indict the bus injury when its effects seem to have disappeared in a reasonable time.[50]

[47]"Les Concerts de la Quinzaine: La Salut Public de Lyon à Saint-Bonaventure," *Le Monde Musical* (January 15, 1890) 4.
[48]William B. Ober, "De Mortibus Musicorum," *Stereo Review* (November 1970) 83.
[49]"Grandes Orgues," *Le Monde Musical* (June 15, 1890) 5.
[50]Ober, loc. cit.

News of Franck's death had scarcely been announced when the opportunistic Eugène Gigout wrote a letter to his old teacher, Camille Saint-Saëns, imploring his help in getting Franck's post:

Paris, November 9, 1890

Mon cher Maître et ami,

Do you think that I might be of service as head of the organ class at the Conservatoire?

The succession to César Franck is a heavy burden.

In any case, I would be obliged for whatever is within your power to do for me in this circumstance and for your advice regarding this matter.

I think I will be supported readily enough on the side of the Beaux-Arts which subsidizes my organ school

But M. Ambroise Thomas, although very friendly, hardly knows me as either a teacher or musician. You alone can be, towards him, the deus ex machina.

Eugène Gigout

Gigout then managed to play the organ at Franck's funeral, even though it would have been more appropriate for the organ to have remained silent. During the offertoire he played Franck's *Cantabile*, unflatteringly described by Louis Vierne as "too fast and without expression."[51]

Franck was buried in the Montrouge Cemetery but his body was exhumed on September 19, 1891 and moved to a marble tomb in Montparnasse Cemetery. A group of pupils, led by Augusta Holmès, raised funds for a monument and commissioned the great sculptor, Auguste Rodin, to design and execute a bronze medallion to be set into the side of a large stele. Rodin fashioned a three-quarter profile bust of Franck below which is a rough treble clef and staff with "Béatitudes" written above it. The medallion was completed in 1891 and installed on the tomb in 1893.[52]

---

[51]Vierne, *Mes Souvenirs* (Paris: Les Amis de l'Orgue, 1970) 26. These were originally published in a series of articles in *L'Orgue* from September 1934 to September 1937.

[52]Danièle Gutmann, "Rodin et la Musique," *Revue Internationale de Musique Française* (February 1982) 105

In 1898 Vincent d'Indy formed a committee with himself as president, which included Massenet, Reyer, Fauré, Pierné, Tournemire, and others, to supervise the building of a Franck monument. By October the committee commissioned the sculptor Alfred Lenoir, to execute a statue of César Franck. The little park in front of Sainte-Clotilde, previously allocated for a statue of Alphonse Daudet, was approved for the Franck project by the Paris city council—which even subscribed 500 francs. In 1904 the beautiful statue of Franck at the organ was dedicated.

Plate 25. César Franck at the Organ, Monument by Alfred Lenoir in the Square Samuel Rousseau

Six Pièces d'Orgue

Introduction to the *Six Pièces*

In attempting an informed performance of the works of César Franck over a hundred years after his death, organists are confronted with two major obstacles: contemporary instruments and a nineteenth-century performance style marked by non-metronomic rhythm and rubato.

For years foreign organists have visited France and basked in the glorious sounds of Cavaillé-Coll organs, have consistently programmed the music written by nineteenth-century composers inspired by those instruments, and yet have seldom required organbuilders to provide them with the proper stops in the proper place for the execution of this literature.

The subject of nineteenth-century performance practice is only recently becoming a cause among organists. In other fields, especially the piano, studies of recordings and students' writings have gone on for quite some time. In *Toward an Authentic Interpretation of the Organ Works of César Franck*[1] I compiled firsthand references to Franck, the organs he played, and the writings and recordings of Charles Tournemire, his student and eventual successor as organist of the Church of Sainte-Clotilde. This study will focus on points of execution including tempi, registration, dynamics, console control, touch, phrasing, fingering, and pedaling.

The *Six Pièces*, Opuses 16–21, were published by Maeyens-Couvreur in 1868 and were reissued by Durand & Schoenwerk in 1880. Franck's subsequent organ music was all published by Durand: the *Trois Pièces* in 1883 and the *Trois Chorals* in 1891. All twelve works were re-engraved and issued in a new, horizontal format in four volumes by Durand in 1956. This has been reprinted

[1]Rollin Smith, New York: Pendragon Press, 1983.

by two American publishers (Kalmus and Dover[2] in excellent, inexpensive editions on fine paper. Since the original, vertical Durand edition is out-of-print, we will refer here to the 1956 edition. The errors in this edition have been collated by David Craighead and Antone Godding and were published in *The American Organist* in April 1985. An emended list of these corrections is found at the end of each chapter.

Durand's new *Édition originale,* as it is fraudulently and confusingly advertised, was necessitated by S. Bornemann's publication, in 1955, of the Franck organ works edited by Marcel Dupré. At the time, Dupré was the most respected organist in the world, for, in addition to being an internationally famous virtuoso and esteemed composer, he was professor of organ at the Paris Conservatoire. Viewed today, his four-volume edition of Franck's organ works promotes some negative features. Dupré added what he considered to be "appropriate phrasing" and "necessary ties between notes," "suppressed all unnecessary ties," indicated "registration . . . and rational dynamics suited to modern instruments," consistently omitted the Hautbois from all foundation stop combinations, eliminated or changed dynamic markings, translated indications from French into Italian, omitted fermatas, and tied all "common notes." The result is that it is impossible to determine what Franck originally wrote. The following list of differences between the Durand edition and Dupré's Bornemann edition of the second movement of the *Fantaisie in C* is sufficient to illustrate Dupré's tamperings with the text.

The beginning registration of the *Allegretto cantando:*

Durand		**Bornemann**	
R.	Flûte, Bourdon, Trompette 8	R.	Trompette
P.	Flûte	P.	Flûte 8
G.O.	Flûte	G.O.	Flûte
Péd.	Flûte 8 et 16	Péd.	Bourdons 16, 8

Inconsistencies appear in Dupré's Bornemann edition in the following measures:

---

[2]Mineola, N.Y., 1987.

Dolce is omitted at the beginning	
8	*diminuendo* should appear in m. 7
9	omits fermata and *crescendo* and *diminuendo* over soprano note
18	omits fermata and *Più f*
21 and 27	omit *p*
49 and 51; 69 and 71	omit *crescendo* and *diminuendo*
59 and 16	omit *rf* over last left-hand eighth note
63–64	omit *Dim.*
74	omits *molto cresc.*
77	omits *Cresc.*
79	omits *f*
81	omits *Dim.*
84 and 89	omit *pp*
87	omits fermata
90 and 99	left hand marked I (G.O.) instead of continuing on Positif
94 and 101	left hand returns to Positif on second eighth note
98	omits *Tirasse du G.O.*
122 and 123	omit *crescendo* and *diminuendo*
124	*Rall.* should appear in previous measure

Even though one may criticize it, Dupré's edition remains a valuable pedagogical tool, similar to the many editions of the works of Chopin and Liszt, filled with imaginative solutions to technical problems.

Other editions of Franck's organ works have appeared which, in the main, interpret the registration to suit instruments of the country of their publication. These include the C.F. Peters' German edition (1919), G. Schirmer's American edition (1923), and the Novello English edition of the early 1950s. Today, organists' interest in historical interpretation makes these nationalistic concerns obsolete. A four-volume oblong urtext edition by Günter Kaunzinger, published in 1990–1991 by Schott includes notes that incorporate textual emendations published in my 1990 series of articles in *The American Organist,* as well as variants between the manuscript and the Durand edition.

Throughout this book the writings and recordings of Charles Tournemire (1870–1939) will be cited. He studied for one year with César Franck in his organ class at the Paris Conservatoire and in 1898 succeeded Gabriel Pierné as organist of Franck's church, Sainte-Clotilde. In his book, *César Franck*,[3] Tournemire discusses each of Franck's organ works, gives suggestions for interpretation and supplies metronome markings. The pertinent chapters have been translated into English and are to be found in the author's *Toward an Authentic Interpretation of the Organ Works of César Franck*.[4] Tournemire recorded Franck's *Pastorale, Cantabile, and Choral III*;[5] these performances will be examined for points of interpretation.

Tempo

In general, tempi can be determined by a composer's metronome markings (lacking in Franck's organ music), the speed at which others have performed the works, examining the score and picking a tempo that "feels right" based on the composer's directions and musical content, analyzing the music for internal relationships, and by consulting historical information about the composer and his students. The intrepid organist will employ all of the above in arriving at appropriate tempi.

As an aid in choosing appropriate tempi in Franck's organ music, there will be listed, in addition to those of Tournemire, the metronome indications of three noted French organists: Marcel Dupré (1886–1971), André Marchal (1894–1980), and Jean Langlais (1907–1991). All were trained in Paris and as-sociated with many students, friends and contemporaries of César Franck. Whatever their artistic differences, each of these men's style was formed by performance practices of the late nineteenth century, thus making their interpretations relevant, and the frequent similarities of their tempi suggest a certain speed at which each piece adapts most comfortably in perform-ance. Dupré includes metronome markings in his Franck edi-tion;[6] Marchal won the Grand Prix du Disque in 1959 for his

[3] Paris: Delagrave, 1931.
[4] Pages 81–94.
[5] Polydor 566059 12" Sides A and B: *Pastorale* (Recorded: April 4, 1930.)
 Polydor 561047 10" Sides A and B: *Cantabile* (Recorded: 1931.)
 Polydor 566057 12" Sides A and B: *Choral III* (Recorded: April 4, 1930.)
 Polydor 566058 12" Side A: *Choral III* (conclusion) (Recorded: April 4, 1930.)
[6] Paris: S. Bornemann, 1955.

recording of the complete organ works of Franck;[7] Jean Langlais's earlier and more representative complete Franck recording was issued by the Gregorian Institute of America in 1964.[8]
Unless otherwise specified, these are the sources for the
metronome markings that will be cited.

Touch

In all of the music of César Franck absolute legato is the
norm. Legato touch was the ideal sought by his contemporaries
and students:

> When there are neither slurs nor dots above the notes it is under-
> stood that the piece should be played in legato style, which is the
> true way [*véritable manière*] of playing the organ. . .
> Alexandre Guilmant[9]

> Legato playing is best suited to the organ, for, by the very essence
> of the instrument, the evenness of all the notes in the same register
> quite naturally calls for precisely connecting these notes one after
> the other.
> Louis Vierne[10]

We know, further, from Karen Hastings's painstaking transcriptions from the Braille of Franck's fingering and pedaling in
his edition of Bach's organ works made in 1887 for the National
Institute for Blind Youths,[11] that he was thoroughly proficient with
finger and foot substitution and glissando, perhaps, even at times,
too much so. This evidence indicates that he not only sought absolute legato but knew how to achieve it.

---

[7]These were recorded at the Church of Saint-Eustache in November and
December 1958 and issued on Erato LDE 3069/70/71; reissued in 1994 on Compact Disc, Erato 4509.9428.2.
[8]M 108/109/110; S 108/109/110. It was copyrighted in 1963, so it was recorded
that year or earlier. It has been reissued on Compact Disc, GIA 272.
[9]Alexandre Guilmant, "La Musique d'Orgue," *Encyclopédie de la Musique et Dic-
tionnaire du Conservatoire*, Deuxième Partie (Paris: Delagrave, 1926) 1157.
[10]Louis Vierne, "Renseignements Généraux pour l'Interpretation de l'Œuvre
d'Orgue de J.-S. Bach," (Paris: Éditions Maurice Sénart, 1924) v.
[11]Karen Hastings, "New Franck Fingerings Brought to Light," *The American Organist* (December 1990) 94–97.

As with all great music that has endured in the repertoire, Franck's organ music is open to many interpretations. The information here is intended as a guide for making appropriate choices in the performance of these works.

CHAPTER II

Fantaisie in C, Op. 16

Composed:	1854–1863
Published:	1868
Publishers:	1. Maeyens-Couvreur, 1868
	Plate no: JB.161
	2. Durand & Schoenwerk, 1880
	Plate no: D.S. & Cie. 2679
	3. Durand & Cie., 1956
	Plate no: D. & F. 13.791
Dedication:	à son ami Monsieur Alexis Chauvet
Manuscripts:	Bibliothèque Nationale, Cons. Ms. 8564 (1),
	8564 (2), October 1863, 8564 (3); Rés F 1418

The *Fantaisie in C* is the first of César Franck's *Six Pièces* and stands as the last of three versions of the work made by him over a ten-year period; its genesis has been detailed by Jesse Eschbach and Robert Bates in their *Fantaisie für die Orgel in Drei Versionen.*[1]

Franck first played this *Fantaisie* during the last week of August 1856 when he demonstrated an organ built for the Cathedral of Saint-Michel in Carcassonne, on exhibition in the erecting room of Cavaillé-Coll's organ factory.

> The interpreter, M. César Franck, an excellent organist, highlighted all the [organ's] riches and tonal resources, first with a knowledgeable performance of serious music, very well written by himself, and then with brilliant improvisations.[2]

This organ was unique for its period in that it had two expressive divisions: a Grand-Récit of eleven stops that included strings

---

[1] Bonn-Bad Godesburg: Rob. Forberg, 1980.
[2] Henry Blanchard, "Auditions musicales," *Revue et Gazette musicale de Paris* (August 30, 1856) 247–48

and 16' 8' and 4' chorus reeds, and an eight-stop Petit-Récit of softer flutes with duplicate Trompette, Hautbois, and Voix humaine.

The second version of the *Fantaisie* is dated October 1863 and may have been the Andante whose "rich sonority was admired . . . [as] played by Franck on the foundation stops"[3] at the inauguration of the organ at Saint-Sulpice in April 1862. Its four movements consist of a new eighty-two-measure *Quasi lento* followed by an eight-measure *Animez beaucoup,* an *Allegretto cantando,* a *Quasi lento,* and an *Adagio.* The version of the *Fantaisie in C* prepared for publication by César Franck joins the opening fifty-six-measure *Poco lento* of Version I to the *Animez beaucoup* and the following three movements of Version II.

After all of this shifting, sorting, adding, and deleting, it is surprising to learn that a third version exists that appends to the initial *Poco lento* of the published version an entirely new *Allegretto non troppo.* Eschbach and Bates speculate that this version, shorter than the published one, may have been prepared by Franck to be played by himself at the inauguration of the organ of the Cathedral of Notre-Dame-de-Paris on March 6, 1868.

Plate 26. Alexis Chauvet

Alexis Chauvet (1837–1871), to whom the work is dedicated, was a fervent defender of the polyphonic tradition and one of the first neo-Classic organists of the French school. Nicknamed "le

[3]Charles Colin, "Réception du Grand Orgue de Saint-Sulpice," *La France musicale* (May 4, 1862) 137–38.

petit père Bach," he played Bach more than any other Parisian organist. He won first prize in the organ class of François Benoist at the Paris Conservatoire in 1860 and some time before that succeeded Franck's brother, Joseph, as *organiste accompagnateur* at Saint-Thomas-d'Aquin. He was organist of Saint-Bernard-de-la-Chapelle by 1863, Saint-Merry in 1864, and La Trinité in 1869. His chronic tubercular condition was aggravated by the nine-week siege of Paris during the Franco-Prussian War and he died the very day France was forced to surrender, on January 28, 1871.

Franck and Chauvet played together on four inaugural organ recitals: at the Chapelle de Jesuits, rue de Sèvres (1862), Saint-Denis-du-Saint-Sacrament (1867), Notre-Dame-de-Paris (1868), and La Trinité (1869).

The freshness of the *Fantaisie* is evident from the outset. We are so far removed from the mid-nineteenth-century Parisian organ world that it is almost impossible to appreciate fully the genius of this music. Nothing like it preceded it and certainly no one up to that time, not even Boëly, understood the organ's serious capabilities as did César Franck. He was the first to realize the potential of Cavaillé-Coll's symphonic organ and to have the talent, originality, and imagination to subdue and submit it to his artistic purposes.

By 1863, the date of the completed manuscript of the published version of the *Fantaisie*, Franck had presided over his new organ at Sainte-Clotilde for almost four years. This and all his subsequent organ works were registered with this forty-six-stop organ in mind. Had this organ not been his model, the choice of stops would have been essentially the same, given the uniformity of the specifications of Cavaillé-Coll's instruments.

Poco lento.

Tournemire	♩ = 66	Without dragging, obviously not strictly [or inflexibly]
Dupré	♩ = 76	
Marchal	♩ = 60–63	
Langlais	♩ = 76	

The registration indicated for this opening movement is as follows:

Registration	Sainte-Clotilde
R(écit). Fonds de 8 pieds et Hautbois	8 Flûte harmonique 8 Bourdon 8 Viole de gambe 8 Basson-hautbois
P(ositif). Fonds de 8 pieds	8 Montre 8 Flûte harmonique 8 Bourdon 8 Gambe 8 Salicional
G(rand)-O(rgue). Fonds de 8 pieds.	8 Montre 8 Flûte harmonique 8 Bourdon 8 Gambe
Péd(ale). Fonds de 8 et 16 pieds.	16 Contrebasse 8 Flûte
Claviers accouplés	Récit au Positif Positif au Grand-Orgue
Tirasses	Grand-Orgue au Pédale Positif au Pédale

To clarify the basic terms:

Fonds de 8 pieds: all 8′ flue stops except celestes.

Péd. Fonds de 8 et 16 pieds: flue stops of 8′ and 16′ pitch. Franck's organ at Sainte-Clotilde had only one rank of open flue pipes at each pitch.

Claviers accouplés: all manuals coupled together at unison pitch.

Tirasses: pedal couplers; from the verb, *tirer,* "to pull," because the manual keys, and all stops drawn on their division, are pulled down. When Tirasse is printed, but no manuals are specified, all are coupled to the pedal.

Because at measure 41 Franck writes, *Ajoutez les jeux d'anches du R* . . . (Add the *jeux d'anches* of the Récit . . .), he would have had to draw them, or "prepare" them, before beginning to play. Twenty years later he would have written *Anches preparées,* the term then used by French organ composers. In addition to the *Fonds de 8 pieds et Hautbois* he would have drawn the *jeux d'anches* (4′ Flûte octaviante, 2′ Octavin, 8′ Trompette and 4′ Clairon) but, because the wind, controlled by the pédale de combinaison, would not yet be admitted to the chest, these stops would remain silent until the combination pedal was depressed.

The *Fantaisie* begins with the most characteristic sound of the Franck organ works: the Récit *Fonds de 8* to which is added the Hautbois. Like the majority of French organs, the Sainte-Clotilde Récit had only three 8′ flue stops (the Voix céleste was not used in ensembles) and an erroneous assumption has been made that Franck added the Hautbois to make a fourth 8′ stop—the corollary being that if he had had more 8′ stops he would not have added the reed. Franck added the Hautbois not to "beef up" the division—it did not add any appreciable weight or body to the sound—but to allow the sound of the Récit to penetrate the tonal texture of the other manuals to which it was coupled so that the opening and closing of the swell shutters created an effective crescendo and diminuendo that permeated the whole organ. This phenomenon works on organs that have enough foundation stops on the other manuals to mask the closed Récit. Without the Hautbois the effect of the coupled Récit in the ensemble would have been negligible.

This is the "basic" Franck sound on which most of his music is played: it is not easy to duplicate on modern instruments and often we must couple at least two manuals, if not all three, to get more stops to interact with the Hautbois. In this instance it may be better to treat the organ as a two-manual instrument, always playing on the Positif to which the Récit is coupled, going to the Great when the Positif is indicated and adding the Great Principal to simulate the effect of the introduction of the third manual.

At m. 17 (*a Tempo*), the hands move to the Grand-Orgue, the left hand playing the tenor, the right hand the alto, and in the Pédale, with all three manuals coupled to it, is heard, on 14 ranks of 8′ pitch, the head of the canon at the octave—a broad sound, indeed!

The pedal line at Example 1, together with the *crescendo* direction

Ex. 1, mm. 39–40

brings up the ever-present problem of the literal interpretation of nuances that appear in the printed score. The swell pedal on mid-nineteenth-century Cavaillé-Coll organs was an iron ratchet pedal that looked so much like a spoon that it was actually called a *pédale à cuillère*. The swell shutters were kept tightly closed by a strong spring so that the organist's foot had to be kept on the pedal to open them for subtle gradations of *crescendo* and *diminuendo*. There were two notches in the right side of the slot in which the pedal moved so that the swell shutters could be held either half-open or fully-open. If the foot were removed from the pedal and it were not hitched into a notch, the swell shutters would slam shut. Ergo: an agile left foot technique was quickly acquired by the expressive organist.[4]

In the pedal passage cited above, the left foot must take over from the right foot on the first beat and the remainder of the passage must be played by the left foot—a maneuver more awkward than difficult. That Franck was well aware of this technical problem, but that his need for the *crescendo* was so strong at this point, is evident in his first version of this *Fantaisie* (Example 2) where, at the peroration he writes a double-pedal on one beat. The pedaling is Franck's:

Ex. 2, *Fantaisie*, Version I, mm. 341–42[5]

Notice that Franck moves the *crescendo* and *diminuendo* to the last measure, so that the right foot could be free to manipulate the swell pedal.

---

[4]When I mentioned to Jean Langlais the impossibility of preserving a legato pedal line in Franck's music when faithfully keeping the right foot on the old fashioned pédale à cuillère, the first prize winner in Marcel Dupré's organ class quipped, "Oh, perhaps you'd like a knife and fork, too!" The witty reply betrayed a greater allegiance to the organ playing rules codified by his teacher, Dupré, than to preserving aspects of a nineteenth-century style inherited directly from César Franck's own students.
[5]Eschbach-Bates, Franck: *Fantaisie für die Orgel in Drei Versionen*, 25.

With the return of the first section at m. 41 the first registrational change occurs: "Add the *jeux d'anches* of the Récit and the 16′ Fonds." The words "*jeux d'anches*" have two meanings and their translation into English, and even their use in French, creates a misunderstanding. It is true that *jeux* (stops) and *anches* (reeds) means, literally, "reed stops." But when we read *Jeux d'anches* in nineteenth-century organ registration directions it refers to the *jeux de combinaison* activated by the *pédales de combinaison* (combination pedals) that control the *ventil* or wind supply to the chest upon which are set those stops designated as *jeux d'anches*, i.e., flue stops above 4′ pitch, including mutations and mixtures, and the chorus reed stops: 16′ Bombarde, 8′ Trompette, and 4′ Clairon. This is true for *all* Cavaillé-Coll organs and the music of Franck, Widor, Vierne, and their students. Some composers were more specific and wrote *jeux d'anches de 8′* (as did Franck in his *Choral III*) or *de 8′ et 4′* but in the music of Franck, unless he specifically indicates a pitch, it means all the stops on that chest. In this instance, at m. 41, it means to depress the *pédale de combinaison* labeled *Anches Récit* which was to the right of center of the Sainte-Clotilde console and generally would have been depressed by the right foot. It would have brought on all previously prepared stops. These would have been:

4′ Flûte octaviante	8′ Trompette harmonique
2′ Octavin	4′ Clairon

When Franck played this piece on the Carcassonne organ he had a 16′ Bombarde on the Grand-Récit; at Saint-Sulpice and Notre-Dame he had not only a 16′ Bombarde but also mixtures and cornets. On most other average-sized Cavaillé-Coll organs he would have had just these four stops to add. Conscientious Franck players now face the dilemma of whether to duplicate the registration available to Franck on the organ at his church or to expand the tonal palette as Franck himself did when playing his music on other organs. Should players choose the latter solution, they must temper their enthusiasm and limit the choice of stops to those which Franck would have used. High-pitched, reiterating mixtures would be as foreign to Franck's music as the sound of Cavaillé-Coll's organ to Bach's.

Having dispensed with the *jeux d'anches*, we have yet to add the *Fonds de 16 pieds* (16′ foundation stops). These include the 16′

Montre and 16′ Bourdon of the Grand-Orgue and the 16′ Bourdon of the Positif.

At m. 41 the upper voices of each hand are tied from the previous measure, the left foot is jumping down to middle C of the pedalboard and the right foot has moved from the expression pedal over to depress *Anches Récit*. Franck would have needed assistance to draw these three stops. In fact, to actualize his precise intent he would have needed two assistants, as the 16′ stops of the Grand-Orgue were on the left side of the console and that of the Positif on the right!

The upper voice of m. 43 is printed:

Ex. 3, m. 43

but should probably agree with m. 3 and the manuscript's m. 43, as well as Version I, m. 345, and Version III, m. 43:

Ex. 4, m. 43

The final eight measures of this movement have eight interpretive indications:

m. 57	The swell box must be fully open on the first beat rest as we begin the *Animez beaucoup* (with great animation).
m. 58	*Ôtez anches du R.* Release the *Anches Récit* combination pedal, thereby silencing any stops on that chest.
m. 59	*Retenez.* Ritard.
m. 60	The swell box must be closed enough on the second and third beats so that the *crescendo* on the fourth beat is audible.
	Express. Expressively…and *crescendo* on beat 4.
m. 61	*Diminuendo*

mm. 62–63	Maintain the basic tempo lest the *ritard* begin too early and its effect be diminished.
m. 63	*Rall.* (Ritard).
m. 64	*Crescendo* on the last soprano note of the fourth beat.

Allegretto cantando.

Tournemire	♩ = 76 Very flexibly
Dupré	♩ = 69
Marchal	♩ = 80
Langlais	♩ = 72

The Trompette of the Récit was Franck's preferred solo stop and it is used here for the first of five times in his major organ works. In spite of its finesse and flexibility the Trompette (harmonique) was quite powerful, but with "...a light, clear, smooth quality."[6] The Flûte harmonique and Bourdon of the same division rounded it out. The Récit solo is both accompanied by and heard in dialogue with the Flûtes harmoniques of the Positif and Grand-Orgue.

Agile left-foot pedal technique is required again throughout this movement. Even in the first pedal entrance:

Ex. 5, mm. 709

the right foot is providing expressive nuances while the left foot leaps down a fourth—subtly articulated rather than detached. Franck's organ works abound in this detail of articulation: a slight separation of the bass notes played with one foot.

Time and again throughout this delightful exercise in invertible counterpoint Franck extends a motivic element by repeating it:

[6]Joseph Bonnet, "Preface," César Franck: *Three Chorals for Organ,* arranged, edited, and annotated by Joseph Bonnet (Glen Rock, N.J.: J. Fischer & Bro., 1948) 2.

Ex. 6, mm. 19–22

He will often vary it dynamically, but he leaves the rhythmic variations to the interpreter. In this example, the characteristic nucleus

Ex. 6a

is to be played with more emphasis the second time. Think of it as though there were a slight fermata over the motif:

Ex. 6b

The most characteristic element of Franck's works is the expanded phrase in which the motif is repeated three times in an ever-expanding range.

Ex. 7, mm. 23–25

The tonal center is E-flat and its is introduced by an ever-enlarging triad: first from the F above, then A♭, and, finally, the climax of the phrase, C. The A♭ should be slightly emphasized; the high C emphasized more. This phrase should be interpreted thusly each time it appears.

Franck had exceptionally large hands that could easily span a twelfth. Reaches such as those in the left hand of Example 8 are not uncommon in his music:

Ex. 8, mm. 28, 30, 112, and 114

There is often a solution for players with small hands. In the above example the last upper left-hand note in each measure can be played with the right thumb:

Ex. 9

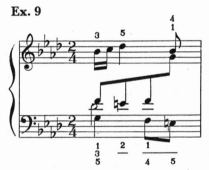

Passages such as Example 10 are unique to the organ:

Ex. 10, mm. 59–61

When two or more voices are played, their tones are sustained as two instruments playing together would be, and yet, because they are being played on the same keyboard, they must use common notes for the same melodic material. The notation of one part must always be compromised for that of the other. At m. 59 the right hand imitates two flutes accompanying the Récit Trompette. The first flute sustains the C♯ while the second executes the countermelody around it. If we repeat the sustained C♯ every time the moving sixteenth-note figuration runs into it, we hear the following:

Ex. 11

This has the effect of destroying the half-step dissonance at A, the whole-step dissonances at C and D, and making B sound:

Ex. 12

With each note articulated we hear the following:

Ex. 13

Under the fingers of a fastidious organist the passage now loses all of its harmonic interest. All close non-chord tones disappear and at D we hear a unison passage with no upper neighboring tones.

The alternate solution is to favor the sustained C♯ and not repeat it each time the sixteenth notes run into it:

Ex. 14

Because of the precision with which Franck's scores are notated we know that he was not unconcerned with the accuracy necessary for cleanly executed performances and, as any good musician, would have let his ear decide the interpretation of a passage. Three of Franck's contemporaries published rules on this point:

Alexandre Guilmant:

> When a part forms an important figuration above or below a sustained part, it will be useful to repeat the note so that the moving voice will be heard.[7]

Charles-Marie Widor:

> The progression of one part running into a neighboring part in no way alters its value. The [C♯] remains tied and the alto merges with the sustained note. Otherwise the effect would be [as at A, B, C, and D] and the listener would be misled.

Louis Vierne:

> Every time the clarity of the text requires it, a tied note must be momentarily let up until the figuration that interferred with it has passed.[9]

Quasi lento.

Tournemire	Simply, emphasize the big chords.
Dupré	♩ = 63
Marchal	♩ = 76
Langlais	♩ = 66

Before beginning the sixteen-measure section that bridges the *Allegretto* and *Adagio,* Franck had to make eighteen registrational

---

[7]"La Musique d'Orgue," 1157.
[8]Charles-Marie Widor, "Preface," *Jean-Sébastien Bach—Œuvres complètes pour orgue,* Vol. I (New York: G. Schirmer, 1914) v–vi.
[9]"Renseignements Généraux," vii.

changes: fifteen stops (five on each manual) had to be drawn and two couplers and a tirasse had to be depressed! General pistons were unknown—listeners were used to long pauses between movements.

To render faithfully the three-measure *diminuendo*, which concludes in the penultimate measure (Example 15), Franck would have played the first two measures (mm. 12–13) with the left foot alone while closing the swell pedal to the first notch, played the first three notes of m. 14 with the right foot, and taken the remainder of the pedal part with the left foot while the right foot returned to the swell pedal to close the box by the beginning of m. 15.

Ex. 15, *Quasi lento*, mm. 12–16

Adagio.

Tournemire	The concluding infinitely calm *Adagio* rejects metronomic rhythm. Thank God! Retrospection . . . contemplation . . . that is the *Adagio*.

Dupré	♪ = 52
Marchal	♪ = 54
Langlais	♪ = 54

Franck's registration for the last movement of this *Fantaisie* is:

R. Voix humaine, Bourdon, Flûte et Gambe de 8 pieds.

P. Bourdon de 16 pieds

Péd. Bourdon de 16, 8 et 32

Accouplement du R. au P.

No mention is made of the *tremblant* (tremulant), and the point must be raised whether or not Franck intended it to be drawn with the Voix humaine for this movement. There can be no doubt that from the devotional character of this *Adagio*, and the fact that the Voix humaine was inseparable from the tremblant in nineteenth-century France, *not* to have drawn the two stops together would have been the exception—as, for instance, in the *Andante* of Saint-Saëns's second *Rhapsodie Breton* where, for a particularly rustic effect, he directs: *Ajoutez la voix humaine sans tremblant* (Add the Voix humaine without the tremulant). Indeed, the Voix humaine *demands* the tremblant, for, as Dom Bédos points out, "without the tremblant it does not truly imitate the human voice."[10] To cite but a few instances in which the finest organ composers of the second half of the nineteenth century called for only the Voix humaine, but assumed its conventional use with the tremblant: Saint-Saëns, *Rhapsodie sur des Cantiques Bretons*, Op. 7, No. 1, *Élévation ou Communion*, Op. 13, *Sept Improvisations*, Op 150, No. 3; Charles-Marie Widor, *Adagio, Symphonie IV;* and César Franck later in his *Fantaisie in A* (1878). These composers were all writing and registering for organs in a country in which the tradition of drawing the two stops together was firmly established and documented through the written instructions of their predecessors Guillaume Nivers (1665), Nicolas Lebègue (1676), André Raison (1688), Jacques Boyvin (1689), Gaspard Corrette (1703), Dom Bédos de Celles (1770), and J.P.E. Martini (c.1850). The organbuilder Aristide Cavaillé-Coll pointed out that the tremblant "is the chief factor in determining the quality of the Voix humaine."[11]

Pedal registration in this *Fantaisie* is a veritable catalog of stop nomenclature. In the first and third movements Franck calls for *Fonds de 8 et 16;* in the second, *Flûte de 8 et 16;* and in the last, *Bourdons de 16, 8 et 32. Fonds* and *Flûte* are synonymous with the 16' Contrebasse and 8' Flûte on the Sainte-Clotilde organ, but the *Bourdons* were stopped flue pipes and, curiously, were not in the pedal division of Franck's organ. The open flue stops gave the pedal line a definition unobtainable from the more nebulous, indeterminate tone of the Bourdon.

Throughout this *Adagio* the left hand doubles the pedal line. The *Tirasse Récit* (Swell to Pedal coupler) was seldom available on French organs in the 1860s. Cavaillé-Coll usually provided it only on his two-manual consoles: the mechanism was easy to build and it increased registrational flexibility. Without the Tirasse, the

---

[10]Dom Bédos de Celles, *L'Art du facteur d'orgues*, Part 3, Chapter IV, No. 16.
[11]Letter of August 21, 1857, in Fenner Douglass's *Cavaillé-Coll and the Musicians* (Raleigh: Sunbury Press, 1980) 367.

Récit could be coupled to either the Grand-Orgue or to the Positif and thus brought down to the Pédale through the Tirasse of *that* division. This duplication of notes is advantageous in a passage such as:

Ex. 16

where the right foot must remain on the expression pedal and the left foot must execute the bass line alone. Because the part is played also in the left hand, an absolute legato line is not missed—it is enough that the sub-octave pitch is provided.

Franck was precise in his tying of notes. The sustaining or repeating of certain notes lends interest to the several repetitions of the theme. For instance, near the end, when the passage goes to the Positif and the 16' Bourdon is added, the inner voices of the manual parts are tied—but not when it is repeated. To try to correct the text or second-guess the composer is unnecessary.

The *Fantaisie in C* is actually a triptych, each of its three main movements being in ternary form. In its approximately thirteen minutes duration it ably demonstrates the organ's potential: the broad foundation tone of the first movement, the clear duo of the *Allegretto* with the Trompette and Flûtes thrown into relief by the full swell of the bridge section, which introduces the ethereal *Adagio* on the Voix humaine. In short, it is a skillfully wrought piece, not technically difficult, and easily comprehended by general recital audiences.

Corrections for the 1956 Durand Edition

P: page; S: score; M: Measure

P	S	M	
3	1	2	tie soprano G to m. 3; slur l.h. to m. 3
3	4	2	*diminuendo* should be marked from m. 2 into m. 3
3	4	3	b. 1, lowest voice should be G (not F)
5	2	5	l.h. last A♭ is an eighth note
5	3	5	r.h. tie A♭s
9	2	7	r.h. add slur from C to F
9	3	6	add registration change: *Ôtez la Tirasse*
10	3	1	pedal tied from preceding score (incorrect only in Kalmus reprint)
12	3	1	add *crescendo* and *diminuendo* indications

Plate 27. Charles-Valentin Alkan

CHAPTER III

Grande Pièce symphonique, Op. 17

Composed:	before September 16, 1863, the date of the completed manuscript.
Published:	1868
Publishers:	1. Maeyens-Couvreur Plate No: JB.162 2. Durand & Schoenwerk, 1880 Plate No: D.S. & Cie. 2680 3. Durand & Cie., 1956 Plate No: D. & F. 13.791
Dedication:	à Monsieur Charles-Valentin Alkan
Manuscript:	Stiftelsen Musikkulturens Främjande, Stockholm, Sweden No. MS 880212 (acquired in 1977).
Performances:	Played by the composer on November 17, 1864, in a recital of is own compositions at Sainte-Clotilde. Played by the composer on October 1, 1878, at the 13th Séance de l'Orgue in the Salle des Fêtes of the Palais de Trocadéro.
Bibliography:	Gary Verkade, "César Franck: *Grande Pièce symphonique:* Some Aspects of Form," *The Diapason* (January 1993) 11–14.

From the *Fantaisie in C* Franck moved, for his second organ work, to the most harmonically remote key, F-sharp minor/major: a tritone. The *Grande Pièce symphonique* is his longest organ work, lasting about twenty-five minutes. It is important to view this work in perspective to understand its place in organ literature. The great nineteenth century organ works in extended form are:

Felix Mendelssohn	*Six Sonatas,* Op. 65 (1844–45)
Franz Liszt	*Fantasy and Fugue on the Chorale "Ad nos, ad salutarem undam"*(1850)
Julius Reubke	*Sonata in C Minor: The 94th Psalm* (1857)
César Franck	*Grande Pièce symphonique,* Op. 17 (1863)

The last three works emerged within little more than a decade, all of them requiring around half an hour of playing time, all conceived in a single movement and all cyclical in their use of thematic material. Of these works, it is unquestionably Franck's which, as Norbert Dufourcq pointed out,[1] is the connecting link in organ music between the classical sonata and the symphony. Indeed, Widor's first *Symphonies,* Op. 13, appeared four years after Franck's work was published in 1868.

Franck entitled this, his first large-scale work in sonata form, a "Symphonic Piece." He did not call it a symphony, and consequently, he gave himself more freedom in its organization, in particular, in the placement of a slow movement before and after the scherzo. The *Grande Pièce symphonique* is cyclical in that the principal theme of the *Allegro* (minor) is transposed into the major for the *Grand-Chœur* movement, is the basis of the fugue subject, and recurs in the repetition of themes at the recapitulation. None of the themes is combined with any other and none is transformed, in the Lisztian-Wagnerian sense, except for the principal theme eventually stated in the major.

The work is divided into four sections, each separated by the composer (as pointed out by Gary Verkade) by double bar lines:

I. An Introduction (*Andantino serioso*), followed by the *Allegro non troppo e maestoso* in sonata form;

II. *Andante* and an *Allegro* in the relative minor;

III. A Beethovenian recapitulation, reminiscent of the introduction to the *Finale* of that composer's *Ninth Symphony,* in which all the themes heard up to that point are briefly recalled; and

IV. *Beaucoup plus largement* (*Grand-Chœur* and Fugue-Final).

[1]*César Franck* (Paris: La Colombe, 1949) 117.

What might be regarded as a preliminary study for this Op. 17 was the *Pièce symphonique* completed September 13, 1859.[2] A relatively short organ work, it nevertheless contrasts an exposition composed of two themes in G minor with a cantabile section, it has a development in which the themes are combined with a jig-like fugue subject, and it concludes with an abridged version of the exposition. It is, in many respects, equal to the larger, more celebrated work which, for this reason, may have been distinguished with the prefix *Grande*.

In dedicating this work to Charles-Valentin Alkan (1813–1888) Franck was paying tribute to a friend and colleague who was the first to write a symphony for a solo keyboard instrument. Nine years older than César Franck, Alkan was born the same year as Wagner and Verdi. His Jewish heritage placed him in a unique position in the French Catholic organ world.[3] Trained as a pianist, he won first prize at the Paris Conservatoire at the age of eleven. Later he won a first prize in organ and pursued a career, not only as pianist and teacher (the wife of Théodore Dubois, Franck's maître-de-chapelle at Sainte-Clotilde, had been his pupil) but also as a performer on the pédalier, or pedal piano, on which he played many of Bach's major organ works. In fact, many of these works were thus heard for the first time in France.

Franck called Alkan the "Poet of the Piano" and their lives intersected many times. He was one of the jurors when Franck competed for the first prize in piano at the Paris Conservatoire and overstepped the rules in the sight-reading examination by transposing the test piece. In 1846 he attended the first performance of Franck's oratorio, *Ruth*. Together, they were in the audience at Saint-Vincent-de-Paul in February 1853, when Jacques Lemmens inaugurated the new organ there. In 1857 Alkan published *Twelve Etudes in Minor Keys*, Op. 39, numbers 4, 5, 6, and 7 of which comprised a half-hour symphony for piano solo. By September of 1863

---

[2]*L'Organiste*, Vol. 2, No. 26.
[3]He was appointed organist of the Paris Temple in 1851, just before the new Cavaillé-Coll organ was completed, but resigned soon afterward. His career as a professional organist was short-lived. See Gérard Ganvert, "Alkan, musicien français de religion juive," *Charles-Valentin Alkan*, edited by Brigitte François-Sappey (Paris: Fayard, 1991) 263–81.

Franck had finished his own symphony for organ, the *Grande Pièce symphonique,* and dedicated it to Alkan. The next year Alkan's *11 Grands Préludes et une transcription du Messie* ("Thy rebuke hath broken" and "Behold and see"), Op. 66, were composed and dedicated to Franck. The volume was published about 1865. Thus, Alkan's dedication appeared first, since Franck's work was not published until 1868. In 1889, the year after Alkan's death, Durand published Franck's arrangement for organ of ten excerpts from Alkan's *Préludes* and *Prières.*[4]

Andantino serioso.

Tournemire	♩ = 69, with grandeur and emphasis.
Dupré	♩ = 72
Marchal	♩ = 76
Langlais	♩ = 80–84

In addition to the *Fonds de 8 pied* (8′ foundation stops) on all manuals, with the Récit Hautbois and 16′ in the pedal, the *jeux d'anches* (those stops activated by the *Anches pédale de combinaison* of each manual) must also be prepared. The Anches are introduced during the four measures preceding the *Allegro non troppo e maestoso* at m. 60.

Each of the three *Quasi ad libitum* passages is marked differently: (1) mm. 6–9 have neither tempo changes nor dynamic markings; (2) mm. 15–20 have a *rallentando* at the end of mm. 16 and m. 19, a *più forte* in m. 17, and a *più dolce* at m. 19; (3) mm. 196–201 of the *Allegro non troppo* have a *rallentando* beginning on the second half of m. 198 (as well as a *crescendo* and *diminuendo*), leading into the *Molto lento* of the last measure.

Does Franck expect the player to interpret a *rallentando* in the first of these passages where none is indicated? Probably, since "*quasi ad libitum*" connotes rhythmic variation, and, with the next

[4]Robert Parkins, in *The Organ Yearbook 1989,* Vol XX, p. 127, described Gérard Billaudot's modern reprint: "The texture of these pieces is highly pianistic with numerous octave doublings and unidiomatic chordal dispositions. Most of them would doubtless sound better played on the piano...The music itself is characteristically banal, but peppered with strange twists of harmony that seem awkward rather than progressive. Most organists will find these works too naive, sentimental, and devoid of real substance to be of much use...."

statement of the principal theme at m. 10, he has written *a Tempo*. A fourth passage (in the *Allegro non troppo*), almost identical to the others, is not marked *quasi ad libitum* (mm. 120–23) and a *ritard* may not have been intended, since the passage leads into an *accelerando poco a poco*.

In the last two passages a pedal point is sustained while the hands play on the Récit. Ostensibly, all pedal couplers are on—an effect that on many organs, whether in France or elsewhere, will need adjustment through the removal, at least, of the Great to Pedal.

On the second beat of m. 35 the right hand joins the left on the Grand-Orgue. Simultaneously, the *jeux d'anches* of the Récit are activated and all of the 16′ foundation stops of the organ are drawn. At Sainte-Clotilde these included the Bourdon of the Positif and the Montre and Bourdon of the Grand-Orgue. Obviously, it was imperative to have a stop-puller, inasmuch as the player could not negotiate all of these changes between two beats.

A counterpart to the "expanded phrase" discussed previously in connection with the *Fantaisie in C* is the triple sequence (Example 1) frequently encountered. From m. 37:

Ex. 1, mm. 37–39

to four measures later:

Ex. 2, mm. 43–45

and continuing directly into:

Ex. 3, mm. 46–48

Pregnant as each of these phrases is with possible interpretative nuance, both the player and listener would become emotionally overwrought and lose the feel for the broad sweep of this work if the performer succumbed to overstatement. It would be better to continue the forward movement of the piece rather than to attempt any momentary interruption. By m. 50 this propulsion has established itself so firmly that the composer ceased the eighth-note figuration altogether and reiterated the four-note motif four times (Example 4), the last two in augmentation.

Ex. 4, m. 50

With Cavaillé-Coll's registrational system based on pedal movements, it is a simple procedure to add successively the Anches ventils of each manual in such a way as gradually to attain full organ (*Ajoutez successivement les jeux d'Anches à chaque clavier de façon à arriver graduellement au Grand-Chœur*). The combination pedals were laid out so that a crescendo was achieved as the foot depressed them successively from right to left. In the space of sixteen beats the organist could build from the initial registration, augmented at m. 35, to full organ, or *Grand-Chœur*, at the beginning of the *Allegro non troppo*.

Allegro non troppo e maestoso.

Tournemire	♩ = 80
Dupré	♩ = 84
Marchal	♩ = 76
Langlais	♩ = 76

Abbé Kurthen, writing in *La Tribune de Saint-Gervais*,[5] perceived a similarity between Franck's declamatory opening:

[5]Abbé W. Kurthen, "César Franck et son œuvre d'orgue," *La Tribune de Saint-Gervais* (April 1913) 105–10; (May 1913) 132–39.

Ex. 5, m. 1

and the "fate" motif in Beethoven's *Quartet,* Op. 135, his last work, composed when Franck was four years old.

Ex. 6, m.

The principal theme of the movement, and the one that recurs five more times, making a cyclical work of the *Grande Pièce symphonique,* is:

Ex. 7, mm. 5–14

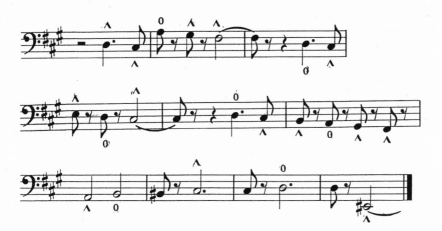

Frank settled the question of phrasing this pedal solo played on the full organ by separating most of the notes with eighth-note rests. The degree of *marcato* or *legato* applied to the other notes will depend completely on the acoustics of the room in which it is played. How the sixth measure of this theme (Example 8) is phrased has been left undecided by the composer. Should it be played as written, i.e., *legato:*

Ex. 8, mm. 11–12

or *marcato?*

Ex. 9

As with so many stylistic alternatives in music, the decision lies with the interpreter.

The theme is immediately restated in the soprano (m. 15) but the same three notes are now harmonized. All of the lower voices are repeated, so they would sound *marcato* anyway, but should the soprano line be played *legato* or, because of the closed-voicing of the chord, be better played thusly?

Ex. 10, mm. 21–22

Again, the player must make the decision.

At m. 25 the hands move to the closed Récit and the theme is developed in three parts. Full organ is retained and there is the question of 16′ tone in the Récit division. Franck's Récit at Sainte-Clotilde had no 16′ stops and, since most of this section lies in the middle or lower octaves of the keyboard, 16′ tone is not essential. Players must remember that if any of the 16′ stops of the Swell are included in the full organ, they should be withdrawn at m. 25 and reintroduced at m. 54.

The only *legato* statement of the principal theme, from m. 58 to m. 74, is accompanied by four-part eighth-note chords separated by eighth-note rests. The previously discussed ascending phrase A-B-B♯ recurs at mm. 64–65 (Example 11). A completely *legato* phrasing of this statement is now appropriate and it is noted that André Marchal and Jean Langlais kept the soprano line *legato* and the lower voices *marcato*, with an unmistakable *tenuto* on the B♯ on the first beat of m. 65.

Ex. 11, mm. 64–65

The reeds of the Grand-Orgue are released at m. 82 (*Ôtez les Anches du G.O.*), removing the upperwork, reeds, and mixtures from that manual. Franck did not indicate the removal of the Anches Pédale but it is difficult to imagine that a battery of 16′, 8′, 4′ pedal reeds would not be overpowering throughout the eight-measure pedal point beginning at m. 98. This is one of those rare instances in Franck's organ music in which a registrational correction is recommended: remove the pedal reeds before m. 98.

The addition and subtraction of the Grand-Orgue reeds between mm. 106 and 111—an orchestral effect, the equivalent of a chord suddenly played by the brass choir—was totally new and unique in organ literature when Franck introduced it. For him, nothing could have been more convenient than, with a movement of the ankle, to depress and release the Anches du G.-O.; the pédale de combinaison was located above the pedalboard's middle D on the Sainte-Clotilde organ console.

While Franck removed the anches from every division except the Récit (*Ôtez tous les jeux d'Anches excepté ceux du R.*) at m. 112, he omitted reference to the tirasses (pedal couplers). With the hands playing on the closed Récit, the five-measure pedal point on low A with all manuals coupled to the pedal will be unsatisfactory on most organs. However, whatever pedal couplers are taken off for this section, they must be put back on at mm. 124–125 in preparation for the pedal entry at m. 155.

Franck incorporated the triplet motif of the *Quasi ad libitum* into this section by developing the principal theme under an accompaniment of broken triads in triplet rhythm. This scherzando section grows out of the *Quasi ad libitum,* first in a solo motif:

Ex. 12, mm. 24–25

then with the addition of a second part, in groups of two-measure phrases. The tempo gradually accelerates to that of the original *Allegro* ♩ = 80. The 16′ stops have not been taken off, so the theme, played on the Positif at m. 133, includes the weight of the Positif 16′ Bourdon.

The right-hand accompanimental triplet figuration is not easy to play, expecially for small hands, as it soon expands from a nervous

Ex. 13, mm. 133–34

to reaches of a tenth:

Ex. 14, mm. 137–40

The difficulty is compounded by the addition of a second voice at m. 150:

Ex. 15, mm. 150–51

Practicing in various combinations of dotted rhythms and in a slow tempo will enable the player to gain both the required relaxation and velocity.

At m. 195 the pedal F♯ is marked *ppp* and is sustained under the *Quasi ad libitum* played on the Récit Fonds et Hautbois. Again, no mention of taking off pedal couplers is to be found in the score. At this point all pedal couplers should be removed.

Andante.

Tournemire	♩	= 60, not strictly observed.
Dupré	♩	= 60
Marchal	♩	= 58
Langlais	♩	= 48

The first slow movement of this symphonic piece is a comfortable andante, not an adagio or lento; notice the similarity of tempi of three of the four organists. The *Franckiste* will not fail to notice that this movement is in B major, a key to which Franck was particularly partial and, as Vincent d'Indy pointed out, "a key invariably favorable to his inspiration."[6] Some of his most notable works were in B major: the *Trio*, Op 1, No. 3 (1841), the *Ballade*, Op. 9, for piano (1844), the *Cantabile* for organ (1878), and the *Larghetto* of the *String Quartet* (1889).

The solo melody of the *Andante* is played on the Cromorne, the only instance in which Franck calls for this stop. It is the traditional French "orchestral" reed. Cavaillé-Coll retained it in his rebuilds of older instruments and maintained its position on the Positif where, inexpressive, its tone was acidic, yet plangent. Franck filled it out with the addition of the 8′ Bourdon and Flûte harmonique and accompanied it with the Fonds et jeux d'Anches (foundation and all stops on the Anches chest) of the Récit. This registration was the equivalent of the full Swell: 8′ Flûte, Bourdon and Gambe, 4′ Flûte octaviante, 2′ Octavin, 8′ Trompette and 4′ Clairon, a mélange that comments as much upon the effectiveness of the swell box as upon the power of the solo stop. Tournemire wrote[7] that Franck frequently improvised on the Clarinette [Cromorne] at Sainte-Clotilde and invariably accompanied it with the foundation stops and Trompette of the Récit. He described the Cromorne's tone as harsh and added that Franck "drowned" (*noyait*) it with the Trompette, Hautbois, and Bourdon of the Récit.[8] We thus have three descriptions of how Franck interpreted *Fonds et jeux d'Anches* as an accompaniment, all of which, in my own experience, work on the organ of Sainte-Clotilde.

The hands play only on the Récit and Positif; the Grand-Orgue with two 16′ stops and four 8′ stops is coupled to the Pédale's 16′ and 8′ open Flûtes. Eight stops provide the bass, further evidence of the tonal idiosyncrasies of the Sainte-Clotilde organ. It goes without saying that such registration will have to be adjusted on the organ at hand. There may be no need to couple the Grand-Orgue to the Pédale and the swell box may not close down enough for the Cromorne/Clarinette to use all of the stops indicated for that division.

No phrase marks appear. Did Franck intend the four-bar phrase to be played as an unbroken legato melody?

[6]d'Indy, *César Franck*, 119.
[7]Tournemire, *César Franck*, 55.
[8]Charles Tournemire, *Précis d'exécution, de registration et d'improvisation à l'Orgue* (Paris: Max Eschig, 1936) 104.

Ex. 16, mm. 1–4

The next four measures provide the answer: mm. 5–6 are played on the Récit, mm. 7–8 on the Positif. Franck felt the melody as two phrases and voiced the second on a contrasting combination. Two-measure phrases continue throughout the movement.

The upper voice in mm. 16 and 36 is notated ambiguously.

Ex. 17, m. 16

Ex. 18, m. 36

Are the second and third beats to be played on the last note of each triplet, as printed, or are they to be played two-against-three?

Properly notated, if they are to be played on the last of each triplet, a quarter rest is missing before each eighth. If they are to be played as two-against-three, an eighth rest is missing.

Since the first beat of each measure sets a pattern of the second eighth note tied to the first note of a triplet, we might assume that the succeeding beats should be interpreted likewise. But, notice in m. 30

Ex. 19, m. 30

that the first beat has an eighth note tied to a triplet and the third beat is notated in triplet rhythm with its last eighth tied to a triplet.

A logistics decision on the part of the engraver (by crowding three voices on one staff (in mm. 16), because he was unable to move the eighth note any further to the left without running into the beams of the lower voice, is improbable since Franck notated these passages in exactly the same way in his manuscript. A different distribution of parts would have provided a possible solution:

Ex. 20, m. 16

While it cannot be said that the conclusion is obvious, the evidence of m. 30 points to a triplet interpretation of the second and third beats of mm. 16 and 36. Since Franck was precise in notating his scores, and was an excellent proofreader, it may be considered that he intended these passages to be played exactly as printed, particularly since he notated passages similarly in the *Fantaisie in A:*

Ex. 21, mm. 54 and 221

Discophiles will note that André Marchal played mm. 16 and 36 as twos-against-threes; Dupré and Langlais, on the third triplet.

An alternate toe pedaling from mm. 9 and 12 is easily executed and eliminates the wasted motion of unnecessary substitution:

Ex. 22, mm. 10–11

Allegro.

Tournemire	♩ = 96, but quite reserved
Dupré	♩ = 120
Marchal	♩ = 104
Langlais	♩ = 100

The "Scherzo Allegro," as Tournemire referred to this *Allegro*, is played on Franck's most bizarre registration: the 8′ Flûte, Bourdon, Hautbois, and 4′ Clairon of the Récit coupled to the 16′ Bourdon, 8′ Bourdon and Flûte of the Positif, a sound reminiscent of the harmonium and one not far removed from Dom Bédos de Celle's formula for a French classic duo's, left hand: 16′ Bourdon and Montre, 4′ Clairon.[9]

The basic touch of this scherzo is *Très lié* (very legato). The 16′ Bourdon of the Positif is on throughout (lacking one in that divi-

---

[9]Dom Bédos de Celle, *L'Art du facteur d'orgues*, Part 3, Chapter IV, No. 3, g.

sion, a 16′ flue in the Swell or Great may be substituted), and the swell box is kept closed, *pp*, throughout the entire movement. This is the only movement in Franck's organ works devoid of expression marks.

In the penultimate measure, the Récit Clairon 4′ was probably taken off by the pédale de combinaison; later, it will be reintroduced with the 8′ Trompette added to it.

Andante.

Franck was obviously so captivated by the beautiful theme of the *Andante* and the key of B major, that, not having exhausted all of its possibilities, he decided to write another movement utilizing this material. Twenty measures shorter than the first *Andante*, this, nevertheless, rivals it in loveliness. His reverie in B major extended to his registration: Voix célestes on the Récit and Positif and coupled together, an orchestral effect not at his disposal when this work was published in 1868. At best he would have coupled his Récit Voix céleste (which extended only to tenor C) to the Positif Salicional and Gambe. He was familiar with the organs of Saint-Sulpice (1862) and the Cathedral of Notre-Dame (1868), both of which had an Unda maris on the Positif as well as a Voix céleste on the Récit, but these were the only two organs at the time with more than one set of undulating ranks.

Franck could have taken off the 32′ pedal stop at m. 8 by playing the three-note chord on beat 3 with the left hand and retiring the stop as the extreme right of the console, but at m. 15 a registrant would have been required to draw it back on.

There is no final solution to playing the following pedal passage *legato:*

Ex. 23, m. 10

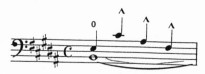

The skip from A♯ to F♯ is hardly noticeable.

Allegro non troppo e maestoso; Andante serioso; Allegro non troppo; Allegro; Poco lento; Andante.

The tempo of each of these themes, presented successively, is the same as indicated in the previous movements.

Just before the fourth section, the *Allegro,* a new set of registration directions is given. The Récit Viole de gambe is removed and the 4′ Clairon added; the Positif Montre, Salicional, and Gambe are removed and the 16′ Bourdon added. Coupler directions include only the Récit au Positif; the Positif au Grand-Orgue is, therefore, removed (it is again drawn two measures before the next Andante but only after the Récit stops have been changed) and with it, the coupling of both the Récit and Positif to the Pédale. With only the Grand-Orgue coupled to the Pédal during the Allegro, the pungent B-minor arpeggiated figuration is supported by a sonorous bass of broad foundation tone.

From the last four-measure statement of the *Andante* on the Récit Voix céleste, Franck built to full organ, initially giving himself three beats of rest to draw stops. Ultimately he put down the pédales de combinaisons and by changing manuals, quickly achieved the *Grand-Chœur.*

Grand-Chœur.

Tournemire	♩	= 80, in a grandiose and solid manner
Dupré	♩	= 120
Marchal	♩	= 116
Langlais	♩	= 116–120

The finale of Franck's symphonic piece might have been entitled *Grand-Chœur and Fugue,* for it begins with an extremely heroic statement of the now familiar principal theme. It is heard for the last time, in the major, harmonized in six-note chords above what Tournemire described as "the beautiful serpentine figure in the pedal."

Ex. 24, mm. 1–5

The tempo indication is confusing: *Beaucoup plus largement qu'à page 3* (Much slower than [the *Allegro non troppo e maestoso*] at page 3). The *Allegro* on page 3 is notated *alla breve* (Tournemire suggested ♩ = 80). The Grand-Chœur is notated in common meter 4/4, and Tournemire's suggested tempo is exactly one-half of the *Allegro:* ♩ = 80.

Irregular pedaling occurs within this brief section, brought on by the key of F-sharp major, and the occurrence of three black keys in succession. The strangest may be the following:

Ex. 25, m. 21

This is a rare instance in organ literature in which the heel plays a black pedal key. This pedaling, suggested by Marcel Dupré, is logical and easily executed because of the position of the right leg and the location of the two black keys on the pedalboard.

Franck was aware of using alternate toes on three consecutive black keys and, because this is not uncommon, a brief digression might not be out of order to examine its execution. Example 26 would, more than likely, be pedaled as suggested by Jacques Lemmens:[10]

Ex. 26, m. 25

Yet Charles-Valentin Alkan (to whom this *Grande Pièce symphonique* is dedicated), in his *Prière in F Major,*[11] (Example 27), a work arranged by Franck for organ in 1889, pedaled a similar passage:

Ex. 27, m. 11

While Franck did not reproduce Alkan's pedaling, it could not have escaped his attention.

Playing with alternate toes on three successive pedal sharp keys is discussed in an organ method by the celebrated American organist, Clarence Eddy.[12] He pedaled the B major scale:

Ex. 28

[10]Jacques-Nicolas Lemmens, *École d'orgue.* (Bruxelles: Schott, 1862). Originally published in two parts in 1850 as *Journal d'orgue.*
[11]No. 11 of *Treize Prières,* Op. 64, for organ, piano à clavier de pédales, ou piano à 3 mains (Paris: Richault, c. 1864) 61.
[12]*A Method for Pipe Organ* (New York: The John Church Co., 1917) 34.

The left toe passes *over* the right foot at G♯ ascending, and the right toe passes *under* the left foot at F♯ descending (particular care being taken to place the left toe far back on the G♯ with the heel very high). Utilizing this system of pedaling, m. 25 would be played as follows:

Ex. 29, m. 25

(*Fugue*).

Tournemire   ♩ = 60
Dupré   ♪ = 120
Marchal   ♪ = 120
Langlais   ♪. = 116

Franck's score had no tempo change indicated, but Tournemire suggested that it be played considerably faster than the *Grand-Chœur*. Players often tend to continue at about the same tempo.

The trill in m. 54 is begun on the principal note.

All three manuals of Franck's organ at Sainte-Clotilde coupled to the Grand-Orgue at the sub-octave. These couplers, as all registrational devices, were activated by the pédales de combinaison. At m. 69, *Péd: des 8ves graves à tous les claviers* (16′ couplers on all manuals), is to be interpreted "all manuals coupled at 16′ pitch to the Great." Of course, this includes the 16′ stops, so there is considerable 32′ tone generated. Franck took this effect into account: notice how little of the music of the last three pages descends below middle C.

For those who have difficulty articulating double notes, (Example 30), or whose right hand tenses with the excitement generated during performance, the following exercises (Example 31), based on the teaching of Alfred Cortot, may be of help. It is imperative to use the same fingering in the exercises as is used in performance of the piece.

Ex. 30, m. 75

Ex. 31

From the *a Tempo* at m. 111 Tournemire advised to "gradually broaden the tempo," yet there is no ritard indicated at the end. This may well have been the effect that Franck intended since we encounter it again in the *Final,* another piece that ends with well-spaced repetitions of the tonic chord.

It is impossible to touch on every facet of performance of so important a work as this, but there is one musical gesture that must be discussed. A noticeable characteristic of Charles Tournemire's playing on recordings is a certain emphasis (an almost imperceptible *tenuto*) given to an eighth note following a dotted quarter and a sixteenth note following a dotted eighth. Rushing these short notes is a common fault; their unhurried articulation is one of the things that distinguishes a truly elegant performance. The two examples that follow are sufficient to illustrate this point in both fast and slow tempi. The asterisk marks those notes that are to receive a slight emphasis.

Ex. 32, *Allegro non troppo e maestoso,* **mm. 5–8**

Ex. 33, *Andante,* **mm. 1–4**

The *Grande Pièce symphonique* remains one of Franck's popular organ works, and Alfred Bruneau's description of it, included in a review of Albert Mahaut's all-Franck recital at the Trocadéro, leaves little else to be said:

> The *Grande Pièce symphonique,* the most imposing and magnificent of the *Six Pièces,* is a vast monument of song, cyclopean in architectural design, and yet decorated with the most delicately carved friezes; a huge cathedral standing before us serene and strong, a scene for human action and triumph.[13]

---

[13]*Le Figaro,* April 29, 1898.

Corrections for the 1956 Durand Edition

P	S	M	
19	3	3	original has no tie in soprano to m. 4
19	3	4	original has no tie in soprano to m. 5
19	3	4	alto E should be E♯; original has no tie in alto to next page
24	3	4	r.h. should be repeat of m. 3 (beat 3 is incorrect)
26	4	4–5	pedal: slur D, C♯, B
28	1	3	no *forte* dynamic indication in original
28	2	9	alto C♯ should be a dotted quarter
28	3	2	original has no tie between soprano F♯s
29	2	1	l.h. tie B from beat 2 to 3
29	3	2	l.h. last triplet eighth note appears to be E♯ in original
30	1	1	tie pedal C♯ from previous page
30	1	3	l.h. tie A♯ to next measure
31	2	3	cautionary F^{x} in alto on beat 4
33	3	8	l.h. last sixteenth note is B (not G)
34	1	1	pedal slur continues from previous page
34	1	2	r.h. first note is B (not D)
35	3	5	fingering: lowest notes in l.h. should be marked 5–5–5
36	1	6	r.h. G should be an eighth note
36	2	1	l.h. tie B from beat 1 to 2
36	2	2	l.h. tie B from beat 1 to 2
36	3	3	l.h., beat 1, lowest note should be D♯ (not F♯)
36	3	4	add *crescendo* mark into first measure next page
37	1	1	slur over upper pedal notes terminating in m. 4, beat 1
39	3	3	P. should be R. instead (both hands are to play on Récit)
39	3	7	In the manuscript *Très lent* is written over the rest on beats 3–4
41	3	1	r.h. last eighth should be C (not A♯)
42	2	7	r.h., b.4, G♯ is tied to b.1 of following measure in the manuscript
42	2	7	alto should have *staccato* dots as in tenor

CHAPTER IV

Prélude, Fugue et Variation, Op. 18

Composed:	c. 1862
Published:	1868
Publishers:	1. Maeyens-Couvreur, Plate No: JB.163
	2. Durand & Schoenwerk, 1880, Plate No: D.S. & Cie. 2681
	3. Durand & Cie., 1956, Plate No: D. & F. 13.791
Dedication:	à son ami Monsieur C. Saint-Saëns
Performances:	Played by the composer on November 17, 1864, at Sainte-Clotilde.
Arrangement:	For orgue-expressif et piano
Published:	1868
Publishers:	1. Maeyens-Couvreur
	2. Durand & Schoenwerk, 1880, Plate No. D.S. & Cie. 2686
Dedication:	à ses élèves Mademoiselles Louise et Geneviève Deslignières
Manuscript:	Bibliothèque Nationale, Cons. Ms. 1835 Donated by Vincent d'Indy.
Performance:	Played by the composer (harmonium) and Vincent d'Indy (piano) on February 7, 1874 at a Société Nationale concert.

This is Franck's most popular organ work, rivaled only by the more dramatic but, in many respects, less technically demanding, *Pièce héroïque*. The appeal of the *Prélude, Fugue et Variation* lies in its primitive, naive, yet penetrating charm. Franck's consummate mastery of trio writing has transformed what could have been a compositional or technical study into a bittersweet essay, admired by players and audiences for the emotion it evokes. The work's popularity is evidenced by its numerous transcriptions, including

Plate 28. Franck (*standing, second from right*) and Saint-Saëns (*playing piano*). Members of the jury examining scores submitted for the City of Paris' first musical competition, February 13, 1878

two by the composer (two pianos, four hands, and harmonium and piano).

The *Prélude, Fugue et Variation* is dedicated to Camille Saint-Saëns, twelve years younger than César Franck, who, like him, was a child prodigy and piano virtuoso, and a prizewinner in the organ class of François Benoist at the Paris Conservatoire. While Franck was organist of Saint-Jean-Saint-François, Saint-Saëns was organist of Saint-Merry, ten blocks away; Franck left to become organist of Sainte-Clotilde only a few weeks before Saint-Saëns went to the Madeleine. They both played on the inaugural recitals of the most notable Parisian organs: Saint-Sulpice (1862), Notre-Dame Cathedral (1868), La Trinité (1869), and the Trocadéro (1878). They were among the founders of the Société Nationale de Musique in 1871, and Saint-Saëns always insisted that he had been responsible for Franck's appointment as professor of organ at the Paris Conservatoire in 1872. Franck's *Quintet* was dedicated to Saint-Saëns and premiered by him. Finally, he was one of the pallbearers at Franck's funeral.

Andantino (Prélude).

Guilmant	$\downarrow \cdot$ = 52
Tournemire	$\downarrow \cdot$ = 60
Dupré	$\downarrow \cdot$ = 63 (Recording $\downarrow \cdot$ = 58[1])
Marchal	$\downarrow \cdot$ = 54
Langlais	$\downarrow \cdot$ = 52–54

In addition to the published organ score, we have additional suggestions for performance of this work from Franck's student, Charles Tournemire, his contemporary, Alexandre Guilmant, and Franck himself, in the form of interpretative directions in a duo arrangement for harmonium and piano.

Guilmant had known Franck since the early 1860s, heard him play many times (they had inaugurated three organs together), and was Franck's first champion as an organ composer, regularly including his music on recital programs. In a survey of organ literature Guilmant wrote as an eyewitness:

[1]HMV D 1843. Recorded on the organ of Queen's Hall, London, on March 17, 1930.

Plate 29. Camille Saint-Saëns in 1879

106

Does it not happen, even today, that modern pieces are often played too fast? A piece like *Prélude, Fugue et Variation* of César Franck is often played *Allegro*, although the composer simply marked *Andantino cantabile!* That is misplaced virtuosity! The composer did not play it like that: the tempo was about ♩. = 52 for the *Prélude* and *Variation*, and ♩ = 72 for the *Fugue*.[2]

The difference between the metronome indications of Alexandre Guilmant and his pupil Marcel Dupré are significant because Dupré based (and advertised) his Franck interpretation on the "authentic" tradition he learned from Guilmant. Yet, his tempi are faster than those given by his maître.

César Franck included considerably more editorial markings in his duo version of the *Prélude, Fugue et Variation* than in the original organ solo. This arrangement for harmonium and piano was a present for his pupils Louise and Geneviève Deslignières, daughters of the headmistress of the girls' boarding school in the rue de Martyrs where he taught piano and was later music supervisor. (Franck's wife, Félicité, had been one of his pupils at this school.) Since he was publishing his transcription for amateurs his pedagogical instincts led him to be more liberal with interpretative suggestions that would have been assumed by more accomplished players. All of these textual variants will be cited.

The melody of both the *Prélude* and *Variation* is played on the Hautbois of the Récit—the only instance in Franck's organ works in which the Hautbois is treated as a solo stop—strengthened by the addition of the Bourdon and Flûte harmonique. The accompaniment, for the most part, is played on the Bourdon of the Grand-Orgue, "a remarkably clear and melodious [*chantant*] chimney flute," wrote Maurice Duruflé of that stop on Franck's organ at Sainte-Clotilde.[3] Twelve measures of the accompaniment in the middle of the *Prélude* and the entire *Variation* are played on the Flûte harmonique of the Positif. In addition to the three stops required at the beginning of the piece, Franck would have prepared

[2]"La Musique d'Orgue," 1171.
[3]Maurice Duruflé, "Preface," Charles Tournemire: *Cinq Improvisations* (Paris: Durand, 1958).

107

the 4′ Flûte octaviante, 8′ Trompette harmonique, and 4′ Clairon for their introduction at the *Lento*.[4]

The exquisite melody presents a fine opportunity to demonstrate the rhythmic nuances which were commonly understood by Franck and his contemporaries. One of the frequently encountered conventions in Romantic music is the contrast of identical passages. The first measure (Example 1) of the *Prélude* is played strictly in time so as to establish the basic tempo, but when it is repeated in the second measure, the first beat can be played with a slight *tenuto* and there can be a slight lengthening of the time between the last note (F♯) and the first note (high B) of the next measure.

Ex. 1, mm. 1–3

A slight *accelerando* accompanies the feeling of impatience in m. 5 but the rising sequence of sixteenth notes culminates in a slight *ritard* on beats 8 and 9 as the theme returns.

Ex. 2, mm. 5–6

[4]This is the only instance where Franck specifies the pitches of the Anches.

Measure 8 differs from m. 3 not only in an addition of accidentals (and a consequent tonal change from diminished chord to dominant seventh) but in a subtle *crescendo* and *diminuendo* over the first four beats. The player will have to make another slight *tenuto* here so that the swell box can make its impression. From m. 11 the tempo and dynamic level increases but the forward drive slackens at *Expressivo* (m. 13) and ritards further as the swell box closes at the *Poco rall.* (m. 14).

Tournemire called attention to mm. 16–19—one of those expanded phrases of which Franck was so fond:

Ex. 3, mm. 16–19

It is performed with a slight emphasis on the C# (1); more emphasis on the E (2).

Measures 28–31 is another pedal passage that must be played entirely by the left foot, the right being occupied in manipulating the swell box.

Ex. 4, mm. 28–31

At. m. 39 (and m. 37 in the *Variation)* we are directed to add an 8' or 4' stop to the Pédale *(Ajoutez un jeu de 8 ou de 4 pieds à la pédale).* Because there was only one 8' flue stop in the Pédale of the organ of Sainte-Clotilde, and it was already drawn, Franck coupled either the Positif or Grand-Orgue to the Pédale for these five measures. Had he wished to add a 4' stop he would have begun with the Grand-Orgue coupled to the Pédale (with, or without, the 8' Flûte of the Pédale also drawn) and had the 4' Octave of the Grand-Orgue drawn but not sounding. Depressing the Anches Grand-Orgue where indicated would bring on the 4' Octave and, through the Tirasse Grand-Orgue, cause it to play in the Pédale. The left hand, playing on the Positif, would not be affected. Whatever method of adding the 8' or 4' stop to the Pédale was adopted, it would have been reversed during the pedal rests at beats 8–9 of m. 43. There is no reason why the organist should not follow the phrasing that appears in the piano score: each measure in the bass begins a new phrase.

The following indications do not appear in the organ solo version of the *Prélude:* they were added to the duo for harmonium and piano.

At the beginning, *Doux et expressif* (softly and expressively) instead of *Cantabile.*

m. 2	*sempre legato*
m. 5	b. 4–6 *crescendo;* b. 7–9 *diminuendo*
m. 7	b. 7–9 *crescendo*
m. 8	b. 1–3 *diminuendo*
m. 10	b. 4–9 *crescendo* culminating in *f* at m. 11
m. 20	bass: *Sostenuto*
m. 36	*Très soutenu*
m. 39	bass: *Marquez un peu la basse* (Bring out the bass a little)

Lento.

Tournemire	according to the performer's inner feelings.	
Dupré	♩	= 58
Marchal	♩	= 48–58
Langlais	♩	= c. 66

Before beginning these nine measures a considerable pause would have been made for registrational changes. Having already

Before beginning these nine measures a considerable pause would have been made for registrational changes. Having already prepared the Anches Récit, Franck would now have drawn the remaining 16' and 8' stops on the Positif and Grand-Orgue, coupled the Récit to the Positif, and Positif to Grand-Orgue. Tirasse Grand-Orgue would have been sufficient to have coupled all three manuals to the Pédale.

No tempo fluctuations appear in the score. The swell box is moved once, from *mf* at the beginning to *f* at m. 5.

In the duo version the *Lento* is played *ff* by the piano and concludes thusly:

m. 7	*Rit.*
m. 8	*Dim.*
m. 9	*p diminuendo* to *pp.*

Allegro ma non troppo (Fugue).

Guilmant	♩	= 72
Tournemire	♩	= 88
Dupré	♩	= 88 (1930 recording ♩ = 116)
Marchal	♩	= 88
Langlais	♩	= 100

While many of Franck's organ works have fugal sections, this is the only movement expressly entitled *Fugue.* Phrasing the subject, a theme Tournemire assures us was a particular favorite of Franck's, must be left to the discretion of the player. Dupré, Marchal, and Langlais take the composer's harmonium score direction literally: *Dolce. Toujours très lié, soutenu et expressif* (Softly. Always very legato, sustained, and expressive) and treat the entire eight-measure subject as one long legato line. Tournemire[5] phrased it:

---

[5]Tournemire, *César Franck*, 23.

Ex. 5, mm. 1–8

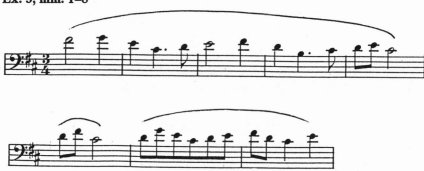

It would not be unreasonable to lift slightly before the F♯ in the third measure.

Those who, as Tournemire wrote, "have lived in the intimacy of Franck's heart," naturally will be inclined to observe the conventional treatment of the expanded phrases in Example 6:

Ex. 6, mm. 5–7

and increasingly sustain the highest note as the intervals grow from a major second to a major third to a perfect fourth. Unless restrained, there is a danger of overworking the subject, but this phrasing is in keeping with the style of the period.

The *Fugue* is registered for the 8′ foundation stops of all three manuals, to which is added the Récit Hautbois. Before beginning Franck would have had to remove only the Anches Récit and the three manual 16′ stops. Although not indicated, the swell box is closed, since the first dynamic mark is a *Cresc.* at m. 36. The addition to the organ score of Franck's dynamic indications in the harmonium score of the duo version in no way runs counter to his intentions. The indications below, from the duo version, are *in addition to* those that appear in the organ solo.

m. 15	*Crescendo*
m. 16	*Diminuendo*
mm. 19–20	*Crescendo*
m. 22	*Diminuendo*
m. 23	*p*
m. 27	Pédale: *Dolce sostenuto*
m. 33	*Cresc . . . . Dim.*
m. 50	*Cresc.* (a measure earlier than in the organ score)
m. 54	*Dim.* begins on b. 3 and extends five measures until
m. 60	b. 1, *p* and *express.*
m. 62	left hand: *Express.*
m. 66	Pédale: *Sostenuto e cresc.*

Franck's fingering at mm. 58–59 (Example 7) does not take into consideration the simple solution of redistributing the inner voices. The left hand's taking the alto C♯, as in Example 8, facilitates the passage by eliminating the awkward passing of the fourth finger over the fifth.

Ex. 7, mm. 58–59

Ex. 8, mm. 58–59 with redistribution of parts

The bass begins the third stretto at m. 66. Assigned to the piano in the duo version, it is played in octaves by the left hand and the last four notes are marked:

Ex. 9, mm. 66–69

The effect is duplicated on the organ by slightly detaching those notes. This has the effect of adding weight to the *En élargissant un peu* (A slight *rallentando* . . . broaden . . . stretch the tempo) without interrupting the flow of the music.

Above m. 77 is written *Ajoutez les Fonds de 16 pieds et les Anches R.* (Add the 16′ foundation stops and the Anches of the Récit). The logical place for these additions is at the end of the measure (before m. 78) rather than during (or before) m. 77. In fact, that is exactly what Franck did in the harmonium score. He began a *Sempre cresc.* at m 77, added the 16′ stops just before m. 78 (both measures can be played by the right hand alone) and added the stops (by the Grand jeu, the harmonium's equivalent of full organ, consisting of 16′, 8′, and 4′ pitches—more or less duplicated on the organ by the addition of Anches Récit) just before m. 79. He then *ritarded* from the second beat of m. 79 and ended the *Fugue ff*.

Andantino (Variation).

Guilmant   ♩. = 52

Tournemire   ♩. = 60 as in the beginning, clearly, unhurriedly and on the tips of the fingers

Dupré   ♩. = 63 (1930 Recording, ♩ = 58)

Marchal   ♩. = 56

Langlais   ♩. = 52–54

For Franck, playing the Cavaillé-Coll organ at Sainte-Clotilde, the transition from the B-minor chord at the end of the *Fugue* to the beginning of the *Variation* was a complicated one, involving considerable time and at least one registrant. Before beginning the six measures of sixteenth notes on the Positif Flûte harmonique, the player, while holding down low F♯ in the Pédale, had to release the Récit au Positif coupler and the Tirasse Grand-Orgue with his right foot, and at the same time push in the other five 16′ and 8′ stops on the Positif. He then could have begun the *Variation* but still would have had to release three more pédales de combinaison:

    1. *Expression Récit* to close the swell box at least halfway so that the expression marks could be observed;

    2. *Positif au Grand-Orgue;* and

    3. *Anches Récit.*

At the same time an assistant took off the 8′ Viole de gambe of the Récit and the five 16′ and 8′ stops of the Grand-Orgue, leaving only the 8′ Bourdon.

More than any other of Franck's organ works, this *Variation* represents the style of the French piano school transferred to the organ, and Reginald Gerig, in his *Famous Pianists and Their Technique* might be describing the exact manner of performing this piece:

> The touch was sensitive, it stayed close to the keys, and it did not press deeply. It also was fluent, deft, immaculate, like a fine etching . . . Behind it was an unruffled emotional spirit which highly valued

such aesthetic graces as elegant, calculated proportions and subtle phrasing.[6]

Most technical difficulties can be overcome by practicing in dotted rhythms, but m. 22 (Example 10) presents a unique problem,

Ex. 10, m. 22

one that is less a matter of moving the thumb around both sides of the C# than in getting the hand repositioned for the last three notes of the figuration:

Ex. 11, b. 1–2   **Ex. 12, b. 2–3**

Those who encounter difficulty with this passage might invent exercises to train the fingers in rapid, lightning-quick movements—reflex actions that, becoming automatic, need not be thought about during performance. These varied rhythmic figurations might be experimented with:

Ex. 13

[6]Reginald Gerig, *Famous Pianists and Their Technique* (Washington: Luce, 1974) 315.

Numerous finger crossings in mm. 25 and 26 can be worked out as in Example 14:

Ex. 14

Addition of 8' or 4' stops to the pedal at m. 37 can be made as discussed at the identical spot in the *Prélude* (m. 39) except that, since the Grand-Orgue is not used in the *Variation*, other 8' registers could be added to the Bourdon to augment it as a solo stop when coupled to the Pédale.

Tournemire suggests a *tenuto* on the first of each sixteenth-note group in mm. 48–49:

Ex. 15, mm. 48–50

The following are additional interpretive directions from the harmonium and piano version of the *Variation:*

m. 1	*Très lié f*
m. 3	b. 3 *Diminuendo* to m. 7.
m. 7	*Doux* (Softly)
m. 11	b. 2 *Cresc.;* b. 3 *Dim.*
m. 16	b. 2–3 *Cresc.*
m. 19	b. 7–9 *Poco rit.*
m. 34	*f Très soutenu*
m. 37	bass: *Soutenu* (Each measure begins a new phrase.)

The *Prélude, Fugue et Variation* is the very essence of French music: clarity of form, simplicity of means, exquisite sense of proportion, intensity of interior life, and true expression of refined feelings, things which Gérard de Nerval said in *Sylvie* were "so naturally French that in listening to them one feels the best of French life and with the greatest pride and the greatest emotion."

Corrections for the 1956 Durand Edition

P	S	M	
51	3		Registration: *P. Fonds de 8 et 16 pieds. Prestant.* (not 4 pieds).
54	2	4	second eighth in soprano should be B (alto remains D)
54	3	1	in original, a dot replaces alto eighth rest, the equivalent of a C♯ eigth note tied from previous measure
59	2	3	l.h. last note of middle group of sixteenths should be D (not B)
61	3	1	l.h. twelfth sixteenth-note is A♯ (not A)

CHAPTER V
Pastorale, Op. 19

Completed:	Manuscript dated September 29, 1863
Published:	1868
Publishers:	1. Maeyens-Couvreur, Plate No: JB.164
	2. Durand & Schoenwerk, 1880 Plate No: D.S. & Cie. 2682
	3. Durand & Cie., 1956, Plate No: C. & F. 13.792
Dedication:	à son ami Monsieur Aristide Cavaillé-Coll
Manuscript:	Bibliothèque Nationale, Cons. Ms. 8562. Donated by Thérèse Chopy-Franck
Performances:	Played by the composer on November 17, 1864 at Sainte-Clotilde.
	Played by Victor Nant on September 3, 1878, at the 7th Séance de l'Orgue at the Trocadéro.
	Played by André Messager on October 8, 1878, at the 15th Séance de l'Orgue at the Trocadéro.

The inspiration for the *Pastorale* may have been the *Allegro moderato* from the *Trente Caprices ou Pièces d'Étude,* Op. 2,[1] for piano by A.P.F. Boëly. Amédée Gastoué noted the striking similarities between its "harmonies and characteristic atmosphere and the first and last movements of Franck's Pastorale."[2]

The *Pastorale* is not program music and has no association with Christmas. It utilizes none of the vocabulary of instrumental motifs created by seventeenth- and eighteenth-century Italian composers for their Christmas pastorales: lilting melodies in triple

---

[1]Paris: Boieldieu jeune, end of 1816 or beginning of 1817; Minkoff, 1986.
[2]Amédée Gastoué, "A Great French Organist, Alexandre Boëly, and His Works," *The Musical Quarterly* (July 1944) 342.

Plate 30. First page of the manuscript of the *Pastorale*

time—usually in 6/8 or 12/8 meter—symmetrical phrases with melodies harmonized in thirds and sixths, and drone basses. Franck's *Pastorale* is bucolic, rustic, and picturesque, but devoid of any literal evocation of a manger scene with posed family, poised angels, adoring shepherds, and bowing magi—an imaginative concept that might have delighted, but surely would have surprised, the composer.[3]

The *Pastorale* is dedicated to Aristide Cavaillé-Coll (1811–99), the most successful and influential French organbuilder during Franck's lifetime, who built or rebuilt some six hundred organs throughout France and whose conception and development of the symphonic organ, including perfection of solo stops, light keyboard action, large swell boxes with infinitesimal possibilities for tonal and expressive nuances, provided the ideal inspiration for Franck and his contemporaries. It is not surprising to find composers paying homage to so powerful and prominent a figure by dedicating pieces to him. Franck's was the first, followed by Guilmant's *Andante con moto* (1865), Widor's *Symphonies*, Op. 13 (1872), and Gigout's *Marche religieuse* (1881).

Plate 31. Aristide Cavaillé-Coll as a young man

[3]As would a recent fantastic interpretation invented by Joël-Marie Fauquet and found in notes for a recording by Belgian organist, Joris Verdin:

Contrary to what one might believe, it was less to Bach's *Pastorale*...that Franck referred when he wrote his own...than to the French romantic organ's imitative tendencies. The city-dweller listening to Sunday high mass would shiver with delight as the organist summoned up the "storms" that were called for by the sensibilities of the times, only to return to calm once more, using the softer stops to conjure up the charms of country life. In Franck's *Pastorale*, reverie gains the upper hand, the storm becoming threatening only in the middle section. Once again, Franck transcends a genre, in which many of his Parisian colleagues confused noise and music.

Cavaillé-Coll had installed a new organ in each of the three churches where Franck played. Unfortunately, at his first church, Notre-Dame-de-Lorette, where he was *organiste accompagnateur,* he played a Somer organ to accompany the choir, rather than Cavaillé-Coll's first organ in Paris, installed in the gallery in 1838; but at his next church, Saint-Jean-Saint-François, he played a quite new Cavaillé-Coll organ, only about five years old. Finally, the Cavaillé-Coll at Sainte-Clotilde, inextricably bound to Franck and his works, was installed in 1859 and played by Franck for thirty years.

Franck participated in the inauguration of seven other Cavaillé-Coll organs in Paris: Saint-Sulpice (1862), Saint-Étienne-du-Mont (1863), Saint-Denis-du-Saint-Sacrement (1867), Notre-Dame Cathedral (1868), La Trinité (1869), the Tocadéro (1878), and Saint-Merry (1878).

Franck and his wife were guests at Cavaillé-Coll's wedding dinner in 1854 and the organbuilder may have been influential in having Franck appointed organist of Sainte-Clotilde towards the end of 1857. An unsubstantiated claim was advanced by Cavaillé-Coll's biographers that he was responsible for Franck's appointment in 1872 as professor of organ at the Paris Conservatoire—supposedly to appease Franck for Cavaillé-Coll's having recommended Widor over him as organist of Saint-Sulpice.

To the composer who created the work, and the organbuilder who created the instrument for which it was conceived, we add the third factor in order to achieve an enlightened performance of the *Pastorale:* a phonograph recording made by Franck's student, Charles Tournemire, on April 30, 1930.

In 1930, at the age of sixty, Tournemire seemed to have undergone a personal Franckian renaissance and, forty years after Franck's death, concerned himself with passing on to posterity his knowledge, feelings, and firsthand impressions of Franck's music. He solidified his legacy from Franck in concrete form; within the year he made 78 rpm phonograph recordings of five of Franck's works on Franck's for-the-most-part unaltered organ at Sainte-Clotilde and, on September 5, finished his book, *César Franck.*

In considering the *Pastorale* we are thus able to compare Franck's performance directions in the score with what Tournemire said in his book and to hear a performance of the piece played by a first generation student of the composer. The music on this recording was performed seventy years after the piece was composed—midway between the middle of the last century and the end of the present one. Those surprised at Tournemire's rhythmic freedom and apparent disregard for the text might note that contemporary critics praised him for his literal interpretations, allowing the music to speak for itself. Such comments merely hint at the freedom of interpretation prevalent among Franck and his confrères.

Andantino.

Tournemire	♩ = 58	(Recording: ♩ = 58)
Dupré	♩. = 60	
Marchal	♩ = 54	
Langlais	♩ = 56	

The *Pastorale* is structured in Franck's much-favored three-part song form, or more specifically, A-B-A^1. Its design is simple: two themes, one rustic in character, the other, more melodic and expressive, answer each other twice at four-bar intervals, then at two-bar intervals and conclude, for the most part, with two-part writing over a twelve-measure dominant pedal point; a central *Allegretto* in A minor introduces an incisive theme which, in passing through different keys, embodies a seventeen-measure fughetta. With the return of the *Andantino* the two initial themes, instead of alternating, are ingeniously combined.

The *Pastorale* presents few technical difficulties for the player. Written for two manuals, it requires but eight stops:

Récit	**Positif**	**Pédale**
8 Bourdon	16 Bourdon	16 Bourdon
4 Flûte	8 Bourdon	8 Bourdon
8 Hautbois		
8 Trompette		

and only two changes of registration—adding and subtracting the Récit Trompette and the Positif au Pédale coupler. The

Pédale registration points to a more generalized stop nomenclature; Franck's organ at Sainte-Clotilde had only open flue pipes in the Pédale—not stopped pipes, or Bourdons. Nevertheless, the composer designated these stops in his registration.

Tournemire's registration on disc differs from that of Franck's: the Hautbois is drawn alone, without the 8' Bourdon and 4' Flûte, and the Récit is uncoupled from the Positif so that, contrary to Franck's directions, the "chorale" passages played on the Positif are heard without expression.

In Tournemire's performance, as the melody rises in mm. 1–2 and 9–10, each upper note is gradually prolonged so that there is a noticeable *tenuto* on the second sixteenth note of the first beat in mm. 2 and 10. At each of the passages played on the Positif, Tournemire slackens the tempo to about ♩ = 44, returning to the Récit *a Tempo*. A *ritard* of at least three beats precedes each fermata but the chords under the fermatas are not sustained any longer than their note values indicate.

Tournemire *ritards* the end of almost every phrase. Specifically, *ritards* not printed in the score are made at mm. 4, 7, 11–12, 15, 18, 22, 37, 39–40, 44, 56, 68, 80 (*poco rit.*), 109, 120, 126, 138, 141, 150, 158, 164, and 166–67.

No phrase marks appear above the chorale-like passages (Example 1) played on the Positif at mm. 5–8 (or the corresponding passage, mm. 13–16). The swell box opens for a *crescendo:*

Ex. 1, mm. 5–7

and then closes abruptly for the *subito pp* at the third beat.

Ex. 2, mm. 7–8

For this sudden *pianissimo* to make its effect all parts must be lifted while the swell box closes. In the corresponding passages in the second *Andantino* (mm. 151–54 and 159–62) the four-bar phrases are under a single phrase mark and no expression is indicated. Tournemire ties the common notes that occur between the lower and upper voices on the third beats of mm. 28–29 and mm. 32–33.

Ex. 3, mm. 28–29

mm. 32–33

At mm. 29 and 33 Tournemire suddenly closes the swell box for an echo effect, opening it slightly for the following measures. A slight *tenuto* is given to the first soprano note in mm. 29, 30, 32, 33 and 34.

Franck closes this movement with the upper voice stated in progressive augmentation:

Ex. 4, mm. 36–40

first in sixteenth notes, then eighth notes and finally in quarter notes. If the player ritards the sixteenth notes (as Tournemire does), the effect of this clever device is lost. It is preferable to let the piece slow itself down.

Quasi allegretto.

Tournemire	♩. = 100	(Recording: ♩ = 120)
Dupré	♩. = 108	
Marchal	♩. = 116	
Langlais	♩. = 108	

The 8′ Trompette is added to those stops already drawn and, with the addition of Tirasse Positif, the Récit stops play through in the Pédale. The swell box is to be opened slightly, since m. 41 is marked *p* and m. 45 begins *pp*. Tournemire plays each measure with increasing volume, then closes the swell box for m. 45. While Tournemire cautions in his book that this section is "generally played at a dizzying speed that completely destroys the balance of the work," he recorded it at ♩ = 120 instead of the ♩ = 100 he recommended. As in the first section, Tournemire's ritards are frequent; here, every six measures. Great emphasis is placed on the left-hand phrase:

Ex. 5, mm. 66–68

Each eighth note is held as long as possible and the last measure is *ritarded* considerably. Measure 69 resumes *a Tempo.*

Beginning at m. 69, and at almost every passage similar to Example 6, Tournemire adds a *sforzando,* immediately followed by a *pianissimo.*

Ex. 6, mm. 69–71

The *legato e cantabile* fugue section that begins with the last eighth note of m. 80 provides relief from the *staccato* section that precedes it. According to Tournemire it should not be played as fast as the preceding section and on his recording he decreases the tempo from ♩ = 120 to ♩ = 100.

At mm. 83 and 93 we again encounter a common note (A) on the first beat and note that Tournemire executes it:

Ex. 7, m. 83

The *Quasi allegretto* resumes at m. 98. The soprano B being tied, the right hand moves to the Positif on the second half of the first beat, following the left hand that moved to the Positif on the first beat. The Récit is still coupled to the Positif and the 16' Bourdon is still drawn on the Positif. Few organists (Dupré among them) can resist the temptation to solo the left-hand melody from m. 127 through m. 147, although Franck specifies that both hands play on the Positif, the right had *sempre staccato,* the left, *cantabile.*

Andantino.

Tempos and registration are the same as those in the first *Andantino.* When the chorale returns at m. 151 (Example 8) it is superimposed over the four preceding measures. What was previously played with two hands is now all taken in the left, while the right hand plays the single-note melody on the Positif 16' and 8' Bourdons to which the Récit is coupled.

Ex. 8, mm. 151–54

This section is easier to play if the hands are reversed. An edition of the *Pastorale* was published by Edwin Ashdown[4] that printed this section:

Ex. 9, mm. 151–52

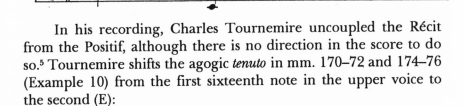

In his recording, Charles Tournemire uncoupled the Récit from the Positif, although there is no direction in the score to do so.[5] Tournemire shifts the agogic *tenuto* in mm. 170–72 and 174–76 (Example 10) from the first sixteenth note in the upper voice to the second (E):

[4]London: Edwin Ashdown, 1941. No editor is credited.
[5]Marcel Dupré directed that all of these Positif solos be played on the Flûte harmonique of the uncoupled Grand-Orgue.

Ex. 10, mm. 170–72

At m. 178 Tournemire omits the high B (dotted half-note) and plays only the lower voice eighth notes. Disregarding Franck's registration, he removes the Hautbois and plays the last measure on the Voix céleste!

Franck's *Pastorale* is a worthy companion to Bach's BWV 590, which Franck later taught when he was professor of organ at the Paris Conservatoire. But while Bach's *Pastorale* is a suite in four movements, Franck's is cast in a Beethovenian three-part form. Noting its song-form, Vincent d'Indy commented upon its special feature, "a completely charming and quite melodic fugal development, comparable to the style evident in the third period of the Master of Bonn."[6]

Louis Vierne wrote that "This artless and tender music, alternating delicate feeling with the profundity of mournful sentiment, reveals the soul of the composer. Such was César Franck, the greatest French musician of the nineteenth century, the finest and saintliest of men."[7]

---

[6]d'Indy, *Franck*, 136.

[7]Vierne, Emended translation of a program annotation for his recital at the Town Hall, Manchester, England, January 8, 1924. Kindly provided by Jean-Pierre Mazeirat.

Corrections for the 1956 Durand Edition

P	S	M	
5	1	1	r.h. lasts two eighth-note chords should have staccato dots below
7	2	2	*simile* does not appear in the original edition nor in the manuscript
7	3	3	tie soprano E to next measure; last alto E lacks eighth flag
8	2	1	l.h. tie A to next measure
8	2	2	slur alto eighths to m. 3
9	1	4	l.h. add dot to D
9	2	5	r.h. fifth chord top note should be F$\sharp$ (not G)
9	3	1	r.h. G-natural not in original edition, but is in the manuscript
12	1	3	fingering: l.h. first sixteenth should be marked 3 as in preceding measure
12	1	4	fingering: l.h. beat 2 lower notes should marked 3–4–5

Plate 32. First page of the manuscript of the *Prière*

CHAPTER VI

Prière, Op. 20

Published:	1868
Publishers:	1. Maeyens-Courveur, Plate No: JB.165 2. Durand & Schoenwerk, 1880, Plate No: D.S. & Cie. 2683 3. Durand & Cie., 1956, Plate No: D. & F. 13.792
Dedication:	à son maître Monsieur Benoist
Manuscript:	Bibliothèque Nationale, Cons. Ms. 8563 Donated by Thérèse Chopy-Franck, June 20, 1947.
Performances:	Played by the composer on November 17, 1864 at Sainte-Clotilde. Played by Albert Mahaut on July 5, 1889, for the organ jury at the Paris Conservatoire. He was awarded first prize.

The *Prière*, Franck's most profound organ work, is dedicated to François Benoist and, perhaps, was inspired by a work of Alexandre P.F. Boëly. Both men were held in high regard as "artists who respect their art and do not prostitute our organs with barcarolles, contradanses, galops, waltzes, and polkas."[1]

Although not a historically established "form," the prière was a genre that few nineteenth-century organ and piano composers ignored. Saint-Saëns published one in 11/4 meter for harmonium in 1858; Jacques Lemmens included one that became quite popular in his *Méthode d'Orgue* in 1862; Franck's, undeniably the greatest, was completed in final draft in 1863; and Charles-Valentin Alkan published thirteen (*Treize Prières*, Op. 64) around 1864.

---

[1]Félix Danjou, "Chronique départmentale," Toulouse: L'Inauguration de l'orgue de Saint-Sernin, *Revue et Gazette musicale* (July 13, 1845) 232.

César Franck, in his *Prière*, has achieved what would seem to be impossible in a piece for a solo instrument: he has maintained a consistently high level of composition and sustained musical interest for nearly a quarter of an hour and, at the same time, created a devotional atmosphere.[2]

A *Larghetto un poco sostenuto* by A.P.F. Boëly[3] may well have served Franck as a model for his *Prière*. An emotionally charged slow movement in C-sharp minor entitled *Style Moderne*, it seemed to Amédée Gastoué "to provide the exact inspiration and atmosphere, even the same harmonies, from which sprang the central episode of Franck's *Prière*."[4]

Plate 33. François Benoist

François Benoist (1794–1878), to whom the *Prière* is dedicated, had been Franck's organ teacher at the Paris Conservatoire. A student at the Conservatoire himself, Benoist won first prizes in piano and harmony and the Prix de Rome in 1815. His return to Paris four years later coincided with the death of Nicolas Séjan, and Benoist succeeded him as organist of the Chapelle du Roi and, two weeks later, as professor of organ at the Conservatoire Royale. He held the latter

[2]The reverence with which the Franckistes approached this *Prière* and testimony to the manner in which the "Franck tradition" was transmitted is exemplified in the following recollection of Jean Langlais: Once I had the extreme audacity to ask the great Albert Mahaut to play for me the *Prière in C-sharp Minor*, a work whose style always seemed extremely difficult to express. "You came too late, my dear," was his reply. And he added, "I promised myself no longer to play after I was seventy-five years old—and here I am." Then I asked "Would you let me play this work for you?" "No, and for the same reason as I just gave, I don't think I have the right to give advice any longer." What unfortunate and admirable wisdom. (Jean Langlais, "Propos sur le style de César Franck dans son œuvre pour orgue," *Jeunesse et Orgue* [Automne 1978] 6.)
[3]*Collection Œuvres Posthumes, Douze Pièces*, Op. 43, no. 8 (Paris: Richault, 1860).
[4]"A Great French Organist, Alexandre Boëly, and His Works." *The Musical Quarterly* (July 1944) 324.

post for fifty-three years—so long that it was jokingly said that three republics and two empires lived and died under him!

Benoist was a marvelous improviser, excelling in extempore fugues on given subjects and, according to Fétis, "was the only organist in France able to hold his own with the Germans."[5] Saint-Saëns, on the other hand, thought him a "very mediocre organist but an admirable teacher . . . [who] spoke little, but as his taste was refined and his judgment sure, everything he said was valuable and important."[6] Four of the dedicatees of the *Six Pièces* (Chauvet, Alkan, Saint-Saëns, and Lefébure-Wély) had won first prizes in Benoist's organ class. Franck succeeded Benoist as professor of organ on the first of February 1872, and it is not unreasonable to assume that Benoist was responsible, at least, in part, for Franck's appointment. Even in retirement Benoist remained active to a limited extent because he was frequently a member of the jury at the Conservatoire's annual examinations for the organ class.

Andante sostenuto.

Tournemire	♩ = 66
Dupré	♩ = 58
Marchal	♩ = 53
Langlais	♩ = 66

The *Prière* is awkward for players with small hands. Its five-part writing is difficult for everyone, but the first thirty-two measures for manuals alone are impossible for many, including Louis Vierne, who drew no pedal stops until m. 33 and played the lowest voice in the Pédale, distributing the four other voices between the hands.[7]

---

[5]Alexandre Cellier; Henri Bachlin, *L'Orgue* (Paris: Delagrave, 1933) 179.
[6]*École Buissonnière* (Paris: Lafitte, 1913) 41.
[7]Vernon Butcher's edition of the *Prière* (London: Novello, 1953) deserves comment. The first thirty-two measures are distributed on three staves, the pedal playing the lowest voice, and the sections written in G-sharp major (mm. 63–96) and C-sharp major (mm. 175–90 and 211–27) have been enharmonically transposed to the more easily read keys of A-flat major and D-flat major. Editorial confusion abounds: all terms are translated into either English or Italian, all registration, phrase markings, and even some ties have to be compared with the Durand edition.

135

Certain progressions are impossible to make legato even for those with Frankian hands. Just as we concede subtle articulations imposed on the bass line when played with one foot (while the other manages the expression pedal), so playing the exposition of the *Prière* as directed by the composer on the manuals alone, imposes a less tidy, more alert effect. Inner voices are impossible to play legato; phrase breaks are forced to be longer as the hands, however skillful, grapple to prepare the next massively-voiced chord; even thumb and finger glissandos are not always perfectly legato. In short, the lack of easy legato may be the effect Franck sought. He could have written this section, as well as the beginning of *Choral I* in E Major, which has less severe problems than the *Prière*, with the manuals coupled to a silent Pédale. That he did not, makes its own statement.

Franck's registration is basic: *Fonds de 8 pieds* (all 8′ flue stops, except the celestes) on all three manuals, the Récit Hautbois included, and the *Fonds de 8 et 16 pieds* in the Pédale. On the organ of Sainte-Clotilde there were thirteen ranks of 8′ pitch (including the Hautbois) drawn on the three manuals that were coupled to the Grand-Orgue. The Récit Trompette is added and withdrawn four times during the *Prière*, twice while both hands are playing. Franck, therefore, would have "prepared" it by drawing the stop that would have remained silent until the Anches Récit pédale de combinaison was depressed.

The subject of common notes, one facet of which was touched upon in the discussion of the *Fantaisie in C*, arises in the first two measures of the *Prière*.

Ex. 1, mm. 1–2

If the lower note is released before it is restruck by the upper voice the effect is as follows:

Ex. 2

Such a detailed repetition of inner voices hardly produces the *molto legato* expected by the composer who qualified his tempo, *Andantino*, with a reference to touch, *sostenuto*.

Fortunately, we have César Franck's own direction concerning the interpretation of this and similar passages. In his Preface to Louis Lambillotte's *Chant Grégorien* Franck wrote:

> When a note is common to several consecutive chords, it must be tied as long as it is part of the harmony.[8]

Thus, following his own instruction, Franck would have tied the lower voice to the upper:

Ex. 3

At mm. 4–5, with the exchange of the two upper voices in each hand, he would have connected them thusly:

Ex. 4, mm. 4–5

[8]Franck, "Preface," *Chant Gregorien* (Paris: Leclére, 1858) iv.

This technique of tying common notes is undeniably the best method of achieving a perfect legato on the organ. Such articulation was universally applied by Franck's contemporaries, such as Alexandre Guilmant:

> When a note is common between two or three chords, it is better to hold it without repeating it, as if it were tied.[9]

and Charles-Marie Widor:

> Two voices succeeding one another on the same note must be tied.[10]

and by his students. Louis Vierne wrote:

> Any note common to two parts must be tied. [11]

and Charles Tournemire:

> When one note passes into another part, it need not be repeated ... it is much better to tie it.[12]

An exception to the tying of common notes between parts occurs when it would conflict with the composer's intentions. For instance, m. 6 (Example 5) is unphrased but is identical to m. 22 in which the third beat begins the first of five six-note phrases.

Ex. 5, mm. 6–7

[9]Guilmant, *"La Musique d'Orgue,"* 1157.
[10]Widor, "Preface," *Jean-Sébastien Bach—Œuvres complètes pour orgue*, Vol. I (New York; G. Schirmer, 1914) v-vi.
[11]Vierne, "Renseignements Généraux," v.
[12]Charles Tournemire, *Petite Méthode d'Orgue* [1937] (Paris: Max Eschig, 1949) 3.

For the ear to detect the beginning of the phrase it is necessary to break between the half-note D♯ and the third-beat B.

If the manuals are coupled to the pedal, the organist has the option of playing one of the manual parts in the pedal. In m. 7, for instance, it is easier to play the lowest voice in the left hand so that the right foot is free to realize the *crescendo* and *diminuendo*. Measures 13–16 can all be played with the left foot, the first C♯ eighth note of m. 16 with the left hand and the second low C♯ eighth note in the pedal. Measure 23 (from the second eighth-note E of beat 1) through m. 25 can be played in the left hand.

The two pedal stops, 16′ and 8′, can be added by hand at m. 32, beat 3.

The melodic line requires a *tenuto* on the first beats of mm. 36, 40, 41 (pedal), and 44.

Note that the soprano's tied-note A at m. 46, beat 1, must be repeated so that the alto's imitation can be articulated.

The climax of this section begins at m. 47, beat 2, where the soprano notes are held almost as two dotted eighths, then *a Tempo* at beat 3. Stress the high A at m. 49, beat 1. The right foot being on the swell pedal executing the *diminuendo* in m. 50, there will be a break in the pedal line between A and the low E at m. 51.

The three rising sequences of three measures each (mm. 51–59) accelerate in tempo as they approach a climax in m. 59, gradually taper off during the following three-measure extension, and finally relax at the *cantando* from m. 63. This sequential passage presages the difficulties of coping with the two-against-three rhythmic patterns that abound in the *Prière*. In this instance the melody is in triple meter and the accompaniment in duple; the reverse will be the case from here on.

The left hand moves to the Positif at m. 63 and the right hand remains on the Grand-Orgue, the indication *Toujours G.O.* is added as a precaution against both hands changing manuals. It is easier if the manual accompaniment to the pedal melody is played by both hands from m. 67, beat 2, through the second eighth note of m. 70.

The sustained D♯ of the accompaniment drops an octave at m. 73. A smooth transition is possible because the right hand intercepts this D♯ at beat 3 (with the Positif coupled to the Grand-

Orgue, the note is automaticaly held down) and the left hand is re-
lieved to change its position on the last C♯ and D♯ of the measure.

Ex. 6, mm. 72–73

The following solutions are offered for uninterrupted manual
changes. The right hand can conveniently play all three parts at
m. 95, beat 3, (Example 7) leaving the left hand free to go to the
Positif and resume playing at m. 96. The G♯ is held on the Grand-
Orgue for two beats.

Ex. 7, mm. 95–96

At m. 108 both hands are again on the Grand-Orgue. The
right hand can intercept the tenor G♯ on what would be the second note of a triplet on the third beat, allowing the left hand to
move to the Positif. As the right hand releases the G♯ and E, they
will already be sustained by the left.

Ex. 8, m. 108

At m. 114 the Anches Récit is depressed, adding the Récit Trompette to the foundation stops and Hautbois. Tournemire advised interpreting this central *Quasi recitativo* "with great freedom."

Translate the direction at m. 120, *Avec une certaine liberté de mesure,* as "with some rhythmic freedom." We can interpret Franck's direction at m. 132, *Toujours avec une certaine liberté de mesure,* to mean "with some rhythmic freedom until further indication to the contrary" i.e., the *a Tempo* at m. 149. Two sections (mm. 120–25 and 132–39) require a slight *accelerando,* a *tenuto* on the first note of the third beat of each section's first three measures, and an indicated *Rallentando.*

Even though *Très mesuré* (m. 149) means "In strict tempo," and is further qualified with *a Tempo,* Tournemire directed the nine measures (from m. 149) to be played animatedly, with a ritard before m. 159. Marcel Dupré marked his edition *Più mosso* ♩ = 76.

The second half of the *Prière* begins at m. 159 in the same tempo as the beginning and on the same registration. Franck's direction for interpretation, *Très-expressif et très soutenu,* is immediately recognized in the familiar Italian, "molto expressivo e legato." The organist needs to be reminded to "sustain" in this section, particularly between mm. 175 and 190, in which large hands or lightning-quick finger substitution is required for the left hand playing in sixths in duple meter, the lower right-hand voice in triplets, and a legato melody in the upper voice on which must be lavished all of those now-familiar rhythmic nuances. Add to

Plate 34. *Prière,* page 8 of the manuscript, measures 174–93

142

these difficulties the two introductions and subtractions of the Récit Trompette by pédale de combinaison, and the player is presented with the fifteen most treacherous measures in all of Franck's organ works.

The right foot's operation of the swell pedal would have necessitated the left foot's execution of the following passage and two detached leaps:

Ex. 9, mm. 183–86

The engraver of the 1956 Durand edition has adjusted the notational ambiguity at mm. 177 and 179 (Example 10), which appeared in the manuscript and in the two earlier editions. In m. 177 the soprano E in the third beat was printed over the last triplet C♯; in m. 179 the soprano E♯ in the first beat was printed over the triplet C♯. This gave the theme, previously stated in mm. 19 and 21 as equal eighth notes, a staggered rhythm. It is assumed that the composer expected similar rhythmic treatment in an exact restatement of his thematic material.

Ex. 10, mm. 177–78

Ex. 10, cont., m. 179

At m. 205 (Example 11) the soprano eighth notes on the second and third beats share their second note-head with the lower accompaniment's triplet rhythm.

Ex. 11, mm. 205–7

The duplet rhythm prevails, in keeping with the rest of the melodic pattern of the *Prière*, and the last notes of the triplets on the second and third beats are assimilated into the second eighth note of each beat.

The right hand moves to the Positif on the first beat of m. 190. It is unclear if the Trompette is to be removed from the Récit before beat 1 or beat 3. Psychologically, its subtraction before beat 3 is better, as the ear is confused by the change in tone color but is immediately satisfied by the melody heard prominently on the Grand-Orgue.

A smooth and seamless transition from the Positif to Grand-Orgue can be achieved between mm. 198 and 199 if the hands are reversed (see Example 12), the right hand being able to take advantage of the eighth rest in the bass staff to move onto the lower manual.

Ex. 12, mm. 197–99

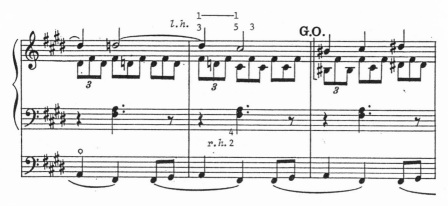

The F♯ in the upper voice of the first beat of m. 214 (Example 13) is tied to the preceding measure.

Ex. 13, mm. 214–16

The corresponding passage (Example 14) at mm. 84–86,

Ex. 14, mm. 84–86

as well as subsequent, sequential statements of this motif, indicates that this F♯ should be played an octave higher. When the *Six Pièces* were published in 1868, the fifty-four-note (C-F) manual compass was standard on Cavaillé-Coll organs, including Franck's own instrument at Sainte-Clotilde; the fifty-six-note (C-G) keyboards of the organs of Saint-Sulpice and Notre-Dame Cathedral were exceptions. The player must decide whether to observe the letter of the composer's "law" and play the F♯ as written (as Dupré and his student, Langlais do) or its spirit and play it an octave higher (as Marchal does).

At the end of m. 233 the Récit is uncoupled from the Positif (*séparez le R. du P.*) and again coupled at m. 240. Both hands play on the Grand-Orgue but, since there was no Récit au Grand-Orgue coupler, the Récit could only be coupled to the Grand-Orgue through the Positif. While the right hand plays a two-measure solo (mm. 244–45) we are directed to *séparez les claviers*. The manuals are uncoupled from each other, not only the Récit au Positif, but the Positif au Grand-Orgue and (on those organs that had one) the Récit au Grand-Orgue. The Pédale is also a clavier so this rather unorthodox registrational directive implies that it, too, is uncoupled from the manuals—Franck had on only the Tirasse Grand-Orgue (according to the registration at the beginning of the piece), so all he had to do was to take it off and the Pédale was instantly reduced from the fourteen eight-foot stops to but one, the 8′ Basse, playing with the 16′ Contrebasse.

Dramatic emphasis may be given to the final declamatory statement of the *Prière* in the following way: a slight *tenuto* is observed on the first eighth note of mm. 246, 247, and 248; the second eighth of the first beat is held quite a bit longer than written by delaying the left-hand chord of beat 2; treat the high F♯ of m. 247, beat 3, as the climax and lengthen it; the denouement of m. 250, the descending A♯ to F♯ to B♯, is played very slowly. While dealing with the emotional upheaval of this passage, the organist must also manage some calculated registrational changes in the accompaniment. Measure 247 reads *supprimez graduellement quelques jeux du P.* (gradually silence some of the Positif stops). As this declamatory passage begins (m. 244), both the solo and accompaniment are *forte*. Since the Positif was unenclosed and accompanied a gradually softening melody, some of the five Positif 8′ stops must be taken off. These would have included, at least, the Montre, Flûte harmonique, and Gambe (leaving the Bourdon and Salicional) and would have been removed on the first beat of mm. 247, 248 and, perhaps, m. 250. This would make the chord on the first beat of m. 251 *pp*. For the last three chords of the piece, *ppp*, perhaps Franck would have taken off the 8′ Salicional, leaving only the Bourdon.

Albert Schweitzer might have been thinking of the *Prière* when he wrote:

Franck composes idiomatically, in a style that seems to spring from the true, fundamental character of the organ itself. Like Bach, he knows intuitively the most natural and effective musical line for the organ: his is always simple and at the same time wonderfully plastic. And the structure of his works is amazingly natural. They give the impression of improvisations which he decided to copy down. The riches of such a natural inventiveness are inexhaustible: hardly any other modern master has succeeded, by means of completely simple registration, in making the tonal riches of the modern organ so effective.[13]

[13]Albert Schweitzer, Notes accompanying his recording of the *Trois Chorals,* Columbia ML 5128.

Plate 35. Last page of the manuscript of the *Prière*

Corrections for the 1956 Durand Edition

P	S	M	
14	1	1	l.h., middle voice, beat 1, E should be a quarter note; beat 2 add F♯ quarter note
14	1	6	l.h. C♯s not tied in original nor in manuscript
14	2	4	l.h. F♯s not tied to next measure in original but is tied in manuscript
14	2	5	l.h. B should be a half note and occur on beat 2
14	3	1	r.h. F♯, should be F^x
15	1	1	l.h. add half note G♯ (octave above bass)
15	3	4	l.h. A not tied to next measure in original, but is in manuscript
16	3	3	l.h. last C♯ is lower voice printed directly below the E in original
17	2	2	l.h. add dot to half note G♯
16	1	3	slur over soprano notes
20	1	4	r.h. tie last E to next score
21	1	1	add *Ôtez la Trompette*
21	1	2	r.h. cautionary A-natural
21	1	4	r.h. tie As
23	3	5	r.h. tie second and third F♯s in alto
24	1	5	soprano cautionary B-natural; l.h. last B♯ not tied to next measure in original but is tied in manuscript
24	2	3	last E♯ in soprano printed directly above alto C♯ in original
24	3	1	E♯ in soprano printed directly above alto C♯ in original
25	1	2	add *forte*
25	2	1	l.h. tie D♯ from preceding score
25	3	4	l.h. beat 3 is an eighth note in both measures
26	3	5	r.h. E♯ half note is dotted in original (it is not in the manuscript, however)
28	2	2	add slur marks connecting alto notes in groups of two

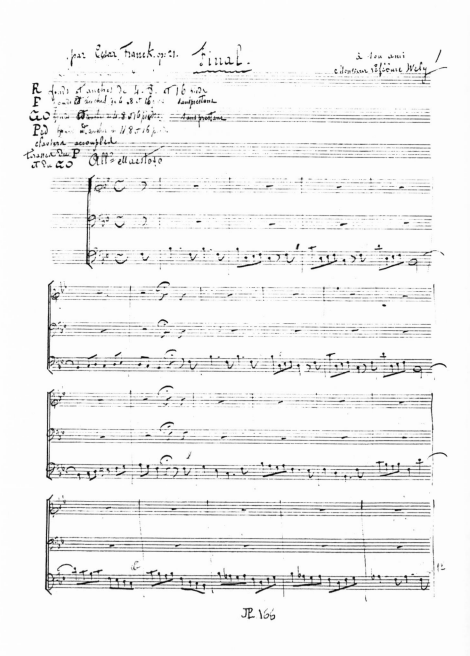

Plate 36. First page of the manuscript of the *Final*

150

CHAPTER VII

Final, Op. 21

Composed:	circa 1859 or earlier
Published:	1868

Publishers:	1. Maeyens-Couvreur,
	    Plate No: JB.166
	2. Durand & Schoenwerk, 1880
	    Plate No: D.S. & Cie. 2684
	3. Durand & Cie., 1956,
	    Plate No: D. & F. 13.792

Dedication:	à son ami Monsieur Lefébure-Wély
Manuscript:	Bibliothèque National, MS 22410, dated 18 7bre 1864 (September 18, 1864)
Performances:	Probably played by the composer on December 19, 1859, at the inauguration of the organ of Sainte-Clotilde. Played by the composer on November 17, 1864, at Sainte-Clotilde.

The *Final* is probably one of the organ solos César Franck played at the inauguration of the Cavaillé-Coll organ at the Church of Sainte-Clotilde on December 19, 1859. The list of pieces performed on the program mentioned an "Improvisation Final;"[1] elsewhere, Adrien de la Fage recognized in said *Final* "the conception and execution of a true master."[2]

A further connection with the inauguration of the organ is the *Final*'s dedication to Louis-J.-A. Lefébure-Wély (1817–1869), who shared the concert with Franck. Acclaimed throughout Europe, Lefébure-Wély reigned as "Prince of Organists"—the most prominent, the most universally recognized and, certainly,

---

[1]*La France musicale* (December 25, 1859) 566.
[2]*Revue et Gazette Musicale* (January 1, 1860) 4.

the most popular French organist of his day. His pedal technique must have been formidable, for among the many works dedicated to him, in addition to Franck's *Final,* were the *Douze Études d'Orgue pour les pieds seulement* by Charles-Valentin Alkan, published in the middle 1860s.

Plate 37. Louis-James-Alfred Lefébure-Wély

Five years older than Franck, Lefébure-Wély had substituted for his stroke-paralyzed father at the organ of Saint-Roch from the age of nine, won first prizes in piano and organ at the Paris Conservatoire, and went on to play at two illustrious Parisian churches, the

Madeleine and Saint-Sulpice. He was a popular virtuoso on the organ, piano, and harmonium, specializing in a kind of cheerful musical insincerity that appealed to a wide and uncritical audience, and though his sparkling salon style was incompatible with the celebration of the divine mysteries, clergy and laity alike were captivated by the originality (and others by the banality) of his talent. Cavaillé-Coll admired him as much for his musical skill as for his ability to sell organs and Lefébure-Wély was always the first asked to inaugurate his newest instrument. Thus it was that he appeared on the same program with César Franck at the inauguration of the new organ in the latter's church.

Allegro maestoso.

Tournemire	♩ = 132	Tempo fluctuations are left to the player's discretion
Dupré	♩ = 112	
Marchal	♩ = 126	
Langlais	♩ = 126–132	

The registration for the *Final* is basic: *Fonds et Anches de 4, 8 et 16 pieds (sans Prestant)* on all manuals and pedal, with the exception of the 4′ Prestants of the Positif and Grand-Orgue. Of the stops of 4′ pitch on the organ of Sainte-Clotilde only the Octave of the Grand-Orgue and the Flûtes octaviantes of the Positif and Récit were on the chest with the foundation stops and would not have been shut off when the Anches pédale de combinaison were depressed.

Although Franck specifically called for both 16′ reed and flue tone on the Récit, his organ at Sainte-Clotilde had neither. The entire piece is written higher on the keyboard to compensate for the sub-octave tone, and if we use only 8′ tone on the Récit, it would sound an octave higher than the other three divisions and, consequently, weaker and disassociated from the ensemble.

The *Final's* effect depends to a great extent on the player adjusting his touch to the acoustics of the room. The legato pedal solos will vary less than the interpretation of the fermatas. In teaching the *Final*, Jean Langlais suggested holding the fermata rests for three beats; each measure then contains six beats instead of four. The duration of the fermatas naturally varies with the reverberation time of

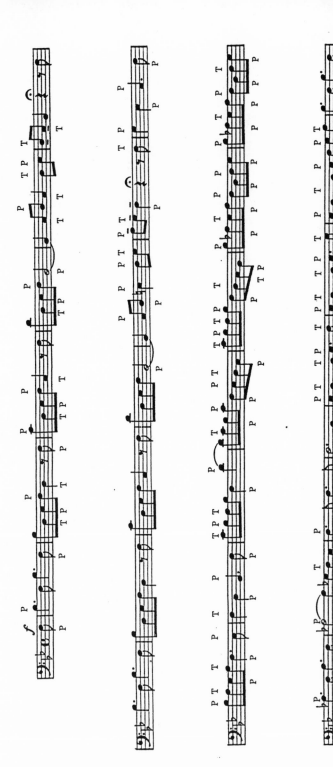

Plate 38. Charles Tournemire's pedaling of the beginning of the *Final*.

P = pointe (toe);   T = talon (heel)

Above staff: right foot; Below staff: left foot

the room in which it is heard and the excitement generated by the player. The *Final* is a virtuoso piece intended to display technical skill. It was written by a keyboard virtuoso who had transferred piano technique to the organ and, for the first time in the *Six Pièces*, had written in the prevailing style of the day—but elevated to a higher plane. The bravura remains, however, and the organist's job is to thrill more than to edify.

Franck has left no indication that the left-hand chords from m. 29 through m. 31 are to be played any other way than legato; he was even particular to add ties to the left hand B♭s in m. 30 (Example 1).

Ex. 1, mm. 29–32

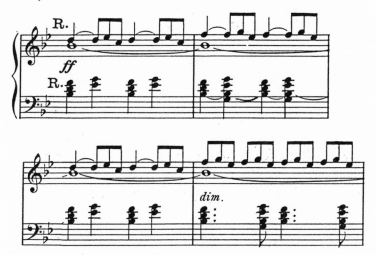

Marcel Dupré articulated them as follows:

Ex. 2, mm. 29–30

Ex. 2, cont., mm. 30–31

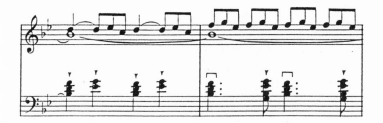

Each phrasing creates a different effect: neither is incorrect. Dupré, who based his Franck edition on Guilmant's teaching, may have heard Guilmant detach the chords. Guilmant may have heard Franck play them this way. Franck may have played them differently on various occasions or may have allowed his students to play them one way or the other—he was a notoriously liberal teacher who allowed consecutive fifths in composition exercises and would certainly not have disallowed a detached chord here and there.

The bass notes in mm. 41–42 (Example 3) are played as duplets against the right-hand triplets; they are not to be played with the last note of each triplet.

Ex. 3, mm. 41–42

But at m. 44 the triplet figuration ritards before the recommencement of the pedal solo so that the pedal D is played with the manual D.

Ex. 4, mm. 44–46

Throughout mm. 125 and 126 Franck wrote *Ôtez graduellement les jeux d'Anches aux Péd. au G.O. et au P.* (Gradually take off the Anches of the Pédale, Grand-Orgue, and Positif).

Ex. 5, mm. 123–26

Thus, with three quick movements of the right foot, the entire organ, except for the Récit, is reduced to 16′ and 8′ foundation stops—most 4′ stops having been silenced with the other ranks on the ventil chests.

If these registration changes are not made until m. 125 the 16′, 8′, and 4′ reed choruses coupled to the pedal will obliterate the mid-range manual writing, and the *diminuendo* made by closing the swell box will be ineffectual. A better solution, and one still following the composer's directions, is to remove the Anches Pédale after m. 119, the Anches Grand-Orgue just before m. 125, and the

Anches Positif just before m. 126. This still allows for the *diminuendo* of the Récit. An alternate plan would be to take advantage of the accented first beats of mm. 123 and 124 and, as the previous chord is released in preparation for the agogic accent, a registrational change could be made.

Marcel Dupré indicated a reduction of the entire organ to 8′ Fonds at the rest on the second beat of m. 119. Not only is this earlier than Franck indicated for the reeds to be withdrawn, but in canceling all 16′ manual tone Dupré, in effect, produced the impression that the piece was being played an octave higher than it was intended to be heard!

From m. 153, Franck reduced the organ. A *poco rallentando* facilitates both hands' change to the Positif at m. 155 and another *rallentando* is not out of order in preparation for the move to the Récit at m. 163. While both hands are playing on the Récit the player has ten measures to uncouple the Récit from the Positif (*Ôtez l'accouplement du R. au P.*) and to take off both the Positif and Grand-Orgue pedal couplers (*Ôtez les Tirasses*). The statement of the second theme at m. 173 is heard on the Pédale stops alone—at Sainte-Clotilde these would have been the 16′ Contrebasse and the 8′ Flûte.

A slight delay of m. 187 points up the statement of the second theme on the uncoupled Positif. Then at m. 199, with both hands again on the Récit, both pedal couplers are again engaged (*Mettez les tirasses du P. et du G.O.*) and the first theme is heard in the Pédale (mm. 201–203) on flue stops only, against the counterpoint of the Récit. With the coupling of the Récit to the Positif (*Accouplez le R. au P.*) between mm. 203 and 206, the 8′ and 4′ reeds of the Récit are added to the foundation stops of the other manuals and pedal.

A *ritard* introduces the statement of the theme on the Grand-Orgue at the last eighth note of m. 214. The first beat of m. 215, slightly held, is *forte;* the swell box closes abruptly for the second beat, *p.* The legato left hand contrasts with the detached eighth notes of the right.

The Anches Positif are added before the last eighth note of m. 235, those of the Grand-Orgue before the last eighth note of

m. 237, and those of the Pédale added so that the two measures of B-flat-major chords (mm. 245–46) are heard on the original registration. An emphatic ritard delays the entrance of the principal theme at the last note of m. 246.

Measure 305.

Tournemire	♩	= 132
Dupré	♩	= 132 *Più mosso*
Marchal	♩	= 108
Langlais	♩	= 160

The only known manuscript of the *Final* was sold at a Paris auction on December 16, 1992. This was the final draft that was sent to the printer and Franck had erased the original registration and written a new one over it. The descriptive catalog noted:

> This manuscript is particularly valuable because it contains the original (unpublished) version of the work's ending. Crossed out in red pencil by Franck, it was shorter than the definitive version and occupied pages 14 and 15; Franck dialogued the Grand-Orgue with the Récit before bringing in one last time the initial soprano motive followed by a thirty-measure stretto leading to the final chords. The new eighty-five-measure ending was rewritten by Franck on new pages numbered 14, 15, and 16; it is a long coda, brilliant and virtuosic.

Dupré, Marchal, and Langlais interpreted the ending of the *Final* considerably faster than the rest of the piece. Tournemire indicated no increase in tempo, perhaps leaving it also "to the discretion of the player." It cannot be denied that a certain static, less-than-virtuosic quality affects the ending if the work is played in one tempo throughout.

Those playing from the Dupré edition—and it cannot be stressed strongly enough that its *only* virtue is its fingering solutions and clever distribution of parts between the hands—are cautioned again about the absence of fermatas. Without them the effect of the low pedal notes at mm. 304, 311, and 318, rising by major thirds from D major, through F-sharp major to B-flat major, is diminished. Most disastrous of all, once Franck has climaxed on B♭ (m. 318), Dupré omits *Très long*!

The manual figurations from m. 305 are traditionally played *staccato*. Jean Langlais told me that Louis Vierne always played them *staccato;* Marcel Dupré marked them so in his edition.

Jean Langlais recommended playing m. 321 m. 321 (Example 6) with the right hand:

Ex. 6, mm. 321–23

At the passage in Example 7 Langlais recounted that Vierne asked Franck if he could play the left hand *staccato* and the right hand *legato*. Franck agreed.

Ex. 7, mm. 336–38

The question naturally arises: is the upper work, i.e. 4′ Prestants (specifically eliminated in the beginning), 2⅔′ Quintes, 2′ and mixtures, never drawn in the *Final?* It seems incredible that Franck would not have added more stops from m. 305 onward. The last dynamic marking is *f* at m. 235, followed by the addition of the Anches Positif, Grand-Orgue, and Pédale. Further additions should be made at the discretion of the performer.

Vincent d'Indy, Franck's organ student, loyal disciple, and bi-ographer, admired the *Final*, finding it

> . . . particularly interesting because of its firm, Beethoven-like structure, its graceful second theme contrasting with the inflexibility of the first and the important development toward the close which leads to a forceful and majestic peroration.[3]

With the *Final* César Franck concluded his *Six Pièces*. He was forty-five when they were published in 1868 and he had been working on the set for at least fourteen years. The hour and twenty minutes of music was the first great contribution to French organ literature in well over a century and the most important organ music since Mendelssohn's. To quote Franz Liszt, one of the early admirers of the *Six Pièces*, "These poems have their place beside the masterpieces of Sebastian Bach."

Corrections for the 1956 Durand Edition

P	S	M	
31	1	1	pedal B♭ should be tied from preceding page
32	1	2	tie l.h. B♭ through entire measure
34	2	2	alto beats 2 and 3 are marked as triplets
35	3	4	tie soprano D to next measure
36	3	8	l.h. chord is G major (B, D, G, B)
37	2	8	l.h. should be D♯, B, A♯, G♯ (beats 2 and 3 are incorrect)
39	1	3	rests in alto match those in left hand
42	1	1	soprano tie to m. 2 not in original
42	1	2	tie soprano E to m. 3
42	1	3	soprano note should be E (not F♯) tied from m. 2; alto beats 3 and 4 are quarters C and A (as in m. 2)
44	3	4	l.h. last half of beat 2 should be D (not C♯)
46	2	4	l.h. F is slured to A♭ in original (possibly a misplaced tie to F in m. 5)
47	2	5	pedal A should be flatted
52	2	5	tie pedal Fs to m. 6

[3]d'Indy, *Cesar Franck*, 137.

Trois Pièces

Plate 39. The northern facade of the Palais du Trocadéro as seen from
the Place du Trocadéro

Introduction to the *Trois Pièces*

In the ten years between the publication of Franck's *Six Pièces* (1868) and the composition and premiere of his *Trois Pièces* (1878), the Parisian organ world underwent a transformation, evolving from Europe's capital of musical frivolity into the world's most influential center of organ playing and composition. Eugène Gigout was appointed organist of Saint-Augustin; within the two weeks that bridged the decades (1869-70), Auguste Durand, organist of Saint-Vincent-de-Paul, founded his publishing firm, Lefébure-Wély died, and Charles-Marie Widor succeeded him as organist of Saint-Sulpice. During the 1870s Alexandre Guilmant succeeded Alexis Chauvet at La Trinité (1871); Franck was appointed professor of organ at the Paris Conservatoire (1872); and Saint-Saëns, for nineteen years organist of the Madeleine, resigned (1877) and was succeeded by Théodore Dubois, who, in turn, was succeeded as maître-de-chapelle by Gabriel Fauré.

The year 1878 saw the completion of a huge Moorish-pseudo-Byzantine structure, the Palais du Trocadéro, built for the Universal Exposition. The central building, the Salle des Fêtes, or Festival Hall, was a 5,000-seat circular auditorium and, across the stage at the front of the hall stood a sixty-six-stop Cavaillé-Coll organ. This was the first large organ in a concert hall in France and, to inaugurate it, a series of fifteen organ recitals was presented. For two months, twice a week at three o'clock on Wednesday and Saturday afternoons, prominent organists were heard in hour-long recitals. Among those performers were several whose names today, a century later, are instantly recognizable: Guilmant (who played the first recital on August 7), Gigout, Dubois, Widor (who premiered his *Sixth Symphony*), Saint-Saëns (who played the first performance outside Germany of Liszt's *Fantaisie on "Ad nos"*) and César Franck (who premiered his just-composed *Trois Pièces*).

Plate 40. Cutaway view of La Salle des Fêtes, Le Palais du Trocadéro

Franck played the thirteenth recital in the series on October 1. He was then fifty-five years old and still known almost exclusively as an organist; indeed, as professor at the Paris Conservatoire, he was at the height of the organ profession. Except for the symphonic poem *Les Éolides,* most of his larger published works were sacred: the *Messe solennelle, Mass in A,* numerous motets, *Ruth, Rédemption,* and the first part of the *Béatitudes.* The *Six Pièces* cannot really be considered "religious" music, except, perhaps, for the *Prière,* and for the fact that their medium confined their performance to churches. With the Trocadéro recital as the intended premiere for the *Trois Pièces,* there can be no doubt that Franck considered these works concert music.

The *Trois Pièces* may have been composed and/or completed within a week: the dates on the manuscripts place them between September 10 and 17; the *Fantaisie,* completed first, was followed by the *Pièce héroïque.* The *Cantabile* was completed last.

166

For his recital at the Trocadéro Franck presented the following program:

Fantaisie

Grande Pièce symphonique

Cantabile

Improvisation

Pièce héroïque

Improvisation

Notice that the *Trois Pièces* were not played as a set, but were interspersed throughout the recital. While a case can be made for performing all three in succession, such may not have been the composer's intent and certainly not his practice. He never again played the *Pièce héroïque* in public, but each of the others he played twice.

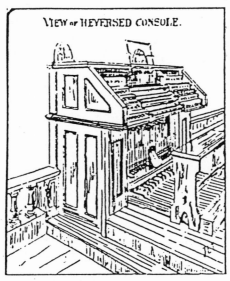

Plate 41. Contemporary Sketch of the Trocadéro's Reversed Console

The specifications of the two organs that most influenced Franck's music appear below. The similarities between the two are striking, the Trocadéro's additional ranks being the ten-stop Solo division, cornets, mixtures, sixteen stops on the Récit, and the very large Pédale.

Sainte-Clotilde	**Trocadéro**
Cavaillé-Coll Organ, 1859	Cavaillé-Coll Organ, 1878
Compass:	Compass:
Manuals, 54 notes: C^1-F^5	Manuals, 56 notes: C^1-G^5
Pedal, 27 notes: C^1-D^3	Pedal, 30 notes: C^1-F^3

* stops controlled by the Anches ventils

I. Grand-Orgue		**I. Grand-Orgue**	
16	Montre	16	Montre
16	Bourdon	16	Bourdon
8	Montre	8	Montre
8	Flûte harmonique	8	Flûte harmonique
8	Bourdon	8	Bourdon
8	Viole de gambe	8	Violoncelle
4	Prestant	4	Prestant
4	Octave*	4	Flûte douce*
3	Quinte*		
2	Doublette*	2	Doublette*
		V	Cornet*
VII	Plein jeu*	V	Plein jeu*
16	Bombarde*	16	Bombarde*
8	Trompette*	8	Trompette*
4	Clairon*	4	Clairon*

II. Positif		**II. Positif expressif**	
16	Bourdon	16	Bourdon
8	Montre	8	Principal
8	Flûte harmonique	8	Flûte harmonique
8	Bourdon		
8	Salicional	8	Salicional
		8	Unda maris
8	Gambe		
4	Prestant		
4	Flûte octaviante*	4	Flûte octaviante
3	Quinte*	2⅔	Quinte*
2	Doublette*	2	Doublette*
III-VI	Plein jeu harmonique*	III-VI	Plein jeu harmonique*
		16	Basson*
8	Trompette*	8	Trompette*
8	Cromorne*	8	Cromorne*
4	Clairon*		

III. Récit expressif

8	Flûte harmonique
8	Bourdon
8	Viole de gambe
8	Voix céleste
4	Flûte octaviante*
2	Octavin*
8	Trompette*
8	Basson-hautbois
4	Clairon*
8	Voix humaine

Pédale

32	Quintaton
16	Contrebasse
8	Flûte
4	Octave
16	Bombarde*
16	Basson*
8	Trompette*
4	Clairon*

III. Récit expressif

16	Quintaton
8	Flûte harmonique
8	Cor de nuit
8	Viole de gambe
8	Voix céleste
4	Flûte octaviante
2	Octavin*
V	Cornet*
I-III	Carillon
16	Basson*
8	Trompette*
8	Basson-hautbois
4	Clairon harmonique*
8	Voix humaine

IV. Solo

16	Bourdon
8	Diapason
8	Flûte harmonique
8	Violoncelle
4	Flûte octaviante
2	Octavin
16	Tuba magna*
8	Trompette harmonique*
8	Clarinette*
4	Clairon harmonique*

Pédale

32	Principal Basse
16	Contrebasse
16	Sous-basse
16	Grosse Flûte
16	Violon-basse
8	Grosse Flûte
8	Basse
8	Bourdon
8	Violoncelle
32	Contre-Bombarde*
16	Bombarde*
16	Basson*
8	Trompette*
8	Basson*
4	Clairon*
4	Baryton*

Pédales de Combinaison

Effets d'orage	Effets d'orage
Tirasse du Grand-Orgue	Tirasse du Grand-Orgue
Tirasse du Positif	Tirasse du Positif
	Tirasse du Récit
Anches Pédales	Anches Pedales
Octaves graves Grand-Orgue	Octaves graves Grand-Orgue
Octaves graves Positif	Octaves graves Positif
Octaves graves Récit au Positif	
	Octaves graves Récit
	Octaves graves Solo
Anches du Grand-Orgue	Anches du Grand-Orgue
Anches du Positif	Anches du Positif
Anches du Récit	Anches du Récit
	Anches du Solo
	Grand-Orgue sur machine
Positif au Grand-Orgue	Positif au Grand-Orgue
	Récit au Grand-Orgue
	Solo au Grand-Orgue
Récit au Positif	Récit au Positif
	Trémolo Positif
Tremblant du Récit	Trémolo Récit
	Expression du Positif
Expression du Récit	Expression du Récit
	Combinaison de la Gr. Pédale
	Combinaison du Solo

CHAPTER VIII

Fantaisie in A

Completed:	September 10, 1878
Published:	1883
Publisher:	1. Durand & Schoenwerk,
	Plate No: D.S. & Cie. 3175
	2. Durand & Cie., 1956
	Plate No: D. & F. 13.793
Manuscript:	No. 20151-1, Bibliothèque Nationale
Performances:	Premiered by the composer on October 1, 1878, at the Trocadéro.
	Played by the composer on March 21, 1879, at the inauguration of the organ of Saint-Eustache.
	Played by the composer on May 27, 1889, at the inauguration of the organ of Saint-Jacques-du-Haut-Pas.

The autograph manuscript of the *Trois Pièces* was given to the Bibliothèque Nationale, Paris, in 1984. It bears Franck's registration notations for the Trocadéro organ and will be referred to in the following discussions of each piece. Franck's notations are given below by measure. Many are the same as, or similar to, those in the Durand edition; those that differ are interesting for the light they shed on Franck's use of the organ, his initial conception of the piece, and how he later adapted that conception to a "standard" organ for a more generalized performance for publication.

Plate 42. First Page of the Manuscript of the *Fantaisie-Idylle*

172

FANTAISIE IN A

Fantaisie-idylle

[Beginning Registration]
S. Tous les jeux
R. Fonds 8 Anches 8 et 4
P. Fonds 8 Anches 8 principal?
G.O. Fonds 8 et 16 sauf violoncelle   Anches 4 8 16
Péd. Fonds 8 16 32 Anches 4 8 16
Claviers accoup.
R. au P.
Tirasses

Measure

1	AR [Anches Récit]
9	ôtez AR [take off the Anches Récit]
13	AR
21	P. [both hands on Positif, instead of Récit].
	ôtez Clairon R.
27	R [both hands on Récit] Ôtez AR
33–34	ôtez Tirasse G.O.
35	ôtez [illegible] G.O. Ajoutez 16p P. [Add Positif 16′]
42	Tous les claviers; AR; Tirasse G.O.
47	ôtez accoup. S [take off Solo au Grand-Orgue coupler]
	ôtez Tirasse G.O.
63	ôtez accoup. P. [take off Positif au Grand-Orgue coupler]
	ôtez Montre 8 G.O.
	8^{ves} G.O. [Octaves graves Grand-Orgue]
	ôtez Tirasse Pos.
85	ôtez Montre 16 du G.O.
	AR
87	Tirasse Pos.
	ôtez 8^{ves} G.O. [take off Octaves graves Grand-Orgue]
91	R. [Both hands on Récit]
	ôtez AR
	ôtez Tirasse P.
102	R. ôtez hautb.
	mettez Vx. hum.
118	R. mettez hautb; Ôtez Vx. hum.
	AR
	Tirasse P.
122	ôtez AR
	ôtez Tirasse P.
133	ôtez hautb; [mettez] Vx. hum.
135	ôtez accoup. R.P. [take off Récit au Positif coupler]
140	ôtez Vx. humaine
144	accoup. R.P. [couple Récit au Positif]; R. hautb.

148   beat 3: AR
162   R. Clairon
       G.O. Montre 8 16; accoup. S. au G.O.; Tirasses
172   Anches R. [at the Trocadéro the jeux d'anches yet to be
       added included 2' Octavin, V Cornet, and 16' Basson]
175   Anches P.
176   A.G.O. [Anches Grand-Orgue]
178   Désaccouplez R. au P.; ôtez A.G.O. et A. Pos;
       ôtez tirasses G.O. et Pos; pédales douce.
189   R. au P.; tous les autres accoupts; Tirasse Pos;
       tous les fonds—anches préparées
195   A. Pos. [instead of m. 194 as in the published version]
196   A.G.O.; Anches Péd.
197   A. S. [Anches Solo]
198   8^{ves} G.O. Right hand: G.O.; Left hand: S[olo]
213   ôtez A. Péd. et 8^{ves} G.O.
214   Ôtez A.G.O. et A. Pos.
228   ôtez Clairon R.
229   ôtez accoup. Pos. et Montre 8 G.O.
230   8^{ves} G.O.; ôtez Tir. Pos.
252   ôtez Montre 16 au G.O.
254   ôtez 8^{ves} G.O.
258   right hand: P.
263   both hands on R[écit]; ôtez hautb.; mettez Vx. hum.
275   no *pp* and no *ôtez la Flûte du P.*

A comparison of Franck's original conception of the *Fantaisie* as he registered it on the Trocadéro organ with his final version that appeared in the published score, reveals several interesting points:

1. Even though the Trocadéro organ had 16' flue and reed stops on the Récit, Franck did not use them.

2. He did not draw the Positif 16' Bourdon at the beginning, adding it only at m. 35. He "prepared" only the Positif 8' Trompette, evidently not intending to include the 16' Basson in the *ff* at m. 175.

3. He specifically excluded the Grand-Orgue Violoncelle, which may have imparted an undesirable quality to the *Fonds* of that division and would have made just one more stop to be taken off at m. 63.

4. Into this ensemble all the stops (*Tous les jeux*) of the Solo are coupled, which, with the 16', 8', and 4' reeds prepared, included three 8' stops and a 16', 4', and 2' stop.
5. Franck's pedal registration specifically includes the 32' Principal Basse but not the 32' Contre Bombarde.
6. In his final version Franck consistently wrote of the Tirasses in the plural, he never took off just the Tirasse Grand-Orgue and left the Positif coupled to the Pédale, as he did so frequently at the Trocadéro.

In the five years between the composition and publication of the *Trois Pièces* Franck simplified his registration, in most instances making it more suitable for a variety of organs, including his own at Sainte-Clotilde. The Solo division was the first to go, couplers and tirasses were kept to a minimum, and many registrational changes were eliminated in favor of changing manuals. The musical result was basically the same as achieved on the great Trocadéro organ, but capable of being realized on organs half its size.

In the manuscript, Franck entitled this work *Fantaisie-Idylle* but for publication shortened that wonderfully evocative title to *Fantaisie*. It is too bad, because it would have been easier to distinguish the two *Fantaisies*—Op. 16 and the present one.

Andantino.

Tournemire	♩	= 88
Dupré	♩	= 72
Marchal	♩	= 72
Langlais	♩	= 69

The *Fantaisie* begins with the 16é and 8é *jeux de fond*s of the Positif, Grand-Orgue, and Pédale, to which are coupled the 8' *jeux de fonds* of the Récit together with the 8' Hautbois, 8' Trompette, and 4' Clairon. The *jeux d'anches* of the Positif, Grand-Orgue, and Pédale are prepared (*préparés*), that is, the stops are drawn but do not sound until the manual's respective Anches pédale de combinaison is depressed, admitting wind into the chest. Since no pitches are assigned, it is assumed that Franck intended all the jeux d'anches to be drawn—those stops designated by asterisks on the stoplists. The manuals are coupled (at Sainte-Clotilde this was accomplished by only two couplers: Récit au Positif and Positif au

Grand-Orgue) and the Grand-Orgue and Positif are coupled to the Pédale.

The tempo, *Andantino,* suggests that Franck wanted more movement than would be indicated by *Andante.* Tournemire's tempo of ♩ = 88 is certainly quicker than that adopted by most organists. The basic tempo, once decided upon, must be adhered to, for it is the single thread that holds the work together. The player must return to the basic tempo at the beginning of every phrase in order to maintain a sense of continuity. If a steady pulse is not maintained, the result will be a rambling, nebulous series of ravishing harmonies with no perceptible form. Because of the registrational, dynamic, and tempo changes indicated by the composer, it is not easy during the course of the *Fantaisie's* thirteen to fourteen minute duration to maintain a musical line.

The phrasing indicated throughout the *Fantaisie* must be scrupulously observed. The left hand's duplication of the pedal part in the unison passages (Example 1) reflects the composer's quest for *legato;* in the last four measures of each passage, while the right foot is closing the swells and the left foot is playing alone, the left hand covers any detached leaps in the pedal.

Ex. 1, mm. 5-8

There is a tendency among even the most accomplished players to "rush" the last eighth note in a measure. Example 2 illustrates this point.

Ex. 2, mm. 24-27

These notes must be held their full value and even "spread" slightly. By following the indicated phrasing, there is a slight lift before mm. 25 and 26 (Example 2), so that the last bass note of each measure is stressed before all parts are released.

In the manuscript the *molto cresc.* is continued through m. 25 right up to what would be, in reality, a *subito pp* at m. 27.

The Tirasse Grand-Orgue is not removed at m. 35 even though both hands are playing on the Positif. In fact, the Grand-Orgue is coupled to the Pédale until m. 102 and on many organs the pedal will be overpowering in those passages where the left hand is on the Postif. When playing at the Trocadéro Franck took off the Tirasse Grand-Orgue between mm. 35 and 43 and again between mm. 47 and 162. This procedure, its precedence documented in the composer's manuscript, will clarify the texture.

Example 3 illustrates a thorny rhythmic problem. Above the left-hand accompaniment figuration of repeated triplets is a countermelody of descending quarter notes, each written directly above the third note of each triplet group.

Ex. 3, mm. 59-60

A two-against-three interpretation of this passage is reasonable because the upper voice is introduced by an eighth rest, and an eighth note begins m. 60. If this countermelody were to be interpreted in triplet rhythm, the rest and the note previously mentioned would have been notated as quarters. Strong evidence, however, indicates that the notes of the countermelody coincide exactly with the third note of each triplet and are to be played just as they appear on the printed page and in the manuscript.

The evidence is found in the previously-mentioned article[1] by Alexandre Guilmant in which, after citing J. S. Bach's *Prelude and Fugue in C Minor*, BWV 546, where a sixteenth note following and barred to a dotted eighth note is played with the third note of a triplet, and quoting the *Foreword* to Nicolas Gigault's *Livre de musique pour l'orgue,* "When there is a sixteenth note above an eighth, they must be played together," Guilmant calls attention to two passages in César Franck's *Fantaisie en la:* Example 4 and the previously discussed Example 3.

Ex. 4, m. 54

This leaves no doubt that Guilmant assumed that the upper voice of the left-hand passage in mm. 59–60 and 226–27 was to fall precisely where it was notated—with the third note of each triplet. Guilmant probably heard Franck play his *Fantaisie in A* at the Trocadéro in 1878 and certainly heard him play it at the inauguration of the new Merklin organ at Saint-Eustache in 1879 when they were among the organists on the recital. (It must be pointed out, however, that Marcel Dupré, who firmly attached his pre-

---

[1]Guilmant, "La Musique d'Orgue," 1162.

eminent position as transmitter of the "Franck Tradition" to his study with Guilmant, has printed mm. 59 and 226 in his edition as twos-against-threes, and not as his maître Guilmant directed!

The pedal part of mm. 61–62 is played with the left foot—the right foot being occupied making the *diminuendo* with the swell pedal—so that the bass notes will be somewhat articulated. At m. 63, the first registrational change Franck would have made would have been to remove the Anches Récit; assistants would have made the other changes. Note that the right-hand solo line included both the 16′ Montre and 16′ Bourdon. At the Trocadéro Franck even brought on the sub-octave coupler (Octaves Graves Grand-Orgue) for this statement of the second theme—producing 32′ manual tone—and kept it on until m. 87. The Récit Hautbois remained on throughout this section, thus making the dynamics more pronounced.

Throughout this passage (mm. 63–87) the rhythm of the melody must be flexibly shaped. A subtle (but not ineffectual) tenuto, or slight delay, introduces the melody at mm. 63, 70, 74, and 78. These are the more obvious examples, but rhythmic nuance is assumed throughout the work.

The *Fantaisie* employs many polyrhythms, particularly twos-against-threes. At mm. 71–72, we meet threes-against-fours, played so that the last two notes of the triplet figuration come just after the second sixteenth note and just before the last. The player must stretch the time on the third beat of these measures so that the triplets sound neither angular nor rushed, but limpid and natural. Keep the left hand very legato, particularly over the bar line.

At mm. 102, 133, and 263, Franck takes off the Hautbois and adds the Voix humaine. It is combined with the three foundation stops of the Récit: an open flute, stopped flute, and a broad-scaled string (Flûte harmonique, Bourdon, Gambe), but no mention is made of the Tremblant. For reasons enumerated in the discussion of the *Fantaisie in C*, Franck understood that the Tremblant would be drawn with the Voix humaine.

No tie joins the last-beat soprano D of m. 134 to the first beat of m. 135; it appears this way in the manuscript. At mm. 268–69, a tie appears in the score but not in the manuscript; at mm. 103–104 and similar places, the tie is consistently notated in the printed score and in the manuscript. A tie should probably be added in those places where it is missing to be consistent.

According to the manuscript, when Franck played this *Fantaisie* at the Trocadéro he took off the Récit 4′ Clairon at m. 21 and did not draw it again until m. 162. Thus, at m. 148, when he writes *mettez Tromp. R.* (add the Récit Trompette), he had no other stop of the jeux d'anches drawn, so that when he depressed Anches Récit only the Trompette sounded. The published score has no indication to remove the 4′ Clairon from the Récit, so, to observe the printed registration at m. 148, the Clairon would have had to be withdrawn by hand sometime after m. 124.

For a perfect legato in the bass of m. 132 (Example 5) play the tenor E with the right hand and, on the second half of the beat, take it over with the left thumb.

Ex. 5, m. 132

Poco animato.

Dupré	♩	= 116
Marchal	♩·	= 112
Langlais	♩	= 112

Très largement.

Dupré	♩	= 72 a Tempo
Marchal	♩	= 69
Langlais	♩	= 58 (m. 206, ♩ = 69; m. 214, = 80)

At the Trocadéro, Franck, after having attained full organ, added the Octaves Graves to the Grand-Orgue for the *Très largement* (mm. 198-214). By playing the left hand on the Solo and the right hand on the Grand-Orgue the theme heard in the soprano was doubled at the octave below, adding a great deal of 32′ tone to the texture.

At m. 206, when the soprano and bass themes are exchanged, the second theme (a descending scale) begins on high E of the pedalboard. Franck gives an alternate reading an octave lower for organs without the required E. By the time of the composition of the *Fantaisie* (1878), the French pedal compass had become standardized at thirty notes (C^1-F^3); it almost seemed old-fashioned to have provided an alternate reading for antiquated instruments— though it was a very real problem for Franck who both taught on one at the Conservatoire and played one at church!

Tournemire considered m. 214 as the return to the initial tempo (*a Tempo* ♩ = 88) "but with an infinitely calm feeling." The same interpretational considerations hold good for this section.

Tournemire suggested taking the last page, from m. 254, at "a very moderate tempo—slowing down until the end." For the last two measures of the piece Franck went to the Positif with both hands. The Récit is still coupled to the Positif but the box is closed (*pp*). Because *ôtez la Flûte du P.* (take off the Positif Flûte harmonique) is printed above the beginning of the measure, it is unclear if it is to be heard in m. 275 and taken off for m. 276, or if it is to be off before the Positif is played upon (in which case it could be removed at the rest in m. 262). Jean Langlais kept the Voix humaine on until the end of the piece. Dupré (and his two students, Jeanne Demessieux and Pierre Cochereau) and Marchal uncoupled the Récit and concluded on the Positif Bourdon alone.

With *Rédemption* and *Les Éolides*, this *Fantaisie* is one of the signal works of Franck's third period (extending, according to d'Indy, from 1872 to 1890). All the elements of the mature composer are present: sensuous chromaticism and alternation and combination of contrasting themes are combined with consummate mastery of the organ's tonal resources and mechanical controls. With youthful enthusiasm, Franck has achieved unfaltering inspiration and an unfailing ease of execution so that each subsequent work will become "radiant with vitality and brimming with beauty."[2]

Corrections for the 1956 Durand Edition

P	S	M	
5	1	2	l.h. fourth sixteenth note is E♭
5	1	3	l.h. fifth sixteenth note should read B (retain G in lower voice); add *diminuendo*
6	2	3	registration: ôtez Hautbois R. (not Anches)
7	3	8	pedal is C, tied to following measure
8	1	1	add dot to pedal C
8	2	5	l.h., beat 3, lower voice should be C-natural (not C♯)
9	2	5	l.h. B♭ is tied from preceding measure as it is tied in the manuscript
9	2	8	l.h., beat 3, tie D to beat 4
11	3	6	l.h. tie F on third quarter to next page
12	2	4	l.h. F♯ tied from m. 3 should be an eighth note
13	1	3	l.h. all G♭s should be G-naturals
13	3	1	pedal is tied from previous score, as in manuscript

[2]d'Indy, *César Franck*, 160.

CHAPTER IX

Cantabile

This piece, characteriszed by a profound and striking emotion, requires no analysis; it is sufficient only to listen to it to hear the song of the Maître's soul.

Albert Mahaut

Completed:	September 17, 1878
Published:	1883
Publishers:	1. Durand & Schoenwerk, Plate No: D.S. & Cie. 3176
	2. Durand & Cie., 1956, Plate No: D. & F. 13.793
Manuscript:	No. 20151-2, Bibliothèque Nationale
Performances:	Premiered by the composer on October 1, 1878, at the Trocadéro.
	Played by the composer on October 28, 1878 at the inauguration of the organ of Saint-Merry.
	Played by the composer on February 29, 1879, at the inauguration of the organ of Saint-François-Xavier.
	Played by the composer on March 21, 1879, at the inauguration of the organ of Saint-Eustache.
	Played by Eugène Gigout on March 25, 1884, on a recital at Salle Albert-le-Grand.

The *Cantabile* is the only one of Franck's major organ works based on a single theme; no other sections contrast with its development. Vincent d'Indy characterized the theme as

. . . suave and devotional . . . that will ever remain the typical prayer of an artist who was also a true Christian. Twice the prayer

Plate 43. First page of the manuscript of the *Cantabile*

184

is heard; and . . . we cannot fail to admire the wonderful canon which, moving with unbroken ease, forms the adornment of the melody. . . . [3]

It has long been a popular teaching piece, and many young organists have been introduced to Franck's music via the *Cantabile*. Yet, it is not free of difficulties, most of which stem from the distribution of voices: the melody played in one hand while the other executes a veritable etude in finger substitution; juggling the three-part accompaniment; trying to keep the voices legato while maintaining correct note values; and all the while, dealing with the chromatic alterations of a key signature with five sharps.

For publication, Franck adopted a conservative registration scheme, suitable for most contemporary three-manual organs. The enclosed Récit 8′ foundation stops together with the Hautbois and Trompette specified for the solo were accompanied by the 8′ Flûte harmonique and Bourdon of the unenclosed Positif. The contrasting chordal passages were heard on the four foundation stops of the Grand-Orgue: Flûte harmonique, Bourdon, Gambe, and Montre. The Pédale was registered strongly. The *jeux de fonds de 8 et 16 pieds* at Sainte-Clotilde were open flue ranks (8′ Flûte and 16′ Contrebasse), while at the Trocadéro Franck chose four pedal stops (16′ Sous-Basse and Contrebasse, 8′ Grosse Flûte, and Bourdon). The Grand-Orgue remained uncoupled and the Positif was coupled to the Pédale throughout.

D'Indy stated that the *Cantabile* "was written by the maître especially to display the warm, expressive quality of the new Clarinette stop, recently discovered by Cavaillé-Coll."[4] Apparently, d'Indy confused the *Cantabile* with the *Andante* of the *Grande Pièce symphonique*, which called for the Cromorne and was performed by Franck on the same program at the Trocadéro. We know that the stop d'Indy heard at the Trocadéro was a Cromorne, not a Clarinette; that Cavaillé-Coll did not "discover" it; that Franck played the *Cantabile* solo on the Hautbois, Trompette, and five other 8′ stops (which registration he wrote on the manuscript); and

[3]d'Indy, *César Franck*, 161.
[4]d'Indy, *César Franck*, 161.

a review of his recital mentions the effectiveness of the melody "thanks to the telling Récit stop employed."[5]

A brief summary of the differences between Franck's original registration at the Trocadéro and that eventually published in the Durand score is of interest. At the Trocadéro Franck reserved the fourth manual (Solo) 8' Diapason and 8' Flûte harmonique for the chordal interludes at mm. 1-2, 6-7, 11, 25-26, and 30-31. The solo melody was played on the Positif 8' Salicional and Flûte harmonique with the Récit 8' Fonds, Hautbois, and Trompette coupled to it. The accompaniment was played on the Grand-Orgue 8' Flûte harmonique and Bourdon. It is noteworthy that Franck coupled the solo combination to the Pédale by means of the Tirasse Positif for the statement of the motif (Example 1), at mm. 6-7, 25-26, and 30-31, and consistently removed the Tirasse Positif as the melody returned to the manuals.

Ex. 1, mm. 1-2

This effect was eliminated for publication. In fact, Franck went to the opposite extreme and did not even couple the Grand-Orgue to the Pédale at these passages, feeling, no doubt, that the Pédale and Positif stops sufficiently balanced the Grand-Orgue. Players disturbed by what, on certain instruments, might come across as incomplete chords, or inadequate pedal tone, might double the pedal-part in the left hand at these chordal passages.

At m. 50 the manuscript reads *ôtez Tremblant* and at m. 65, *tremblant*. For the premiere of the *Cantabile* Franck had the tremulant on the solo stops for the entire piece except for the canon between mm. 51 and 65. He must have had second thoughts about this effect, for it was deleted at the time of publication.

[5]"Nouvelles Musicales de l'Exposition," *Revue et Gazette musicale de Paris* (October 6, 1878) 321.

Non troppo lento.
Tournemire   ♩ = 69 (Recording, Polydor 561047   ♩ = 76)
Dupré   ♩ = 69
Marchal   ♩ = 58
Langlais   ♩ = 69

It is incongruous that the composer drew four 8′ stops on the unenclosed Grand-Orgue and then wrote *p* for a dynamic in the first measure! This indication is more applicable to the Positif in the third measure.

Notice how Franck began each new phrase on the Récit either *mf* or *f* and then ended with a *diminuendo*. Players must remember to open the swell box each time they go to the Grand-Orgue in order to prepare for the next entrance of the melody. The importance of faithful observation of the dynamic marks was pointed out by Louis Vierne in his description of hearing Eugène Gigout play the *Cantabile* at Franck's funeral:

> Unbearable distress seized us when, at the offertory, we heard coming from the Grand Orgue the maître's own *Cantabile*, played too fast and without expression.[4]

The left hand's upper voice in m. 7 was originally (in the manuscript) an A♯ for three beats (as at the corresponding progressions in mm. 2 and 26). For publication, Franck changed it to an A-natural going to an A♯.

The upward leap of a minor seventh occurs five times. The first two times, in m. 9 (Example 2) and in the left hand in m. 33, it is in the middle of a phrase.

Ex. 2, mm. 8-10

---

[6]Louis Vierne, *Mes Souvenirs* (Paris: Les Amis de l'Orgue, 1970) 26.

Its next three appearances, during the canon of the middle section, (right hand, mm. 58 and 59, Pédale, m. 59), Franck began a new phrase with the upper note on the third beat. The player must be aware of the two different phrasings applied by the composer and interpret each as indicated. Charles Tournemire phrased them identically on his recording, lifting before the upper note each time it occured.

A better legato may be achieved, especially by players with small hands, in the accompaniment in mm. 18 and 67, by taking the upper note in the left-hand staff on beat 2 with the right thumb.

The third beat of m. 19 (Example 3), a repetition of m. 17, will be played with *tenuto*. The passage continues with an *accelerando* through mm. 20-22 and concludes with a *tenuto* at beats 3 and 4 of m. 23 and a *rallentando* in m. 24.

Ex. 3, mm. 16-24

The corresponding passage from m. 67 through m. 73 should be interpreted the same way as mm. 18-24 (see Example 3).

The Récit was coupled to the Positif (*accouplez le R. au P.*) at m. 43 and automatically coupled to the Pédale through the Tirasse Positif. The left hand, playing on the Grand-Orgue, retains its independent line. A canon at the octave begins at m. 51, the antecedent being the upper of the three right-hand voices. The consequent, beginning in the bass at m. 52, stands out all the more as the Grand-Orgue is coupled to the Pédale (*mettez la tirasse du G.O.*). The left hand's counterpoint comes to the fore, heard on four unenclosed stops.

The 1956 Durand edition added the tie between the left hand As connecting the second and third beats. The tie appeared in the manuscript but was missing in the original edition.

The soprano note of the fourth beat of mm. 61 and 63 must be tied to the alto voice of the first beat of mm. 62 and 64 (Example 4). These notes are treated as common notes in order to preserve the *legato* indicated by the phrasing.

Ex. 4, mm. 61-64

There are numerous instances (such as in Example 4) where the fingers of the left hand can reach to the upper manual to achieve a legato execution.

Marcel Dupré solved the fingering difficulties of the middle section by coupling all manuals to the Grand-Orgue at m. 43 and moving the right hand to that manual at m. 60, beat 3; the inner parts are then comfortably distributed between the hands. Both hands move to the Positif at m. 63 and the right hand returns to the Récit (as in the Durand edition) at m. 65. Although this alters the composer's precise directions, his conception remains unchanged (the canon has ceased in the right hand at m. 60) and Dupré's solution can certainly be considered as a viable compromise for players with small hands.

For a work featuring a melody played on a solo combination, the ending of the *Cantabile* is unconventional. On the second beat of m. 87 (Example 5) Franck suddenly introduces a second voice in the solo line.

Ex. 5, mm. 86-89

Then, in the next measure, he adds a third voice. Perhaps it was this disappearance of the solo line that encouraged Charles Tournemire on his recording to change the right-hand registration to the Voix humaine at the second beat of m. 86. (André Marchal changed to a Voix céleste on the second eighth note of m. 87.)

For his second piece written as a solo with accompaniment (the first being the *Andante* of the *Grande Pièce symphonique*, Franck again chose the key of B major. This time, though, he foreshadowed the extended solos of the *Choral I* in E Major and the *Choral III* in A Minor and featured the Récit Trompette for the solo voice.

Charles Tournemire, trying to describe the *Cantabile*, lapsed into a flight of almost untranslatable prose:

> The *Cantabile* is a masterpiece: the soul's unsatisfied desire—a saint's inner supplications—incessant pleas—faith in divine mercy. This page, one of Franck's most remarkable, presents a simple melody, softly contoured, like the shore of a lake. One of the most beautiful canons blooms in full clarity. The totally concentrated peroration is the most perfect expression of suavity.[5]

While few organists would venture to attribute so metaphysical an interpretation to this, the shortest of Franck's twelve major pieces for organ, none would deny that, in spite of its brevity, the *Cantabile* may well be his most inprired and, perhaps, his most beautiful organ work.

Corrections for the 1956 Durand Edition

P	M	S	
15	1	7	l.h. slurs over beats 1–3
16	1	6	l.h., beat 3, C♯ not tied to m. 7 in first edition (1883), nor in manuscript
16	3	5	r.h. A-natural half note not slurred to beat 4 in first edition, nor in the manuscript
17	2	4	pedal add tie to m. 5
18	1	1	l.h. two B♯s not tied in first edition, nor in the manuscript
18	1	3	l.h. two As not tied in first edition, but they are in the manuscript
18	1	4	slur alto B to next measure A♯ half note (not in the manuscript)
18	2	3	beat 1, C♯ not tied to m. 4 in first edition, nor in the manuscirpt
19	2		r.h. slurring not indicated in first edition until m 5; l.h. slurring not indicated in mm. 5–6
19	3		l.h. slurring not indicated in first edition in mm. 1–2; l.h. mm. 3–4 marked with one long slur, instead of two short ones. No slurs in the manuscript.

[7]Tournemire, *César Franck*. Translated in Smith, *Toward an Authentic Interpretation...*, 85.

CHAPTER X

Pièce héroïque

Completed:	September 19, 1878, Paris
Published:	1883
Publisher:	1. Durand & Schoenwerk, Plate No. D.S. & Cie. 3177
	2. Durand & Cie., 1956 Plate No: D. & F. 13.793
Manuscript:	No. 20151–3, Bibliothèque Nationale
Performance:	Premiered by the composer on October 1, 1878, at the Trocadéro.
Bibliography:	Winslow Cheney, "A Lesson in Playing Franck—Measure-by-Measure Outline of Technical Details Involved in Attaining an Artistic Interpretation of *Pièce héroïque*," *The American Organist* (August 1937), 263–67. This article is cited because of its reference to R. Huntington Woodman, Franck's only American student, and its noteworthy performance suggestions.

An apocryphal anecdote intimates that César Franck intended the *Pièce héroïque* as a tribute to the French army defeated in the 1871 Franco-Prussian War, its ending in the major mode being a great hymn of joy exalting the soldiers of France, crushed in arms but morally victorious. Camille Saint-Saëns composed a *Marche héroïque* in 1871 in memory of his friend, the painter Henri Regnault, who was killed in the war, and this work may have become confused with Franck's *Pièce héroïque*, which, undedicated, has nonetheless inspired program annotators with vivid imaginations for fictionalized history. No evidence exists to suggest that the work has a programmatic intent and one cannot help recalling the words of Arturo Toscanini to his orchestra

Plate 44. First page of the manuscript of the *Pièce héroïque*

194

about the opening bars of Beethoven's *Fifth Symphony:* "See those notes? That's not Fate knocking at the door—it's *Allegro con brio!*" Similarly, the *Pièce héroïque* is not, as Charles Tournemire panegyrized, "a hymn of spiritual triumph in which struggle gives way to gentle pleas for help and leads to victory and joy." It is *Allegro maestoso.*

Two additonal secondary sources will be cited in discussing the *Pièce héroïque:* Marcel Dupré's recording (the earliest phonograph record of a Franck organ work) made on June 21, 1926 for His Master's Voice[1] on the 1893 four-manual, fifty-four-stop Hill organ in Queen's Hall, London; and Joseph Bonnet's (1884–1944) edition that appears in Volume V of his *Historical Organ Recitals.*[2] Bonnet won first prize in Alexandre Guilmant's organ class at the Paris Conservatoire in 1906, one year before Dupré. He had been Tournemire's assistant at Sainte-Clotilde during his student days, was a lifelong friend and colleague of Louis Vierne, a conscientious scholar, and a consummate virtuoso whose lineage in the Franck "tradition" is quite valid. Additional technical details, including Joseph Bonnet's metronome marking, were kindly provided by William Self, who studied this work with Bonnet in 1928.

Allegro maestoso.

Tournemire	$\quad$ = 96
Bonnet	$\quad$ = 80
Dupré	$\quad$ = 80 (Recording: $\quad$ = 92)
Marchal	$\quad$ = 76
Langlais	$\quad$ = 96

As usual, Franck's registration is uncomplicated: all the fonds and anches of the Récit, 8' foundation stops on the Positif and 16' and 8' foundation stops on the Grand-Orgue and Pédale. All divisions except the Récit have *jeux d'anches préparées,* but at what pitches? The manuscript clarifies the composer's intentions: Récit and Positif have the 4' and 8' reeds, Grand-Orgue and Pédale, 16', and 4'—a registration that would have been appropriate for

---

[1]No. D 1115.
[2]Joseph Bonnet, *Historical Organ-Recitals, Volume V, Modern Composers: Franck to Reger* (New York: G. Schirmer, 1929) 3-13.

either the organ at Sainte-Clotilde or the Trocadéro, where Franck premiered the work.

The left hand trill (Example 1) found in mm. 6, 26, and 143

Ex. 1, mm. 6–7

is played as follows:

Ex. 2

At the brisk tempo of around ♩ = 96, this is the maximum number of notes that can be articulated comfortably.

Franck wrote *lentement* above m. 7 (see Example 1) and its counterpart, m. 70 (but not, oddly enough, at m. 27), in the manuscript. Perhaps he felt such an interpretation would be misunderstood or, if printed, exaggerated, so he omitted it in the published score. Organists should keep this nuance in mind, however, and experiment with a slackening of the tempo here, as the composer did.

From the distribution of the parts in m. 21 (Example 3), it is obvious that the soprano F♯ is played on the Grand-Orgue and the three lower voices accompany it on the Positif. This can be realized by the right hand playing on two manuals at once, reaching up to the Positif to play the last half of the second and third beats.

Ex. 3, m. 21

It is not inconceivable that Franck played it this way, but in all probability he played the thirds on the Grand-Orgue (detached, as indicated in the editions prepared by Bonnet and Dupré, and as taught by Langlais and Marchal) and the bass, which he was particular enough to include above a one-measure phrase, *legato* on the Positif. In the similar place at m. 158 Franck indicated *staccato* for the thirds in both the manuscript and the published score.

R. Huntington Woodman (1861–1943), "who studied this composition in Paris with César Franck himself, said that Franck was particular about having (the eighth notes in m. 27) played in a crisp, short, staccato."[3]

Ex. 4, m. 27

[3]Winslow Cheney, "A Lesson in Playing Franck—Measure-by-Measure Outline of Technical Details Involved in Attaining an Artistic Interpretation of *Pièce héroïque*," *The American Organist* (August 1937) 264.

In the manuscript a *crescendo* is indicated throughout m. 33. Its deletion in the published version suggests Franck's considering it impractical inasmuch as the right foot had to depress the Anches Positif and the left foot had to prepare the pedal entry. Yet, it could be executed on organs where the effect would be heard, by closing the swell box part way as the hands move to the Grand Orgue and opening it throughout m. 33. The *f* in m. 34, missing in the manuscript, appears to be incorrect since the Positif Anches, added to the Grand Orgue, certainly equal more than the *f* in m. 32.

Measure 34.

Marchal ♩ = 72
Langlais ♩ = 88

Tournemire suggested playing this section *insistant,* that is, stressing the chords. Dupré, on his recording, played mm. 36–37 on a secondary manual; in his Bornemann edition, he marked the left hand *legato* (mm. 36–37) while keeping the right hand *marcato.* Winslow Cheney described in detail how to achieve a thrilling climax for this section:

Ex. 5, mm. 44–47

Assuming that a strong rhythmic momentum has been developed from m. 33 through m. 44, hold back on b. 2 of m. 45 just a little; on b. 3 hold back much more, making the third beat as large as possible without breaking the rhythm. Then play the first two beats of m. 46 right in time, making only the slightest ritard on b. 3. Try it over a couple of dozen times to get just the right feel. If you get it just right it certainly puts a dynamic kick into the high

F$\sharp$ climax chord in m. 47. Further, I believe it's a little more heroic sounding than the broad ritard. *But,* a strong rhythmic development from m. 33, or at the very latest, m. 38, is the fundamental essential. I have heard this device used by some orchestral conductors with excellent effect.

Then, too, let us observe another thing about this climax. Measure 45, where we are making the ritard, is a duplicate of m. 44. Therefore, let us be sure that m. 44 is exactly in time, to provide good contrast, and to heighten the effect of the ritard when it comes in m. 45. Then our idea of holding back the rhythm in m. 45 is only to let it drive on forward again in m. 46, sweeping through to the climax in m. 47, with only the slightest ritard at the end of b. 3, m. 46.[4]

Bonnet treated the F$\sharp$ chord on the first beat of m. 47 as an eighth note, rather than a sixteenth, to insure its receiving full emphasis.

Charles Tournemire suggested playing the left-hand part from m. 47 very *legato* and evenly and, from m. 60, making a cadence of the descending line that precedes the return to the initial theme at m. 65.

According to the manuscript, Franck went to the Récit with both hands at m. 79.

Measure 80.

Tournemire	less quickly
Dupré	$\quad \downarrow$ = 72
Marchal	$\quad \downarrow$ = 60
Langlais	$\quad \downarrow$ = 80

At. m. 80 the 4′ stops are removed from the Récit, the Grand-Orgue is reduced to 8′ Flûte harmonique and Bourdon, the 16′ Bourdon is added to the Positif, and the Positif is uncoupled from the Grand-Orgue. Both the Grand-Orgue and Positif remain coupled to the Pédale, however, and because the Récit is still coupled to the Positif, it, too, is carried through to the Pédale. This means that the *quasi tympani* effect that pervades this section, is quite prominent. Those organists who object to the Trompette of the Récit heard in the Pédale may wish to follow a precedent set by the composer at the Trocadéro: he marked the manuscript at this

[4]Ibid.

point: *ôtez les tirasses, mais laissez tous les jeux aux Péd* (take off the tirasses but leave all the pedal stops). He then added the Tirasse Positif in m. 107 and Tirasse G.O. at the beginning of m. 113. Joseph Bonnet left all the pedal couplers off until m. 144. Dupré, contrary to the composer's intentions, reduced the organ to 8′ Fonds at this point, with only the Récit coupled to the Pédale, so only 16′ and 8′ stops are heard.

The *p* indication in the manuscript will make the *crescendo* and *diminuendo* in mm. 82–83 more effective than the *mf* in the published score.

Bonnet tied the left-hand F♯ on the second beat of m. 81 to the first beat of the following measure.

At m. 108 we are instructed to *mettez tous les jeux d'anches du R.* (add all the jeux d'anches of the Récit), which at Sainte-Clotilde would have included the 4′ Flûte octaviante, 2′ Octavin, and 4′ Clairon, and at the Trocadéro would have been 2′ Octavin, Cornet, and 16′, 8′, and 4′ chorus reeds. In the manuscript Franck added only the 4′ Clairon. The 4′, 8′, and 16′ fonds are again added to the Grand-Orgue, along with the Positif au Grand-Orgue coupler.

Tournemire directed that the section beginning at m. 109 be played "progressively animated and restless," the equivalent of an *accelerando*. First, it is important to establish a steady tempo at m. 108, then develop an *accelerando* that will continue until the climax of the section at m. 125. The pedal eighth notes B–F♯ can be played with alternate toes since the swell pedal is not required until m. 119, where the minor third in the pedal part is easily managed by the left foot.

Marcel Dupré devised a clever means of making the octave leaps from mm. 111–20 legato: the upper left-hand note on the first beat in mm. 111, 115, and 119 is taken with the right thumb; the upper left-hand note on beat 2, mm. 112, 116, and 120 is played by the fifth finger of the right hand.

The two lower right-hand voices in m. 118 are tied to the following measure in the manuscript. These ties are missing in the score.

Franck marked *lentement* in his manuscript between mm. 138–39. This was eliminated in the published score, but is an important example of the nuances that Franck added as he played his music.

At the *Très largement ff*, m. 151, Tournemire suggested "with grandeur." At m. 157 a *rallentando* is required, and a slight *accelerando* on the last half of m. 158 leads back to an *a Tempo* at the beginning of m. 159. Winslow Cheney gave the following advice for interpreting the next five measures:

> Pick up the tempo just a little through m 160 and m. 161, and make a good-sized ritard in m. 163. . . and don't hold onto b. 3 unduly. Do most of the enlarging on b. 2. The idea is to carry the listener along from m. 159 through m. 163, then suddenly leave him up in the air for the rest of measure 164.[5]

Più lento (Manuscript: *Lentement*).

Dupré   ♩ = 72 (Recording: ♩ = 63–69)
Marchal   ♩ = 50
Langlais   ♩ = 60

From m. 165 through m. 172 Bonnet and Dupré played all manual chords detached and the pedal *legato*. Marchal and Langlais played the soprano line *legato* in mm. 167–68.

From mm. 173–78 the first three soprano notes of each phrase are played *legato*, the rest of the chords, detached; the pedal, still *legato*. Dupré and Marchal ignored the dots on the half notes in the Pédale at mm. 175 and 178.

There is no reason why the pedal solo at mm. 179–83 must be played *legato* from beginning to end as Marchal and Langlais interpreted it. Three alternate phrasings are not without interest. Dupré, on his recording, phrased it as in Example 6.

Ex. 6, mm. 179–83

---

[5]*Ibid.*

Plate 45. Measures 175–92 of the manuscript of the *Pièce héroïque*

This is a subtle variant of the pedal phrasing (Example 7) adopted by Charles Courboin (1886–1973), the Belgian-American organist who enjoyed an enviable and much-deserved reputation as a Franck interpreter during the three decades following World War I.[6]

Ex. 7, mm. 179–83

Joseph Bonnet, on the other hand, by using alternate toes, created phrases in entirely different places: between the two notes played with the right foot.

Ex. 8, mm. 179–83

As originally composed and performed at the Trocadéro, the *Pièce héroïque* had an additional two measures inserted between mm. 185–86, and all of the concluding chords had a B as the highest note instead of D♯. In Plate 47 we see how Franck originally conceived the ending. Rather than adopt a new tempo, Bonnet executed a *sempre stringendo* beginning at m. 224 and extending to m. 231, where he added *molto* to Franck's *Rit.*

While rejecting the programmatic intent of the *Pièce héroïque,* there is no denying that it is rich in those elements that make it a consummate Romantic organ work. Its menacing, sinister, growling theme contrasts dramatically with the contemplative middle section, and the contest between minor and major tonalities, translated by many listeners as evil battling with good, ends triumphantly in B major. Its repeated chords and arpeggios have been criticized as pianistic, but their effect has never detracted from the work's popular

[6]His phrasing can be heard on a recording (Victor DM 695) made on October 22, 1939 at the American Academy of Arts and Letters in New York City.

success. It is all the more surprising then that this is the only one of the *Trois Pièces* that Franck never played again after its premiere.

Ex. 9, Franck's original ending.

Corrections for the 1956 Durand Edition

P	S	M	
20	1	6	l.h. no slur under first three notes
21	2	2	tie soprano F♯ to m. 3
21	2	4	original may indicate ties of soprano F♯ to m. 5 (as at 20–1–4 and 23–3–3; original shows incomplete tie between F♯s); it is tied in the manuscript.
21	2	7	tie alto F♯ dotted half note to next score
22	2	4	l.h., b. 4, E-natural should be E♯
23	1	4	tie pedal F♯ to m. 5
23	3	3	tie soprano F♯ to m. 4
23	3	4–6	l.h. slurs not in original
24	2	4	l.h., b. 2, ties to m. 5 not in original, nor in the manuscript
24	3	3	l.h. last eighth is G♯ (not G-natural)
25	3	1	add *diminuendo* indication; alto E does not tie to m. 2, nor in the manuscript
25	3	1–2	l.h., b. 1, triplets slurred (C♯-G♯ and A-E)
25	3	2	B in last chord not tied to m. 3 in original, or in the manuscript
27	2	1	r.h., b. 2, second sixteenth should be G♯ (not G)
27	2	3–4	and beats 1 and 2 of m. 5, l.h. no slurs in original
27	3	3–5	no pedal slurs in original nor in the manuscript
27	3	4	tie soprano B to m. 5
28	2	1	r.h. no slurs in original
28	2	5–6	r.h. no slurs in original
28	3	1	r.h. no slurs in original

Plate 46. First page of the manuscript of *Choral I* in E Major

Trois Chorals

The *Trois Chorals pour Orgue* have a unique spontaneity of spirit and perfection of form. And, in addition to their other qualities, they have yet another, the greatest of all: a spirit of dedication. Franck's works, like those of Bach, reveal the profound piety of the artist who wrote them.[1]

Albert Schweitzer

. . . in the *Trois Chorals* is found the purest and most complete expression of Franck's genius as a composer: they take their place beside the organ works of Bach among the masterpieces written for the instrument. Deriving more from the later Beethoven quartets than from the chorale preludes of Bach, they are, in a sense, variations on a chorale-like theme, but welded into wholes unimagined by the earlier composers of *partite.*

Felix Aprahamian

[1]Note accompanying his recording of the *Trois Chorals*, Columbia ML 5128.

Plate 47. Augusta Holmès

Introduction to the *Trois Choral*s

The *Trois Chorals* for organ were César Franck's last works. They were composed, as was his custom, during summer vacation and were completed within a two-month period: *Choral I*, August 7, 1890; *Choral II*, September 17; and *Choral III*, September 30. Unlike the nine pieces already discussed, these are works Franck did not have the opportunity to "teach": he died on November 8, 1890, and they were not published until the following year. He did play through them on the piano at his home with at least two students. Louis Vierne wrote that "he played them to us himself on the piano, with [Guillaume] Lekeu playing the bass, on Thursday, October 2, 1890,"[2] two days before his first class at the Conservatoire. Around the same time Charles Tournemire also heard Franck play them over, it being his job to play the pedal part "à *la main*."

Vincent d'Indy wrote that Franck "wished to drag himself once more to his organ at Sainte-Clotilde in order to write down the proper combination of stops."[3] It might be wondered why, since the registration of the *Chorals* is the same *Fonds et Hautbois, Anches Récit*, etc., as in all of his other music. Much of the registration in the manuscripts available for study is incomplete and, in the case of the *Choral II* in B Minor, erased and written over by an editor.

None of the manuscripts, whether first or final drafts, bears the name of a dedicatee, yet, upon publication by Durand, each *Choral* was inscribed to a different person: I. à Eugène Gigout; II. à Auguste Durand; and III. à Augusta Holmès. Vincent d'Indy said that it was by mistake that these names appear and that Franck had really dedicated the *Chorals* to: I. Alexandre Guilmant; II. Théodore Dubois; and III. Eugène Gigout.[4] Léon Vallas was more specific, writing that, for personal reasons, Franck's son, Georges,

[2]Vierne, *Mes Souvenirs*, 23.
[3]d'Indy, *César Franck*, 58.
[4]d'Indy, *César Franck*, 198.

replaced the first two names with those of Durand and Holmès. The Franckists, perfectly aware of their maître's intentions, wrote and told the truth to the three original dedicatees.[5]

Others contend that all three *Chorals* were dedicated to Augusta Holmès. Perhaps not even examination of manuscripts still in the possession of the Franck family would confirm this. Between the two sets of dedicatees one name remains constant: Eugène Gigout, albeit on two different *Chorals*. Gigout prepared the manuscript of the *Trois Chorals* for publication[6] and Marcel Dupré said that he had seen the final proofs of the *Chorals* at Durand's publishing house signed by Gigout, approving them for final publication.[7] A comparison of the handwriting in the manuscript of *Choral II* with Eugène Gigout's autograph, however, indicates that none of the registration is in his hand. What may have been Franck's original directions were erased, rewritten, and translated into English by an unidentified editor.

Two editions of the *Trois Chorals* are recommended for their informed editorial annotations but should be used only in conjunction with the Durand edition. The first is an edition by Joseph Bonnet,[8] completed in 1942 and published in 1948, four years after Bonnet's death. Bonnet's interpretative and technical suggestions are all useful. The only drawback is that the registration was adapted to a standard American organ of the 1930s. A 1973 edition by Maurice Duruflé is a reprint of the 1956 Durand edition with Duruflé's "revisions and annotations" consisting of dynamic and rhythmic suggestions added in parentheses. Like Bonnet and Dupré, he offered some clever solutions to technical difficulties, making it worth the exorbitant price.

---

[5]Léon Vallas, *La véritable histoire de César Franck* (Paris: Flammarion, 1950.) Translated by Hubert Foss as *César Franck* (New York: Oxford University Press, 1951) 233.
[6]Gabriel Fauré, *Hommage à Eugène Gigout* (Paris: Floury, 1923) 17.
[7]Christiane Trieu-Colleney, *Jeanne Demessieux* (Paris: Les Presses Universelles, 1977) 135.
[8]César Franck: *Three Chorals for Organ*, arranged, edited, and annotated by Joseph Bonnet (Glen Rock, N.J.: J. Fischer & Bro., 1948).

CHAPTER XI

Choral I in E Major

Completed:	August 7, 1890
Published:	1891
Publisher:	1. A. Durand & Fils.
	Plate No: D.S. 4414
	2. Durand & Cie., 1956
	Plate No: D. & F. 13.794
Dedication:	Eugène Gigout (or Alexandre Guilmant, or Augusta Holmès)
Manuscript:	Pierpont Morgan Library, New York City
Performance:	Played by Albert Mahaut at the Trocadéro in June, 1899.
Bibliography:	Ernest Bücken, "Die Musik des 19 Jahrhunderts," *Handbuch des Musikwissenschaft 1928* (Leipzig: Röder, 1928) 281. Plate XVII reproduced the first page of this manuscript, then in the collection of Alfred Cortot, Paris. (It was credited to Alfred Coctot!)
	Amy Dommel-Diény, *L'Analyse harmonique en examples de J.-S. Bach à Debussy.* Fascicule 11: César Franck (Paris: Éditions A. Dommel-Diény, 1973). Pages 43–91 contain an extended analysis of the *Trois Chorals.*
	Philip Gehring, "Master Lesson: Franck's *Choral I,*" *The American Organist* (April 1980) 44–45.
	Karen Hastings, "From Manuscript to Publication: Implications for Performance Practice in the *First Choral* of César Franck," DMA term project, Stanford University, June 1987.
	Robert Rayfield, "Rhythmic Conventions in the Performance of César Franck's *Three Chorals,*" *MUSIC* (June 1975) 29–33.

Kathryn Eleanor Schenk, *Heinrich Fleischer: The Organist's Calling and the Straube Tradition.* Ph.D. dissertation, University of Minnesota, 1989. Pages 377–394 contain a facsimile of Fleischer's "transcription" of *Choral I* with several imaginative examples of part redistribution.

Charles Tournemire, *César Franck* (Paris: Delagrave, 1931). Chapter Vbis, "Les *Trois Chorals*," pp. 27–36, appears in English translation in Rollin Smith's *Toward an Authentic Interpretation of the Organ Works of César Franck* (New York: Pendragon Press, 1983) 85–94.

The Franck family spent summer vacations at Nemours with Mme. Désiré Brissaud, a cousin of Franck's wife. It was during this time that Franck completed his first *Choral* on August 7. At the end of August Franck wrote to a friend:

> I have written a long organ piece that I have entitled simply *Choral.* A chorale it is, indeed, but with plenty of fantasy. Then I've also done fifty pieces for harmonium, about half the promised volume. I am hoping next to compose two other organ chorals, the second half of the harmonium book, and a sonata for piano and cello.[1]

A fourteen-page manuscript of *Choral I,* probably the second draft, was for many years in the autograph collection of the great French pianist, Alfred Cortot, it having been inscribed and given by Franck to Clotilde Bréal, Cortot's wife. After his death in 1962 it was acquired by Robert Lehman who donated it in 1972 to the Pierpont Morgan Library in New York City. The differences and similarities between this manuscript and the Durand edition have been scrupulously analyzed by Karen Hastings in her paper, "From Manuscript to Publication," and those interested in pursuing the subject further are referred to that source.

---

[1] Vallas, *César Franck,* 230.

Moderato.

Tournemire	♩ = 69	
Bonnet	♩ = 50	(In the 1920s and '30s he suggested ♩ = 60).
Dupré	♩ = 56	
Marchal	♩ = 56	
Langlais	♩ = 63	
Duruflé	♩ = 60	

There is a broad range of tempos among the six organists cited above: from ♩ = 50 to ♩ = 69. A variation of twenty beats a minute is not inconsiderable. William Self, who studied with Joseph Bonnet between 1928 and 1940, mentioned that during that time Bonnet suggested ♩ = 60 for this *Choral*, apparently feeling it slower as he grew older. One must bear in mind that the quicker the tempo the more flexibility the performer will have with rubatos and ritards. At ♩ = 50, a *rallentando* can be interminable; frequent ones, deadly.

The registration is *Fonds de 8* on all three manuals with the addition of the Hautbois on the Récit. The Pédale, with *Fonds 8 et 16*, is uncoupled until m. 195, beat 3.

While the first sixty-four measures of six-part harmony are written for manuals only, it is convenient to couple all manuals to the pedal with no pedal stops drawn and, playing the lowest voice in the pedal, to distribute the other parts comfortably between the hands. Tournemire, Vierne, Bonnet, and Dupré all did so, and it cannot be denied that such an arrangement keeps a passage, such as Example 1, effortlessly *legato*. A manual-only interpretation should be considered, nevertheless, for the reasons outlined on page 136 in our discussion of the *Prière*.

Ex. 1, mm. 30–34 (Original Durand edition printed on two staves)

Bonnet's and Dupré's editions print the beginning of *Choral I* on three staves. Those passages on the Récit are less awkward and can be played without pedal by most players, but for those with small hands, all couplers, except those of the Récit, must be removed when playing on that manual.

Ex. 2, mm. 30–34 (Bonnet's edition printed on three staves)

There is no dynamic indication until the *crescendo* at m. 31. Thus, the swell box should be closed before the *crescendo* but, knowing Franck's proclivity for expressive dynamics, it is not idiomatic to play the first part of the *Choral* without nuance. Bonnet and Duruflé, in their respective editions, have inserted *crescendos* and *diminuendos* compatible with Franck's usage in his other works. Both add a *ritard* at m. 45 but neither indicates a fermata on the second beat of m. 46, demanded by Tournemire, from whom both trace their style.

Four of the five fermatas in *Choral I* appear in the first draft manuscript.[2] Although the manuscript is devoid of dynamic marks, as well as most phrasing and tempo indications, the fermatas appear to have been part of Franck's creative process.

Undoubtedly, a tie is missing in m. 36 between the alto, beat 3, and the next measure. Throughout this section, when the right-hand octaves are repeated, the lower notes are tied.

---

[2]Hastings, "From Manuscript to Publication...", 42

Ex. 3, mm. 36–40

The "real" theme of *Choral I* begins on the third beat of m. 46. Franck was quite specific that the Gambe be removed from the foundation stops of the Récit so that the Voix humaine is heard with only the Flûte harmonique and Bourdon. This is emphasized because, in his book, Charles Tournemire wrote that Franck delighted in using the Voix humaine with the Gambe and Voix céleste (coupled to the Positif 16′ Bourdon).[3] It is therefore remarkable that Franck never wrote a piece in which he specified this registration, and in this instance he specifically wanted the Gambe taken off.

At the risk of too closely associating Franck with the organ's most maligned stop, the Vox humana, it is important to realize that into whatever language it is translated, it is a legitimate and, historically, very old organ voice. As the Voix humaine, it was particularly favored by César Franck who used it with discretion not only in the *Fantaisie in A*, but also in his first major organ work, the *Fantaisie in C*, and his last, two of the *Trois Chorals*, confiding to it some of his most sublime thoughts. If an organ lacks this voice, it is necessary to substitute something else. The Voix céleste should not be the player's first choice: save for the "voix" it has nothing in common with the tremulous nasal quality of the short-length reed stop. The Voix céleste was available to Franck but he used it only once if frequency is a determinate, the Voix humaine was preferred.

Karen Hastings, observing the absence of ties in the Morgan Library manuscript, suggested that Franck composed this *Choral* at

[3]Smith, *Toward an Authentic Interpretation...*, 25.

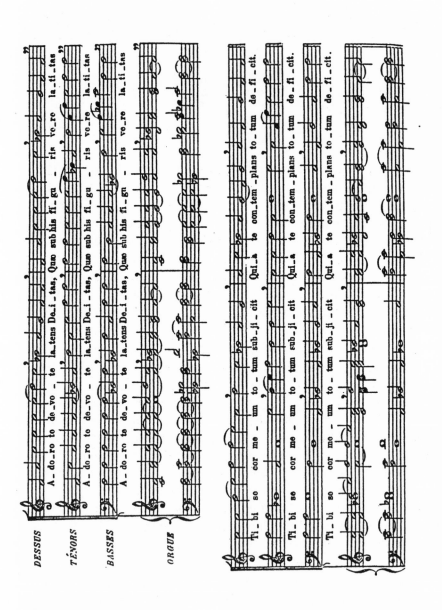

Plate 48. Franck's harmonization and accompaniment of the hymn, *Adoro te devote*. Note the repeated notes.

the piano, "where repeated notes would have helped sustain a fuller harmony," and later, when he played it over on the organ, added slurs and ties.[4] Even so, an intimate acquaintance with Franck's music, and his organ music in particular, leads one to suspect that many more ties are missing from the Durand edition. For instance, in Example 4 only two ties are printed: two common notes in m. 53, beat 2, bass, tied to the upper bass part in beat 3, and m. 54, beat 3, bass, tied to the upper bass part in m. 55, beat 1.

Ex. 4, mm. 53–55

In the space of slightly more than two measures, eight accompaniment notes are repeated—not common notes, but repeated notes within the same voice. Players will have to decide if, indeed, there are too many repeated notes in succession and if this passage, as it appears in Example 5, "edited" by Marcel Dupré, is an improvement. A glance at Franck's harmonization of *Adoro te devote* (Plate 48 on page 216) will illustrate the composer's preference.

Ex. 5, mm. 53–55

[4]*Op. cit.*, 38.

This first variation is obviously the same tempo as the beginning *Moderato*. Tournemire cautioned against hurrying this variation, saying *insister:* to emphasize or stress it. Duruflé added a precautionary *p* in preparation for the *crescendo-diminuendo* in m. 67.

Faithfully observing Franck's dynamic markings imposes an articulation in the pedal line of Example 6 where the right foot must remain on the swell pedal to make the *crescendo* and *diminuendo* while the left foot leaps a fourth, fifth, sixth, and octave within three measures

Ex. 6, mm. 69–72

The alto F♯ on the third beat of m. 79 is tied to the next measure in the manuscript; its omission in the original Durand edition was corrected in that of 1956.

Players who encounter difficulty with the left hand passage between mm. 80 and 86 might experiment with Heinrich Fleischer's suggestion and reverse the hands. The left hand playing the theme on the Récit from the third beat of m. 80, the right hand remaining on the Positif.[5]

Measure 87 is again *a Tempo*. The Trompette was subtracted and the Tremblant added by pédales de combinaisons, but the Hautbois, Voix humaine and 32′ stop knobs, inconveniently located at opposite ends of the stop jambs, had to be moved by hand. Unlike m. 46, there is no mention of withdrawing any other foundation stops that may have been added to the Récit. According to custom, only the Bourdon (and, if indicated, the Flûte harmonique) would have been left on with the Voix humaine and Tremblant. The manuals are still not coupled to the pedal, but a very soft 32′ stop is added to that division's *Flûte 8 et 16*.

In this Voix humaine section (mm. 87–105), the chorale theme is interspersed with arabesques based on the figuration of

[5]Kathryn Eleanor Schenk, *Heinrich Fleischer: The Organist's Calling and the Straube Tradition*. Ph.D. dissertation (University of Minnesota, 1989) 381–82.

the first variation. Only in mm. 93–94 and in the last nine measures does the pedal duplicate the lowest left-hand notes. If the Récit au Pédale *were* added for the sake of facility, it would only be practical from m. 97 onwards.

Example 7 illustrates a clever fingering solution for the awkward Positif interludes in mm. 95 and 96. Joseph Bonnet suggested that the chord divided between two manuals (m. 96, beat 3) "will be more easily played in closing the right hand third and fourth fingers towards the palm."[6]

Ex. 7, mm. 95–97

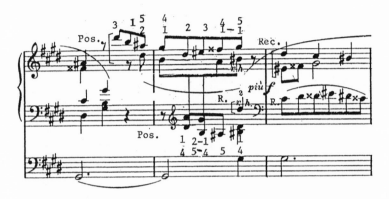

The bass notes (duplicated in the left hand and pedal) E♯ to F-natural in m. 99 are tied in the manuscript and in the first edition. The tie is missing in the Dupré and Duruflé editions.

Maestoso (*Largo* in manuscript).

Tournemire	with much freedom and imagination
	(*beaucoup de fantaisie*)

	♩
Dupré	= 88
Marchal	= 58
Langlais	= 72
Duruflé	= 76

[6]Bonnet, César Franck: *Three Chorals for Organ*, 6.

During the rest under the fermata at m. 105 the pédales des anches are activated in order to bring on the 16′ and 8′ reeds on all manuals (claviers) and the Pédale (also a clavier). An assistant would have already drawn the 16′ and 8′ foundation stops on the Positif and Grand-Orgue while the organist was playing on the Récit. Tirasses are not mentioned, but even without them, the Pédale on Cavaillé-Coll's instruments is adequate to balance the tone of the manuals. Dupré and Duruflé (and Bonnet, through the addition of the Crescendo Pedal) added the pedal couplers for this and the subsequent *Largo*.

Poco animato.

Dupré	♪ = 126
Marchal	♪ = 66
Langlais	♪ = 76
Duruflé	♪ = 80

The swell box must be partly closed at the beginning of m. 112 so that its *crescendo* can be realized in the next measure.

The second *Poco animato* (m. 121) is harmonically the same as the first but a major third lower, and the pedal point appears an octave lower in the Pédale. Because of this the Pédale reeds and the manual couplers obliterate the manual figuration. Removing the Anches Pédale and leaving only the Tirasse Récit provides the perfect solution—but Franck did not have a Tirasse Récit. While it is possible to play the low B an octave higher in the left hand (as at m. 12) it must be assumed that the composer, by writing it in the Pédale, expected it to be heard on 16′ tone. But, without a Récit au Pédale it would be 16′ tone without a reed! To realize Franck's intention the Récit must be coupled to the Pédale at the beginning of m. 121.

Measure 126.

Tournemire	a little faster (*vivante*)
Bonnet	*senza rigore*
Dupré	♩ = 56 *Tempo I°*
Marchal	♩ = 60
Langlais	♩ = 69
Duruflé	♩ = 63 *Moderato*

Franck used the same registration for this second variation as he used for the first—and which he would use again for the *Adagio* of *Choral III:* the *jeux de fonds de 8, Hautbois et Trompette* of the Récit, accompanied by the *Flûte et Bourdon de 8* of the Positif. The Positif can remain coupled to the Grand-Orgue and the direction at m. 147 can be considered precautionary and disregarded.

The editions of Bonnet and Duruflé are useful performance guides for interpreting the *Trois Chorals,* particularly if used together. For instance, in twenty measures we see how the one concentrates on rhythmic inflection and tempo fluctuation while the other is more concerned with dynamics.

Measure	Bonnet	Duruflé
128	b. 3, *poco rit.*	
129	b. 1, *a Tempo*	
	b. 3, *poco rit.*	
130	*a Tempo, sempre cantabile*	*mf*
132	*senza rigore*	*dim.*
133	b. 3, *poco rit.*	
134	*a Tempo*	
135		b. 2, *f*
136	b. 2, *poco rit.*	
137	*a Tempo ma senza rigore*	
139		*poco dim.*
141		*p*
147	*a Tempo*	*a Tempo*

In a split second before the second half of the first beat of m. 147 Franck called for two registrational changes (not including the Positif au Grand-Orgue): *Accouplez Récit au Positif* and *Ôtez Tromp. du Récit* (couple the Récit to the Positif and take off the Récit Trompette). With a very leisurely *ritard* on the first beat, it would be possible for either the player or an assistant to push in the Trompette (the second inside stop knob on the left side of the Sainte-Clotilde organ) but the player would have to depress the pédale de combinaison to couple the Récit au Positif. The two Es in the pedal will have to be taken by the left foot (the right being engaged with the combination pedals). If the Trompette were withdrawn by hand it would still be necessary to silence the Anches

Récit and to draw all of the stops on that chest (i.e., 4', 2', 8' Trompette, and 4' Clairon) in preparation for their introduction at m. 195.

The left hand's imitative phrases played on the Grand-Orgue at mm. 148, 150, 157, and 159 can be fingered in such a way as to facilitate the right hand's playing two four-note chords. If the Grand-Orgue passage begins with the third finger, the second finger is free to reach up and play the lowest note of the right-hand chord on the second half of the second beat. Example 8 illustrates this, as well as m. 157, which must begin with the left thumb.

Ex. 8, mm. 157–59

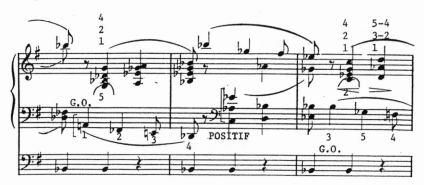

Franck was aware of the difficulty in keeping the accompaniment *legato* when he wrote out the fingering for the close harmony in mm. 174 and 186. However, his solution is not as clever as that of Maurice Duruflé "Example 9" who reached up with the left hand from the Grand-Orgue and played the lower treble-staff notes.

Ex. 9, mm. 174–75

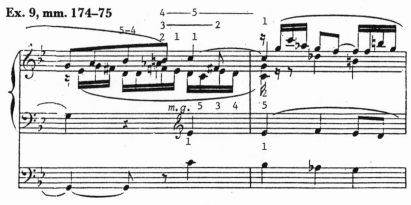

When the counterpoint is inverted at m. 182, the left hand moves to the Positif, but there is no indication what the right hand is to do. Bonnet, following traditional French registrational practice, kept the right hand on the Positif and noted that "the theme being in the soprano stands out perfectly well and would sound too loud and unbalanced if played on the Grand-Orgue."[7] On the contrary, the treatment of mm. 170–81 requires the use of the Grand-Orgue to make the tenor, surrounded by the three other parts, "more noticeable . . . ."[8] There is no doubt that with both hands playing on the same manual, numerous fingering problems are automatically solved by the right hand playing some of the left hand's notes.

Ex. 10, mm. 182–84

An argument for playing the right hand on the Grand-Orgue is just as valid, in that Franck was very particular to maintain the independence of the soprano voice in his manuscript, to the extent that he uncomfortably squeezed three voices, all of different rhythmic value, onto one clef with a plethora of ledger lines. Had he considered the four parts played together, he might have spread the part-writing more conveniently over both staves.

At m. 187 Duruflé suggested playing the high G♭ (see Example 11) with the second and third fingers. This avoids a rhythmic interruption while the left hand changes octaves within a thirty-second of a beat.

[7]Bonnet, César Franck: *Three Chorals for Organ,* 12.
[8]Ibid.

Ex. 11, mm. 186–8

There is a tiny sixteenth note on the second sixteenth of the second beat of m. 192 (Example 12). This is an alternate note for the high F, but, unlike m. 80 (right hand, beat 2) where the small alternate D is written for players with hands too small to reach a tenth, this F might be considered as a way of maintaining the sixteenth note motion.

Ex. 12, mm. 191–93

It could also be considered evidence of Franck's intention that the right-hand melody be played on the Grand-Orgue, since, if both hands were on the same manual, the right hand could easily play notes beyond the reach of the left hand. Wherever the soprano F is played, it would not be repeated since it is the theme; the left-hand high F is already sounding, being coupled to the Grand-Orgue.

If the right hand goes to the Grand-Orgue at m. 182, it must, in another unwritten manual change, move back to the Positif on the second sixteenth of m. 194. At the same time an assistant must draw the Positif 16′ Bourdon and the player must add the Tirasse Grand-Orgue (Tirasse Positif is unnecessary since the Positif is already coupled to the Grand-Orgue and would play through to the Pédale). The swell box should be closed to mask the introduction of the reeds and to execute the *crescendo* that begins in m. 197.

An obvious engraving error in m. 196 (Example 13) has been corrected in the new Durand edition and in all other editions of the *Chorals*. The second sixteenth in the right-hand part, beat 3, was written imprecisely in the manuscript.

Ex. 13, m. 196

While most of the note-head is in the first space, it is not centered as is the F♯. Though it could easily be misread by an engraver, it should, undoubtedly, be an E to agree with m. 201.

Ex. 14, mm. 200–201

Tournemire suggested that this section from m. 196 to the final statement of the *Choral* be played with increasing warmth and intensity.

Players will find m. 200 (Example 14, opposite) easier to play if the hands are reversed.

The right hand's leap from high F♯ to the F♯ two octaves below and then its leap back up on another manual will prove unnecessary with the parts redistributed as in Example 15.

Ex. 15, mm. 200–201

Poco animato (m. 218)

Dupré	♩	= 72
Marchal	♩	= 88
Langlais	♩	= 100
Duruflé	♩	= 100

Rather than adopt a new tempo, Bonnet executed a *sempre stringendo*. beginning at m. 224 and extending to m. 231, where he added *molto* to Franck's *Rit.*

The manuscript has a C♯ in the soprano on the second beat of m. 225. As Karen Hastings points out, "either reading is possible within the chromatic dissonant context,"[9] and many players may prefer the C♯ to the C-natural in the Durand edition.

[9]Hastings, *op. cit.*, 28

Ex. 16, mm. 224–25

For the two measures leading up to the *tutta forza* climax of the *Choral* (Example 17), both Dupré and Duruflé played all lower parts *marcato*, but Dupré played the soprano *legato* while Duruflé played it *staccato*.

The last chord in m. 232 (Example 17) is lacking what has come to be interpreted as a natural sign before the A.

Ex. 17, mm. 231–32

The sharp sign before the first A in the measure was not canceled in either the manuscript or the Durand edition.

Tutta forza (m. 233ff.)

Bonnet	*Maestoso*	
Dupré	♩ = 63,	*Maestoso*
Marchal	♩ = 60	
Langlais	♩ = 63	
Duruflé	♩ = 72	

The last page and a half of *Choral I* is subject to as many diverse interpretations as there are organists to play them. Bonnet played all the chords detached:

Ex. 18, mm. 233–35

Dupré, Marchal, Langlais, and Duruflé played only the chorale melody legato—in both hands—and played the other voices *marcato*. The pedal remains *legato*.

Ex. 19, mm. 233–35

The pedal B in m. 246 is tied to the following measure in the manuscript, but not in the Durand edition. Neither Bonnet nor Duruflé tied it, but Dupré did—to agree with the C in mm. 249–50.

The alto B (Example 20) on the second half of the first beat of m. 248 reads B♯ in the manuscript. With the B♯ it is an exact sequential repetition[10] of m. 245 (in fact, mm. 248–50 are sequentially the same as mm. 245–47). Again, the player must decide to add the accidental or not.

[10]Ibid.

Ex. 20, mm. 248–50

The reappearance of the theme of the first variation at the *a Tempo* (m. 255) can be treated either *legato* (Marchal, Bonnet, and Dupré) or *staccato* (Duruflé).

Franck indicated no *rallentando* for this *Choral.* Bonnet added an *allargando molto* in the penultimate measure, and Dupré an *allargando* in the same measure; Duruflé began his *rallentando* a measure earlier, at m. 257.

In the program notes for André Marchal's recording of Franck's organ works, Norbert Dufourcq wrote:

> Speaking of his *Choral I* in E Major, Franck said to Vincent d'Indy: "You will find that the *Choral* is not what you expect. The real chorale evolves during the course of the prelude." By way of an exordium in variation form, which is to lead the listener through a labyrinth of minor tonalities to the theme's blazing apotheosis in the major, Franck develops the six verses of a great hymn, which eventually, through modulations into remote keys, loses itself in a new theme, that of the harmonized *Choral.*

Corrections for the 1956 Durand Edition

P	S	M	
2	2	8	soprano B♭ is not tied to next score: what appears to be a tie here is merely a slur mark.
3	1	1	l.h. remove dot from C♯
3	3	3	l.h. add dot to half note E
4	3	5	alto F♯ is not tied to next measure in original; it is tied in the manuscript
6	2	1	l.h. E♯ is tied to F-natural in the manuscript
7	1	2	r.h. second sixteenth is G♭ (not F)
9	1	4	slur under lower l.h. voice as in following measure
9	1	4	slur under lower l.h. voice as in following measure
9	2	1	pedal E tied from preceding score; dot missing
10	1	1	l.h. first eighth note A should be a sixteenth
11	1	4	r.h., beat 3, add alto quarter note D

11	3	3	fingering should read: 5_____5_____
			  4_____3
			  3 2 1 1 2 1

12	3	2	phrase mark that ends on b. 3 should carry over to the next measure
12	3	4	tie pedal B♭s
13	1	2	phrase mark that ends on b. 3 should carry over to the next measure
13	3	2	second sixteenth of beat 3 should surely be an E (as in Bonnet and Dupré editions)
16	3	4	pedal tie to next measure should surely be added (as in similar situation three measures later); it is tied in the manuscript

CHAPTER XII

Choral II in B Minor

Completed:	September 14, 1890
Published:	1891
Publisher:	1. A. Durand & Fils., Plate No: D.S. 4415
	2. Durand & Cie., 1956 Plate No: D. & F. 13.794
Dedication:	à Monsieur Auguste Durand (or Théodore Dubois, or Augusta Holmès).
Manuscript:	in the possession of Emory Fanning, Middlebury, Vermont
Performance:	Played by Albert Mahaut at the Trocadéro, June 30, 1898.
Bibliography:	*Facsimile of the Autograph Manuscript* with Introduction and Annotations by Emory Fanning. Privately printed, 1981 (available from Emory Fanning, 46 High Street, Middlebury, VT 05753).
	Emory Fanning, "*Chorals II and III:* Two Franck Autographs," *The American Organist* (November 1990) 112–14.
	Amy Dommel-Diény, *L'Analyse harmonique en examples de J.-S Bach à Debussy.* Fascicule 11: César Franck (Paris: Éditions A. Dommel-Diény, 1973). Pages 56–75 contain an extended analysis of *Choral II.*
	Olivier Latry, "A Masterclass on César Franck with Olivier Latry," *The Sydney Organ Journal* (June-July 1994) 17–25. A transcript of a tape-recorded masterclass held on April 15, 1994 at the Sydney Conservatorium of Music.

Those who play all three *Chorals* know the difficulty of choosing a favorite. Usually it is the one they are working on at the time.

The first may be the most "masterful" owing to its length, number of themes, variety of invention, skillful use of invertible counterpoint, and the surging buildup to the magnificent climax. The third, shorter than the first two, though technically less difficult, impresses the listener with its virtuosity and is especially memorable for its beautiful *Adagio*. The second *Choral* is the most severe. Its initial passacaglia with three complete variations gives it a magesterial stateliness, and the two Voix humaine sections evoke the very essence of the composer Tournemire called the "Fra Angelico of Sound." The opening fugue of the second section could only have been written by the "French Bach" (Busoni's appellation), and the solemn peroration leaves no doubt that this great work is all seriousness, and, as Daniel Gregory Mason wrote of Franck's music, "it sings constantly; it almost never dances."

Maestoso.

Tournemire	♩ = 76	
Bonnet	♩ = 72	(He recommended a tempo of ♩ = 66–69 to his students during the 1920s and 1930s.)
Dupré	♩ = 76	
Marchal	♩ = 60	
Langlais	♩ = 72	
Duruflé	♩ = 76	

Five of the organists cited are basically in accord on the initial tempo, but, because of the inherent forward movement, by the second statement of the theme at m. 17, Langlais has accelerated to ♩ = 80 and Marchal to ♩ = 69. At the beginning of the third statement, m. 33, Marchal's tempo has increased to ♩ = 76 and Duruflé's to ♩ = 80.

Franck was uncompromising in his part writing, giving no consideration to players with hands smaller than his own. However, he was not adverse to rearranging the harmony for students who had difficulty with wide stretches. Robert Baker, a former pupil of R. Huntington Woodman (who studied with Franck in 1888), told the author that numerous passages in Woodman's scores were rewritten by Franck himself to accommodate Woodman's small hands.

Joseph Bonnet, who had small hands, was particularly sensitive to the difficulties faced by students unable to reach all the notes in Franck's organ music. For instance, in Example 1, the hands span two and one-half octaves.

Ex. 1, mm. 35–36

Bonnet has redistributed the parts (Example 2) so that, while the voice leading is not what Franck desired, the harmonies are complete and the outer voices remain intact.

Ex. 2, mm. 35–36

For players with Franckian hands, Example 3 provides an excellent solution to this technical problem.

Ex. 3, mm. 35–36

From m. 41 through m. 44, the second half of the third statement, Tournemire said to play the pedal *legato,* the left-hand
chords detached, and the octaves in the right hand as *cantabile* as
possible (Example 4). Dupré and Duruflé indicated this in their
editions; Bonnet did not.

Ex. 4, mm. 41–44

Bonnet added pedal octaves from m. 49 through m. 55, sug-
gesting them "in view of a better balance with the manuals and of
more effectiveness."[1] It must be borne in mind that Bonnet's edition was intended for American organists playing instruments of
the 1920s and 1930s with deficient pedal divisions; octaves would
not have been necessary on a French organ with the Positif reeds
coupled to the Pédale.

[1]Bonnet, César Franck: *Three Chorals for Organ,* 19.

Organists playing this *Choral* for the first time are cautioned about one of the more frequently misread chords in organ literature: in the third beat of Example 5 the right hand plays B—not C-natural.[2]

Ex. 5, m. 54

The fourth and last statement of the passacaglia is in the subdominant, and the accompanimental triplet figuration phrases itself: Franck has slurred the chords that fall on the beat—the other chords are detached. Although Franck did not indicate it, many players take the left-hand triplets from m. 57 through m. 64 on a secondary manual. The overlapping of the parts is less confusing and if the right-hand octaves are not played absolutely *legato*, the excuse can be made that Franck did not include them under a phrase mark. Dupré played the left hand on the Récit; Bonnet and Duruflé played both hands on the Grand-Orgue.

Cantabile, m. 65.

Dupré	♩	= 72
Marchal	♩	= 76
Langlais	♩	= 80
Duruflé	♩	= 76

---

[2]When Jean Langlais pointed this out to André Fleury (who played the C-natural) after the latter played this *Choral* on a recital in the early 1980s, Fleury said, "You know, I've played it that way for sixty years and until now no one has ever noticed it."

A smooth transition into the *cantabile* at m. 65 was impossible for Franck. Even with a lift at the end of m. 64, he still had to release two pédales de combinaison (Anches Grand-Orgue and Anches Positif) and to push in the 16′ Montre and Bourdon of the Grand-Orgue. In addition, the swell box must be at least partially closed during m. 64 (in the manuscript Franck wrote *Fermez la boîte du Récit* and then, inadvertently, crossed it out) in order to observe the *cresc.* at m. 75.

The pedal duplicates the left-hand bass voice (except for the first two measures where it plays an octave lower) until m. 80. The tirasses have not been removed and players can simplify the manual part considerably by eliminating the lowest voice and dividing the alto part between the hands.

The right-hand F♯ on the third beat of m. 72 is not tied in either the manuscript or the Durand edition. Ties do occur at a similar passage on the third beats of mm. 218, 220, and 222.

Tournemire considered the "little divertissement" beginning at m. 80 to be in the spirit of Buxtehude, and wrote that it was to be executed very freely, "*légèrement rubato*—a slight *rubato* imposes itself. Such was the interpretation of the composer." Dupré indicated that the left-hand C♯ is to be repeated when the bass voice enters on the same note on the third beat.

It will be noted that not all of the repeated notes in the chords of b. 1 and b. 2 in mm. 97–105 are tied. They appear thus in the manuscript. The addition of ties is certainly stylistically correct and the reader is referred to the discussion accompanying examples 4 and 5 (p. 217) in the previous chapter.

Measure 115.

Bonnet	*Cantabile sostenuto*	
Dupré	♩	= 60
Marchal	♩	= 50
Langlais	♩	= 50
Duruflé	♩	= 58

In preparation for this, one of the most sublime passages in all organ music, the tirasses are removed during the second "petite divertissement" beginning at m. 105. The player could conceivably add the Pédale 32′ Bourdon at the eighth rest which precedes this. Nothing else can be done before the first beat of m. 115, however, and it is the many passages like this that refute the oft-made accusation that the lengthy pauses throughout all of Franck's music were influenced by his having to change registration when playing the organ. In reality, he infrequently changed stops at a fermata; when he did he usually did not leave enough time to do so conveniently. Here, Franck did not write *rallentando*, although players will surely make one in m. 114, and yet he had to make the following registration changes:

Retire:	Récit 8′ Hautbois and 8′ Gambe
Draw:	Récit 8′ Voix humaine
Depress:	Tremblant Récit with the right foot

Lacking a Récit au Pédale coupler at Sainte-Clotilde, and to safeguard his music against such a deficiency in other instruments, Franck doubled the bass part in the left hand and Pédale. With a Tirasse Récit (Récit to Pédale) it is possible to eliminate the left hand's duplication of the bass part, thus reducing the manual voices to four parts.

On the other hand, if there is no soft 32′ pedal stop, the manual parts might be played as written with the pedal part played an octave lower. Of course, the low B must be played an octave higher (as written) but the effect is justified.

Measures 118–22 contain a reference to a similar melodic phrase in Franck's *Symphonie* in D Minor, completed in 1888. A comparison of Franck's use of the two motifs (Examples 6 and 7) is interesting because, in spite of what we remember of the *Symphonie* each time we hear the *Choral*, more differences than similarities are revealed: key, time signature, rhythm, harmony, and even melody.

Ex. 6, *Symphonie* in D Minor, mm. 365–68 (transposed)

Ex. 7, *Choral II* **in B Minor, mm. 118–22**

These twelve measures are divided into four phrases of varying length. A slight lift of the soprano voice before each phrase is sufficient to define the beginning of the next. Before the last phrase, however, all voices are repeated, thus creating a natural space. There is an apparent error in the Durand edition: the dot following the right-hand's lowest voice, middle B, in m. 122 (and also in m. 281) does not appear in the manuscript.

Move the *diminuendo* on the third beat of m. 119 into m. 120. It is so written in the manuscript and agrees with mm. 278–79.

Largamente con fantasia, mm. 127 and 136.

Bonnet	♩ = 66
Dupré	♩ = 84
Marchal	♩ = 76
Langlais	♩ = 88
Duruflé	♩ = 66

At any time after m. 106 the requisite registrational changes on the Grand-Orgue and Positif can be made: 16′ Fonds added and the jeux d'anches introduced. Before m. 127 the Voix humaine and Tremblant are taken off and the Anches Récit added. The direction to redraw the Hautbois and Gambe is missing: it is understood to do so.

We cannot fail to note that for this tutti section Franck removed the 32′ stop in the Pédale!

Joseph Bonnet has provided the following fingering solution for the ascending figurations:

Ex. 8, mm. 139–41

When the hands move to the Récit on the fourth beat of m. 141 the swell box remains open; it then closes for the indicated *diminuendo*. The left hand ties in the two upper voices should extend from m. 142, b. 1 to m. 144, b. 1.

I° Tempo ma un poco meno lento.

Dupré	♩ = 80
Marchal	♩ = 88
Langlais	♩ = 88
Duruflé	♩ = 88

The short fugue begins *"Tempo I,* but a little less slowly." All the jeux d'anches and 16′ manual stops are retired; the Récit Hautbois remains on, as do the manual and pedal couplers. Knowing that Franck "heightened the tempo in episodes of Bach fugues,"[3] it is idiomatic to increase the tempo a bit more for the fugal section of this *Choral.*

Charles Tournemire spoke of this fugue's "rarely surpassed elegance worthy of J. S. Bach." It is based on two subjects: the first eight measures of the passacaglia and a countersubject that is later extensively developed.

There is no accidental before the B in m. 157, beat 3 (Example 9), in either the manuscript or the Durand edition. Dupré and Duruflé played it as a B♭.

---

[3]Rowland W. Dunham, "From Yesterday No. 2: Franck, Libert, Widor," *The American Organist* (December 1954) 403.

Ex. 9, mm. 155–58

In mm. 170–74 Bonnet suggested playing the left-hand voice (Example 10) on the Great (Grand-Orgue) to bring out the canonic imitations.

Ex. 10, mm. 170–74

Emory Fanning pointed out in his facsimile edition that m. 191 was originally written as:

Ex. 11, mm. 191–94

Franck later pencilled in the first three accidentals in the left hand and the A♭ in the right, thus altering the harmony to what now appears in the Durand edition:

Ex. 12, mm. 191–94

Plate 49. Charles Tournemire's own copy of *Choral II* detailing how he
arranged mm. 175–90.

Tournemire recommended playing on two manuals the passage in which the theme appears in E-flat (Example 13) in the
upper left hand voice. "A complex arrangement, to be sure, but

the clever organist with a sure technique ought to be able to overcome this great difficulty. The result will be an extraordinary il-
lumination of the melody."[4] Just how much emphasis is required
on a theme that is so familiar and that has been stated so often is a
decision left to the player.

Ex. 13, mm. 180–81

Joseph Bonnet has provided precise indications for thumbing
the theme on a lower manual (Example 14). Those who wish to experiment with Tournemire's suggestion may follow Bonnet's
elaborate, but feasible, scheme.

Ex. 14, m. 180

[4]Smith, *Toward an Authentic Interpretation...*, 90.

Ex. 14 continued, mm. 181–83

Measure 195.

Bonnet   *sostenuto*

Duruflé   ♩ = 76

The tempo may well slacken a bit and, as Tournemire suggested, "the playing ought to be penetrating and profound."[5]

Observing the *crescendo-diminuendo* in Example 15 would have been almost impossible for Franck with the pedal part written nearly beyond the reach of the left foot—especially on a flat pedalboard. Today, with the centrally positioned swell pedal, it is possible to move it with the left foot and to play mm. 198–99 with the right foot.

Ex. 15, mm. 197–201

[5]Smith, *Toward an Authentic Interpretation...,* 90.

The unconventional pedaling in m. 199, the heel playing a black key, is identical to that suggested by Marcel Dupré in the *Grand-Chœur* of the *Grande Pièce symphonique*, m. 21. It maintains the *legato* of the main theme and at the same time imbues it with expression.

Measure 226.

Tournemire   The buildup must be played freely. Let's throw the metronome away. . . .

Bonnet   *un poco più mosso ed agitato*

Dupré   ♩ = 80, *più animato*

Marchal   ♩ = 96

Langlais   ♩ = 100

Duruflé   ♩ = 92, *poco animato*

All the new organs Franck is known to have played during the decade leading up to the composition of the *Trois Chorals* had manual compasses of fifty-six notes (C^1-G^5). So it is noteworthy that he was still publishing *ossias* for instruments with, by then, an antiquated compass of fifty-four notes (C^1-F^5). His own organ at Sainte-Clotilde had such a compass and this obviously influenced his scoring of the passage below. (Unlike the published version, the manuscript has G-natural as the fourth small sixteenth note of b. 3.

Ex. 16, mm. 233–34

Many players will find the descending figurations in Examples 17 and 18 easier to play if divided between the hands.

Here the wide leaps are eliminated and the hand is able to position itself for the next measure.

Ex. 17, mm. 239–41

Ex. 18, m. 245

In the reverberant buildings for which this music was conceived, the many repeated notes in the right hand of Example 19 add considerable rhythmic vitality to the texture—especially since the left hand is playing on a louder manual.

Ex. 19, mm. 246–47

In an acoustically dry setting the effect is extremely choppy. Dupré has added numerous ties connecting notes within the same voice (not to be confused with notes in common between different voice parts):

Ex. 20, mm. 246–47

While the effect is neither what Franck wrote in the manuscript nor what was published by Durand, in a dead room it in no way interferes with the composer's intentions.

Duruflé began a ritard in m. 256; Bonnet and Dupré in m 257.

Measure 258.

Bonnet	*a Tempo. Maestoso*
Dupré	♩ = 76, *Tempo I°*
Marchal	♩ = 72
Langlais	♩ = 80
Duruflé	♩ = 80, *a Tempo*

Bonnet had his students make a decided break in the pedal after the first eighth note in m. 258, ostensibly to add the pedal reeds.

Beginning at the *molto rall.* in m. 270 Franck was specific about how to reduce the organ. The Récit Hautbois and Gambe must be taken off by an assistant; likewise, the Pédale reduced to "very soft stops." Franck did not say to add the 32' again. A fastidious editor has followed the manuscript to the letter and omitted the Voix humaine from the Récit, as did Franck, leaving but one direction: *Tremblant.* The Voix humaine should, of course be, included.

Organists have always found it irrestistable to solo the left-hand eighth notes in mm. 285–86 (Example 21). Duruflé played them on the Positif and Bonnet on the Great or Solo.

Ex. 21, mm. 285–88

Certainly all who have heard or played this second *Choral* will agree with Albert Schweitzer that it is "the most unpretentious and most deeply felt of the three." It likewise distills the essence of Franck,

> composed idiomatically, in a style that seems to spring from the true, fundamental character of the organ itself. Like Bach, he knows intuitively the most natural and effective musical line for the organ; his is always simple and at the same time wonderfully plastic. And the structure of his works is amazingly natural. They give the impression of improvisations which he decided to copy down. The riches of such a natural inventiveness are inexhaustible: hardly any other modern master has succeeded, by means of completely simple registration, in making the tonal riches of the modern organ so effective.[6]

---

[6]Note accompanying his recording of the *Trois Chorals*, Columbia ML 5128.

Corrections for the 1956 Durand Edition

P	S	M	
18	2	6	first chord is F#-A-D-F#
18	2	7–8	l.h. bass line should have two-note slurs, as in tenor
19	1	1–3	l.h. bass line should have two-note slurs, as in tenor
20	2	4	r.h., beat 2, tie first two G#s in alto
20	3	1	original omits slurs over chords on beat 3
21	1	3–4	r.h. slurs not in original
21	3	3	l.h. add dot to tenor F#
21	2	4	remove dot from alto C#
23	2	5	tenor, add tie between second C# of b.1 and b.2 as in 22-2-1.
24	3	1	r.h. dotted half note B is tied from previous measure in the manuscript
24	3	2	r.h. half note B is not dotted in manuscript
24	3	4	l.h., tenor, tie B to next measure as in the manuscript
25	2	1	r.h. add quarter rest to match that in bass clef
26	1	4	l.h. original contains slur mark up to tied D in m. 5
26	2	8	l.h. legato slur from b.1 to b.1 of following measure as in manuscript
26	3	2	*Cresc.* indication begining on the second half of b.1 in the following measure in the manuscript
26	3	4	r.h. add dot to half note G
27	1	4	*Cresc.* extends to b.2 in the manuscript
28	2	7	*Cresc.* begins at b. 2 in the manuscript
29	1	7	l.h. F# half note should be A
29	3	1	alto, add eighth note B on beat 2, add eighth note C# on beat 3— each followed by an eighth rest
29	3	2	r.h. chord is F#-A-D#-F#
30	1	4	The manuscript reads *Ôtez Anches G.O.* at the beginning of this measure (not the next)
30	2	1	no *diminuendo* in original
32	2	3	l.h. B not tied to B in m. 4 in original edition, but it is tied in the manuscript
32	2	6	l.h. D-natural (not D#)
32	3	1	r.h. half note B is not dotted in the manuscript
32	3	3	Although the manuscript has no tie from this B to that in the following measure, it is analogous to 24-3-4 and should be added.

CHAPTER XIII

Choral III in A Minor

This organ *Choral* is really a toccata, both in the brilliant virtuosity that dominates it and in its form, which freely alternates the brilliant sections with more pensive ones. It is these latter sections that present the chorale melody in various guises and combinations. Even more than the two preceding *Chorals pour Orgue*, this gives the impression of an improvisation.[1]

Albert Schweitzer

Completed:	September 20, 1890
Published:	1891
Publisher:	1. A. Durand & Fils., Plate No: D.S. 4416
	2. Durand & Cie., 1956, Plate No: D. & F. 13.794
Dedication:	à mon élève Augusta Holmès (or Eugène Gigout)
Manuscript:	First draft in the possession of Emory Fanning, Middlebury, Vermont.
Performance:	Played by Eugène Gigout, March 12 and 13, 1898, at the inauguration of the Cavaillé-Coll organ in the Salle Poirel of the Nancy Conservatoire.
Bibliography:	Emory Fanning, *"Choral II* and *III:* Two Franck Autographs," *The American Organist* (December 1990) 112–14.
	Amy Dommel-Diény, *L'Analyse harmonique en examples de J.-S. Bach à Debussy.* Fascicule 11: César Franck (Paris: Éditions A. Dommel-Diény, 1973). Pages 67–91 contain an extended analysis of *Choral III.*

[1]Note accompanying his recording of the *Trois Chorals* Columbia ML 5128.

Quasi allegro.

Tournemire	♩ = 100 (Recording: = 112)
Bonnet	♩ = 96
Dupré	♩ = 100
Marchal	♩ = 108
Langlais	♩ = 108
Duruflé	♩ = 108

Franck's last *Choral* begins with the following registration: *Jeux de fonds et jeux d'anches de 8 p. à tous les claviers* (8' foundation and reed stops on all manuals), 8' and 16' foundation and reed stops in the Pédale, *Claviers accouplés* (manuals coupled: i.e. Récit au Positif and Positif au Grand-Orgue) and *Tirasse Grand-Orgue.* Lacking at present a final manuscript version and with only the 1891 Durand edition as reference, it has long been conjectured that this registration is incomplete—perhaps not originating with Franck at all, but with an editor—and should, at least, be augmented with more upperwork. Such an argument is substantiated by the fact that, save for the addition of 16' foundation stops, this is the same registration with which the piece concludes. Jean Langlais, nevertheless, insisted that this registration was quite right for the organ at Sainte-Clotilde, though conceded that its effect was less than desirable anywhere else.

Joseph Bonnet stressed the precise observance of all note values throughout this work:

> It is important to give the left-hand notes and all rests their exact values and to play these opening measures in strict and very firm time. The entire effect depends on this.[2]

The *Largement* passages, Tournemire informed us, are to be played with *grandeur.* Bonnet, Dupré, and Duruflé added 16' tone for these sections, though there is no indication to do so. Dupré, ever the pedant, marked these passages *Doppio lento* (half-tempo), or ♩ = 100.

[2]Bonnet, César Franck: *Three Chorals for Organ,* 31.

The ascending figuration in mm. 5 and 14 (Example 1) is facilitated if the second sixteenth note of the second beat is taken with the left hand.

Ex. 1, m. 14

To observe Franck's very precise notation, observe the sixteenth notes on the third beats of mm. 5, 14, and 52.

In mm. 7, 16, and 18, the fermata is over the rest. To emphasize this, do not elongate the eighth notes that precede it. At mm. 16 and 18 Jean Langlais advised counting "three-four-five" to complete the measure and to take the fermata into account.

Bonnet solved the difficulty of the *Largamente*, mm. 15–18 (Example 2), by taking the first note of the third beat with the left hand, and playing the pedal in octaves.

Ex. 2, mm. 15–18

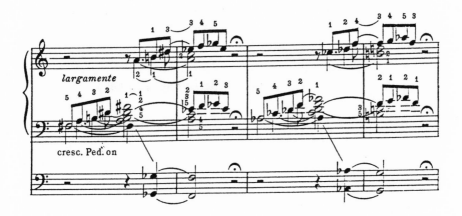

On his recording of *Choral III,* one can hear Charles Tournemire's frequent practice of stressing non-chord tones. In the *Quasi allegro* passage (Example 3) following the *Più largamente* (m. 19) he singled out unaccented passing tones (marked with asterisks) and played them *tenuto:*

Ex. 3, mm. 20–22

In his book he referred to this as a "cadenza" and suggested it be played animatedly.

It is imperative to sustain the entire chord of the fourth beat of mm. 23, 24, and 25 until the first note of the right hand of each succeeding measure is played.

Measure 30.

Tournemire	Place a fermata over the A-minor chord on the first beat. Generally, one goes on—and it is a grave error. (Recording: ♩ = 84)
Bonnet	*a Tempo* (♩ = 96)
Dupre	♩ = 92 *Cantabile*
Marchal	♩ = 100–104 (1948 Recording: ♩ = 84[3])
Langlais	♩ = 96–100
Duruflé	♩ = 92

[3]Lumen 32078/9; Lumen 326998/9.

Tournemire insisted that the exposition of the *Choral*[4] (m. 30) was to be played in the original tempo. However, on his recording he, like the other organists cited, slackened the tempo.

In mm. 33, 43, and 59 prolong the first two quarter notes of the inner voices to emphasize the soprano note. Likewise, make a *tenuto* on the soprano third beat of mm. 61, 62, 74, and 75.

The only way to make mm. 34 (Example 4), 46–47, 60, 78–79, 177, and 189 absolutely *legato* is to play the lower note of the right hand's quarter note thirds also with the thumb. The thumb is sustaining the lower whole note as well.

Ex. 4, mm. 34–35

The execution of the left-hand eighth notes in mm. 46 and 78 is impossible for players with small hands. Bonnet suggested playing the five lower notes in the pedal (Example 5) with the Swell to Pedal coupler and no stops drawn.[5]

---

[4]The dissimilarity between the A-minor theme of Franck's *Choral III* and the melody of a once-popular *Noël*, "Trois anges sont venus ce soir," by his student, Augusta Holmès (1847-1903), hardly warrants Rollo Myers's assertion that Franck "incorporated one of her best known songs" into this work. ("Augusta Holmès: A Meteoric Career," *The Musical Quarterly* [July 1967] 373.) The fact is that the Noël was not composed until after Franck's death!

There is, likewise, little to support Charles Tournemire's theory that *Choral III* was influenced by Bach's *Prelude in A Minor*, BWV 543—a theory suggested by the rhythm and the first four notes being identical.

[5]Bonnet, César Franck: *Three Chorals for Organ*, 34.

Ex. 5, mm. 45–47

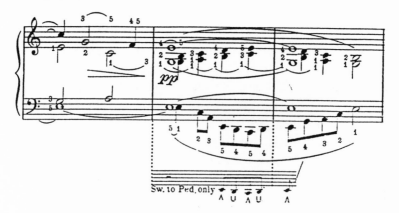

A tempo qualification for mm. 53–56 and 91–96 has been omitted—if one were intended. Should these broken arpeggios be *Largamente,* as in all similar passages, or are they to be played in the same tempo as the sixteenth-note toccata figuration which they follow?

Bonnet and Langlais said, "same Tempo"; Tournemire said, "*sempre largamente*"; Dupré, "*doppio lento*"; and Duruflé indicated them at ♩ = 80—midway between his tempo for the *Quasi allegro* and *Largamente* sections.

A consistent feature of Charles Tournemire's recorded performance is his habit of rhythmically prolonging notes of shorter duration in phrases with notes of mixed time values. In Example 6 the passing notes in the fourth beat are considerably lengthened, although the rest of the measure is played in tempo.

Ex. 6, m. 64

There is no reason to play the left-hand passages between mm. 80 and 86 on another manual, except that it is possible to do so. An elegant effect is obtained if the swell box makes a *diminuendo*

to *mf* through mm. 87–88 and then closes abruptly for a *subito* **pp** at m. 89, echoing the preceding measure.

The right hand passes *under* the left on beat 3 of m. 90, allowing the left hand freedom of motion to pass *over* and strike low A at m. 91.

Adagio.

Tournemire	♩	= 76, very freely (Recording: ♩ = 80)
Bonnet	♩	= 60
Dupré	♩	= 84
Marchal	♩	= 84–92 (1948 Recording: ♩ = 72)
Langlais	♩	= 84
Duruflé	♩	= 84

Tournemire gave sound advice for interpreting this, the most iridescent and tranquil slow movement in all of Franck's organ music: it is to be played

> . . . without ever hurrying and with great freedom. This is a solo [*récit*]. César Franck played this section *rubato* and to play it metronomically would be heresy and absolutely contrary to his intentions.

The soprano D on the second beat of m. 96 (Example 7) is often questioned.

Ex. 7, mm. 95–97

The absence of a fermata on any other parts of the second beat leaves three alternatives for its interpretation.

1. As written, the D is held the length of its fermata on the Positif and then restruck on the Récit. The time it takes to change

the Positif and Pédale stops, however, is considerably longer than is allotted by the quarter note that introduces the *Adagio*. And it is an unpleasant effect to hear the Trompette and loud 8' stops being taken off while the D is held on the Positif.

2. Dupré releases the D with the chord beneath. Tournemire, on his recording, does too, but since it is the end of a side we cannot be sure if he might not have done otherwise if there were no interruption.

3. Doubling the D on the Récit, so that, as the chord is released, the D is sustained and the stops for the accompaniment can be changed. Some organists tie this D to the fourth beat and make a diminuendo into the first beat of m. 97.

The registration of the Récit is unchanged and the Positif is reduced to 8' Flûte and Bourdon and the Pédale to soft stops (*jeux doux*). The Tirasse Grand-Orgue must be taken off—an obvious editorial omission.

The key to the tempo of the *Adagio* may, perhaps, be found at its conclusion. The initial theme of the *Choral* returns (m. 146) with the marking: *Le double plus vite (movement du commencement)*. This indicates that the *Adagio* should be played twice as slowly as the tempo of the *Quasi allegro*. According to Bernard Gavoty, Louis Vierne played *Choral III* at a very rapid tempo and felt that the majority of organists played the *Adagio* much too slowly, being led astray by the word "Adagio." Vierne always insisted that his students calculate the tempo of the *Adagio* in proportion to that of the Allegro.

The six organists whose interpretations have been considered all began the *Adagio* considerably slower than half the tempo they adopted at the outset, but they all began to accelerate from m. 131, and so, by m. 142, achieved a tempo very nearly half as fast as they began. Duruflé, for instance, increased the tempo at which he began the *Adagio*, $\quarternote = 84$, to $\quarternote = 108$ at mm. 140 and 144, with the result that he concluded the *Adagio* at exactly one half the tempo of the beginning of the *Choral*.

The interpretative elements discussed previously, in particular, tempo alteration in all of its guises (melodic, polyphonic, rhythmic, and harmonic), can be applied to the first 18 measures of this cantilena as a case study in Franck style. Recall Tournemire's remark,

"C'est un récit,"[6] and that he actually meant *more* than just a solo melody—one that combined the declamatory as well as the lyrical, and certainly one in which the melody was preeminent (in a sung recitative the rhythm would freely follow the accentuation of the words) and the accompaniment was completely subordinate to it. The following interpretive suggestions are based on Tournemire's recorded performances, not only of this *Choral*, but also of the *Pastorale* and the *Cantabile*.

m. 97 The tempo is established in this measure, so, except for a slight *tenuto* on the suspensions of the first, second, and fourth beats, the rhythm must be steady.

m. 98 Slightly prolong the first sixteenth note, or slightly delay the second sixteenth note, of beats 1, 2, and 3. Make a slight *tenuto* on the third and fourth sixteenth notes of beat 3. Slightly delay the tenor B in beat 4, and hold the soprano's last G♯.

m. 99 There is a slight *accelerando* in the accompaniment from the second half of beat 1 through beat 3 with an *a Tempo* as the solo enters on beat 4. The swell box must open on beat 3 for the *più f*.

m. 100 Prolong the first sixteenth note of beats 1 and 3; the rest in tempo.

m. 101 Make a slight *accelerando* to beat 3 and then stress the high A. The *a Tempo* returns during beat 4.

m. 102 There can be an *accelerando* through beat 3 and a slight *ritard* in beat 4 leading to an *a Tempo* in the following measure.

m. 103 Slightly prolong the first eighth notes of beats 1 and 3 and stretch the arpeggios of the last three sixteenth notes of beats 2 and 4. Make a slight *tenuto* on the last sixteenth note (high F♯) as it moves into the *molto espressivo e dolce*.

m. 104 Make a slight *tenuto* on the third sixteenth notes of beats 2 and 4 (B♭ and G♯).

m. 105 Make an *accelerando* throughout this measure as the *crescendo* increases and the pitch rises; then, an abrupt *a Tempo* at

[6]Tournemire, *César Franck,* 35.

m. 106 beat 1 on the *subito pp*. Stretch beat 3 slightly and rubato on beat 4.

m. 107 Slightly prolong beats 1 and 2 so the repeated notes do not sound measured. Throughout this section Tournemire (on his recording) consistently stretched the rising figuration that begins on the second of a group of four sixteenth notes:

Ex. 8, m. 107

The accompaniment, however, he plays in tempo.

m. 108 Use *tempo rubato* in the right hand while maintaining the pulse with the left. Make a slight *tenuto* on the high F♯ of beat 3.

m. 109 While maintaining the tempo with the left hand, make a slight *tenuto* on the last three sixteenth notes of beats 1 and 3 (Example 9), as did Tournemire.

Ex. 9, m. 109

Duruflé moved the *diminuendo* from the previous measure to beat 2 so that beat 3 is an echo of beat 1.

m. 110 *Accelerando* through this measure with slight *tenutos* on the first sixteenth notes of beats 2, 3, and 4 and a slight *ritard* leading into

m. 111 Following Tournemire's example (Example 10), slightly emphasize the two high As in beats 1 and 3; *ritard* during beats 3 and 4 to prepare for the return of the theme.

Ex. 10, mm. 111

m. 112 *a Tempo.*

m. 113 During the *diminuendo* make a slight *tenuto* on the high notes of each beat with the longest on the last two sixteenth notes of beat 3. Stretch beat 4.

m. 114 Begin with the first of three eighth-note Gs that fall to F♯. Two options might be: (1) slightly emphasize the first of each group of eighth notes (the G♯ and the two G-naturals), returning to strict tempo afterwards, or (2) as Tournemire did (Example 11), keep the eighth notes in strict time, slightly lengthening the sixteenth notes.

Ex. 11, m. 114

m. 115 Make a slight *tenuto* on beat 1 but *a Tempo* on the second eighth note through beat 2 so that the *rallentando* can be effected through beats 3 and 4 and the next measure. This must be a barely perceptible *rallentando* initially, or the tempo will die by the end of m. 116.

On the second beat of m. 117 the Récit Trompette is taken off by the Anches Récit pédale de combinaison and, with the *Fonds et Hautbois*, this manual now becomes the accompaniment to the tenor theme played on the Positif. During mm. 17 and 18 an assistant adds some stops to the Positif (*ajoutez q.q. jeux de fonds de 8 au Positif*)[7] which, on the organ of Sainte-Clotilde, would have included the Montre, Gambe, and probably the Salicional. The Récit is again coupled to the Positif. The Positif could have remained coupled to the Grand-Orgue, the registration of which remained unchanged since the beginning.

[7]q.q. is an abreviation for *quelques* (some).

From m. 119 to m. 146 Tournemire encouraged students to "let yourself go and allow the theme to broaden."

Bonnet suggested that mm. 118–24 are easier for small hands if the order of manuals is reversed so that the solo is played above, rather than below, the accompaniment.[8] His edition offers several clever thumbing solutions to difficult passages.

The Pédale in m. 119 is marked *moins douce* (less softly). On Franck's organ at Sainte-Clotilde nothing could be done because the only 16′ and 8′ stops of that division were already drawn; if the Positif were coupled to the Pédale, the left-hand solo line would be less prominent. Still, it was the composer's intent that the pedal phrases in mm. 119–20 and 122–23 should stand out and not over-power the manuals with the sustained notes in mm. 127–30. When both hands move to the Grand-Orgue with the last eighth note in m. 130, all manuals are again coupled to the Pédale.

Bonnet, however, cautioned against adding the Tirasse Grand-Orgue (Great to Pedal) until the climax at m. 142, beat 2. "Indeed, the effect . . . is quite unsatisfactory even when the full Great comes in at m. 140, beat 2."[9] The Tirasse Positif (which would couple both the Récit and Positif to Pédale) would be suffi-cient for the bass line of this section and would prevent the long pedal points from covering up the manual passages.

From m. 131 Bonnet also suggested a *poco a poco animando* that increases the excitement. There is a *ritard* at the end of m. 139 to point up the entrance of the chorale theme in the minor.

Tournemire directed in m. 142 to

> . . . play the pedal theme very pronounced (*très marqué*), non-legato: orchestrally, very trombone-like. This is how the composer himself played: the great chords daringly, obtaining a great sonority from the instrument.[10]

Dupré, Langlais, and Duruflé detached each of the manual chords in mm. 144–45.

---

[8]Bonnet, César Franck: *Three Chorals for Organ*, 39.
[9]Ibid.
[10]Smith, *Toward an Authentic Interpretation...*, 93.

Le double plus vite (Mouvement du commencement). Twice as fast (same tempo as the beginning).

Tournemire	♩ = 100 (Recording ♩ = 116–120)	
Bonnet	♩ = 96	
Dupré	♩ = 108	
Marchal	♩ = 112 (1948 Recording ♩ = 116)	
Langlais	♩ = 104	
Duruflé	♩ = 108	

At m. 147 both hands play on the Positif, to which, Tournemire reminded us, the Récit is coupled. Duruflé suggested removing the Tirasse Grand-Orgue, while Dupré took off all the pedal couplers.

Tournemire suggested that at mm. 157 and 164 the swell box should be three-quarters open as the chorale enters on the third beat. Duruflé marked this *mf subito.*

From m. 168 Tournemire interpreted agitatedly: *con fuoco. Ritard* the first two beats of m. 173 to prepare for the final statement of the chorale, which Tournemire said to play

. . . majestically: *fff, largement.* Detach the melody and to do not connect the inner parts—shorten them a little.[11]

Measure 192.

Tournemire	*très largement, più largo*	
Dupré	♩ = 88, *Largamente*	
Langlais	♩ = 84	
Duruflé	♩ = 92	

Bonnet marked the left-hand octaves *marcato molto* (mm. 190–92); Langlais gave students the option of detaching them or not, as they wished, but he, Dupré, and Duruflé all detached the open-fifth chords in mm. 190–92.

There are differing opinions about the interpretation of the last two measures. Bonnet connected the pedal line from m. 197 through the last measure and added a fermata to each of the penultimate notes. Dupré, while connecting the manual parts of the

[11]Smith, *Toward an Authentic Interpretation...*, 93.

last two measures, marked the last two pedal notes with left toe signs, thus detaching the bass part before the last chord. Langlais was very insistent about connecting all parts of the last two measures. Yet, Tournemire, while connecting the pedal D to the A in the last measure, made a distinct break in the manual parts before the final chord.

Louis Vierne considered that with this Third Choral "Franck's genius never reached a greater height. Here inspiration takes on a hitherto unknown grandeur and serenity whose majestic architechtural proportions reveal the transcendent musician."[12]

Corrections for the 1956 Durand Edition

P	S	M	
34	2	1	first l.h. note is a sixteenth
34	3	1	first l.h. A add dot; tie b. 3 A (not F♯) to next measure
34	3	2	l.h. should duplicate soprano (E♭, F, G♭, E♭) an octave lower as in m. 4
35	2	3	r.h. ties not in original; l.h. no quarter note stem on F; no upper eighth note stem on E in original
36	2	5	extend slurs to m. 6, beat 1
37	1	2	l.h. first B should be a sixteenth note
37	2	1	l.h. add dot to second eighth note G♭
42	1	2	r.h. A tied from beat 2 to 3 not in original
42	2	1	l.h. tie A♯ to B♭ (beat 1 to 2); l.h. last D♯ tied to m. 2
42	2	3	beat 4, r.h. D♯ belongs on common stem with alto F♯
42	3	3	r.h., beat 1, all three notes are eighth-notes
45	2	3	l.h. should have slurs for all three voices
45	3	1	l.h. should have slurs for all three voices
46	3	3	l.h. should have a slur between quarters E and E♭
49	3	4	r.h. add dot to second eighth note F
44	3	3	l.h. top not of chord on second half of b. 2 and 4 should probably be C (not D♭)

[12]Vierne, Emended translation of a program annotation for his recital at St. Anne's Priory Church, Liverpool, England, January 10, 1924. Kindly provided by Jean-Pierre Mazeirat.

Introduction to Tournemire's
Annotated Scores

The information on the following pages is compiled from Charles Tournemire's performing scores, a bound volume containing the original Durand editions of Franck's twelve major organ works and the 1890 Richault edition of the *Andantino* in G Minor. It was given in 1964 by Mme Tournemire to Allen Hobbs, organist of Holy Ghost Church in Denver, Colorado, presently permanent curator of the organ of the Cathedral of the Immaculate Conception in Denver. The volume is among the books and scores comprising the Jean Langlais Collection, presented by Hobbs to Duquesne University, Pittsburgh, in 1990 and housed in the Gumburg Library.

Tournemire's markings, in black, red, and blue pencil, consist primarily of registration and stop changes for various organs that he played during his career. Different colors during each piece signify a different recital. When the three colors were used up, Tournemire erased all the registration and began again. Thus, we are able to distinguish several registration schemes for several works. Lack of markings in the *Fantaisie in C*, *Prière*, and *Choral I* in E Major, indicate that Tournemire either did not play them or had other copies of these works. Other notations of interest include the pedaling of numerous passages of the *Final*, a few examples of fingering at the end of the *Final* (mm. 307–08, 314–16), some thumb glissandos, finger substitutions, and fingerings in the *Fantaisie in A*, elaborate fingering of mm. 180–87 of the B-minor Choral arranged for thumbing the theme in the inner voice, and timings in the *Fantaisie in C* and the *Prélude, Fugue et Variation*, indicating that Tournemire may have either recorded or broad-casted them.

There are several cues for registration changes to be made by stop-pullers: Pierre Moreau (*Fantaisie in A*, m. 196), "B.B.", Tourne-mire's second wife, Alice, whom he called "Bébé" (*Fantaisie in A*, mm. 213 and 261), Raymond Petit (*Choral III in A Minor*, m. 134); and black pencil notations in the *Grande Pièce symphonique* and the *Choral III in A Minor* for Felix Aprahamian, who drew stops and turned pages for Tournemire at his two London recitals in February, 1936.[1] On February 22 Tournemire played Franck's *Choral II* in a recital for the Organ Music Society at St. Alban's Church in the Holborn district of London[2] on one of "Father" Willis's masterpieces which, Aprahamian informs us, both Lynnwood Farnam and André Mar-chal had played without assistance, but which gave Tournemire con-siderable trouble. On February 24 he broadcast a recital for the BBC in the Concert Hall at Broadcasting House playing Franck's *Grande Pièce symphonique* on a Compton unit organ which, with all the stop borrowings and the luminous stop-key console, caused him even more difficulty—in particular, the placement of the Choir manual below the Great (see his note, "En bas jouer au Choir" at the beginning of the Allegro of the *Grande Pièce symphonique*, and "en bas Choir" in measure 68 of the Beaucoup plus largement). Felix Aprahamian told Allen Hobbs that the recital disintegrated into such chaos that the station was forced to take it off the air and, feigning "technical difficulty," to substitute another program.

Registration for an unidentified Dutch organ (Rugp[ositief], Spitsfluit, and Gedekbass) appears in the *Cantabile* while indications in Flemish in *Choral III* refer to the studio organ of the Belgian or-ganist and composer, Flor Peeters. On May 16, 1938 Tournemire joined Flor Peeters in a broadcast recital inaugurating Peeters's new electric-action studio organ recently built by Joseph Stevens of Duf-fel. Although neither played Franck's music, later in the day they each played a recital for invited guests, Tournemire playing

---

[1]Felix Aprahamian, "Charles Tournemire en Angleterre," translated by Jac-queline Englert-Marchal, *Charles Tournemire, Cahiers et Mémoires*, No. 41 (Paris: Les Amis de l'Orgue, 1989) 64.

[2]Built in 1893, the three-manual, fifty-two-rank organ was destroyed in a German air raid during the Second World War.

Franck's *Choral III in A Minor*. The organ had the following specification[3] and almost all of the stops are clearly identified in the score:

Hoofdwerk	Zwelwerk	Pedaal
8 Prestant	8 Rohrfluit	16 Subbass
8 Holpijp	8 Spitsgamba	8 Bass
4 Zingend Principaal	8 Vox Coelestis	4 Fluit
2 Zwitserse Pijp	4 Blokfluit	
Cymbel II–III	2⅔ Nasard	
	2 Woudfluit	
	1⅗ Terts	
	8 Schalmei	

Tournemire renamed some of the stops in his score, such as "Bourdon" for Holpijp, "Chalumeau" for Schalmei, and "Chantant" for the Zingend ("singing") Principaal.

It is difficult to identify the organs connected with some of the French registrations: the Positif or Grand-Chœur Cor-de-nuit, Positif 16' Quintaton, Récit Diapason, and "Chamade" are not found together on any particular organ.

Here follows the unique elements of Tournemire's various interpretations of each piece and then, for those interested in pursuing the subject, we print the complete annotations found in the scores.

The *Grande Pièce symphonique* is among the most extensively annotated works and Tournemire seems to have played it on a variety instruments. In particular, we note that:

> he added only the Choir 16' Lieblich Bourdon at m. 35. The rest of the 16' manual stops were not introduced until mm. 50, 52, and 54;
>
> the Crescendo Pedal (*progressivement péd. Rouleau*) was used for the *crescendo* in mm. 58–59 and the *diminuendo* in mm. 176–77;
>
> the pedal theme beginning in m. 64 is marked "*moyenne;*"
>
> at m. 178 he removed the tirasses (Franck left them all on).

[3]John Hofmann, *Flor Peeters: His Life and His Organ Works* (Fredonia, N.Y.: Birchwood Press, 1978) 36.

265

he added the Tirasse Swell [*sic*] at m. 214, Tirasse
Positif (m. 230) and an Hautbois to the Pédale (m. 231)
to bring out the canon begun in the soprano;

the accompaniment of the *Andante* is played only on the
Swell 8' Rohr Gedeckt, while the pedal part is heard
only on the uncoupled 16' Subbass. The Clarinet is on
the Choir. When both hands go to the Swell (mm. 15–
16 and 23–26) the Geigen 8' is added to the Rohr
Gedeckt;

the *Allegro* is played on the Choir with the Solo coupled;

the second *Andante* is played on the Solo Vox Angelica and
Viola da Gamba with the left hand theme at mm. 5–6
and 9–15 played on the Choir 8' Dulciana, Violoncelle,
and Echo Flute;

the *crescendo* in the *Très lent* from mm. 44 to 46 is again made
with the *Péd. Rouleau;*

the fugue (m. 36 of the *Beaucoup plus largement*) is begun
"moins fort" and the Choir Tuba 8' solos out the left
hand theme from m. 69 until m. 99 when both hands
play on the Great;

fff is reached at m. 111.

Indications in the score suggest that Tournemire recorded, or
prepared for recording, the *Prélude, Fugue et Variation:* he has written timings (4' at the end of the *Lent* and 4' at the end of the
Fugue), a circle within a circle to indicate a side-change, and at the
end of the *Variation,* "3 faces," referring to "three sides." Unfortunately, the recording was either never made or never released.
The Positif Clarinette is indicated for the solos designated by
Franck for the Récit Hautbois. Tournemire added the 8' Bourdon
to strengthen the Pedal between mm. 39–43 of the *Prélude* and
mm. 37–41 of the *Variation.*

The *Pastorale,* which Tournemire did record, has a side-change
symbol before the last note in m. 109. Because he calls for a Positif
16' Quintaton throughout, it is probable this registration does not
refer to the organ of Sainte-Clotilde. He consistently wrote an **R.**
after the printed **P.** to indicate that the manuals were coupled and
added the Tirasse Positif when playing on the Positif, thus bringing
the Récit Hautbois into the Pédale. When the Trompette is intro-

duced at the *Quasi allegretto* (m. 41) he strengthened it with the 4′ Clairon and 2′ Octavin, removing them for the fughetta in m. 80. The 2′ is again added for the passage between mm. 98 and 109. The 4′ and 2′ were probably added again at m. 121 since they are removed at m. 142. Registration for the last *Andantino* calls for the Récit Voix céleste against the Positif 16′ Quintaton and 8′ Cor-de-nuit, alternating every other phrase from m. 181 with the G.-O. 8′ Bourdon.

A few departures from the registration in the printed score of the *Final* include taking off the 16′ Basson after the first pedal solo before going to the Récit; having only the Tirasse Récit for the four pedal notes from m.159; adding all three Tirasses at m. 185 and going to the Positif on the second eighth note in m. 185; adding the G.O. Prestant for the left hand theme at m. 214 and the Octavin at m. 226.

Tournemire's handwritten registration annotations for the beginning of the *Fantaisie in A* conform with Franck's, though he specifies "mixt." with the *anches prép.* At the stop reduction at mm. 63 and 230, in addition to the anches III., he removes the 16′ stops of manuals I. and II., the Montres of I. and II., and the Gambe 8′ of all three manuals. He adds the Récit Gambe at m. 87, removes the Hautbois at m. 96, and adds the Céleste to the Voix humaine at mm. 102 and 133, leaving it on at m. 40 when he takes off the Voix humaine. For the following general *crescendo*, Tournemire has crossed out *mettez Tomp. R.* at m. 148 and moved its introduction (together with the 4′ Clairon) to m. 150. Throughout, he adds and subtracts the Récit 4′ Flûte, and 2′ Octavin by hand, independent of the Récit Trompette and Clairon. Although he does not indicate the removal of the Récit au Positif coupler, he indicates the last two measures to be played on the Bourdon alone.

There are two independent registrations for the *Cantabile* for two different organs (one being Flor Peeters's studio organ), but in both Tournemire adds the Tirasse Grand-Orgue when playing the chordal passages on the Grand-Orgue and then removes it when the hands move to the other two manuals. At the beginning of m. 51 confusion arises with a black pencil indication for the right hand to be played on the G.O., while an erased "–III./II." (in blue) appears above the staff and a "I. – Montre" is written below in red. As on his recording, Tournemire removes the solo reed from the Récit at m. 86 and ends the piece on the Éoline céleste.

On the first page of the *Pièce héroïque* two separate registrations are again written, one in blue, the other in red, the latter calling for both a Kéraulophon and Diapason on the Positif. Tournemire removes the Tirasses and the manual couplers for the section beginning at m. 80 (not indicated in the printed score, but played similarly by Franck at the work's premiere at the Trocadéro), playing the right hand on the Hautbois alone, (or with the Flûte) and the left hand on the 8' Bourdon only (or together with the 8' Flûte and Gambe). At m. 107, while both hands are playing on the Récit, he couples it to the Positif and adds all the foundation stops of 8' and 4'. He is quite specific about the build-up, adding the anches Récit at m. 112, the Positif Diapason during m. 112, the Positif 16' stop at m. 121, anches Positif at m. 125, and then removing the last two aditions for m. 129.

All the notations in the score of the *Choral I* in E Major correspond to Tournemire's analysis of the work that appeared in his book, *César Franck*.

The *Choral II* in B Minor begins with a notation, "Les III. Tirasses," a reminder that on more recent instruments, including the rebuilt Sainte-Clotilde organ, the Récit did not couple through to the Pédale via another manual but required its own tirasse to be depressed. When Tournemire adds the anches G.O at m. 57, he indicates also the addition of the 4' Prestant and Mixture of the Positif. The addition of a natural sign before the left hand's G at the beginning of m. 59 reveals that Franck's student was also prone to play it as a G♯. Tournemire took off the anches Récit variously at m. 69, b.1, m. 72, b.3, or m. 80, b.2. He again removed the anches Récit at m. 105, b.3, but left the 4' Flûte and 2' Piccolo. He was also precise about breaking before the third beat of mm. 83 and 105. In England he apparently had no Voix humaine and so played mm. 115–126 on the Swell Salicional and Vox Angelica.

Tournemire cancelled all pedal stops and tirasses in order to bring out the pedal entry at m. 163 on the Pédale Trompette. He then took it off before the second beat of m. 170, adding the Pedal

16' and 8' Fonds and Tirasse Positif. With great difficulty and much practice he brought out on the Positif the theme between mm. 180 and 187, playing the accompaniment surrounding it on the Récit. Markings throughout the score indicate that Tournemire followed Franck's registration quite closely, adding stops by hand, and with the help of, usually, two stop-pullers. From m. 272 the organ is quickly reduced with stops removed on each beat until m. 274. The Salicional and Gambe are drawn on the Positif in order to solo the left hand voice from m. 285.

All of the registration is erased in the *Choral III* in A Minor. From what is visible we note that Tournemire was not shy about beginning it on a full ensemble with even the Cymbal drawn–particularly on the inaugural recital of Flor Peeters's studio organ. He also added the Octaves graves and 16' Bourdon at every *Largamente* section. It is evident that he used the Octaves graves from m. 142 or 143 and began the *Le double plus vite* (m. 147) on the 8' and 4' foundation stops only. Super octave couplers were added on the third beats of mm. 183 and 185 and the 16' Bombarde on the third beat of m. 190.

I am grateful to Ann Labunsky of Duquesne University School of Music for bringing these scores to my attention and arranging for them to be placed at my disposal for examination and to Allen Hobbs who answered many questions encountered in studying Tournemire's scores.

PRÉLUDES ET PRIÈRES

de

C. V. ALKAN

CHOISIS ET ARRANGÉS POUR L'ORGUE

par

CÉSAR FRANCK

Organiste du G.^d Orgue de Ste Clotilde
Professeur au Conservatoire National de Musique.

Plate 50. Franck's signed autograph inscription to Charles Tournemire
of his edition of Alkan's *Préludes et Prières*,
"à mon élève bien affectionné" (affectionately to my dear pupil)

CHAPTER XIV

Charles Tournemire's Annotated Scores of Franck's Organ Works

Underline = registrations that have been erased, but are
still legible.
~~Strikethrough~~ = registrations that have been crossed out.
Italics = original printed markings in the score.
Handwritten annotations in the score appear in **bold** type.
In general, spelling has been corrected, punctuation and
accents added, and all stop names capitalized.

Fantaisie in C

No marks except where **4 1/2** is written above the beginning of
m. 27 of the *Allegretto cantando* and above the end of m. 16 of the
Quasi lento.

Grande Pièce symphonique

Markings are in black pencil unless otherwise noted.
G.   **Fonds 8**
P.   **Fonds 8**
R.   **Fonds 8, Hautb. (sans Diap**[ason]**)**
Péd. **8, 16**
      Claviers acc[ouplés]
      Préparés anches G., anches R., anches Péd., anches Pos.
A notation in red: **Hautb. 8 (Tirer le H**t.
[Hautbois] **à la main)**

Registration for BBC recital, London, February, 1936 (in black):

Gén. 1 :

Swell	**Fonds 8**
Great	**Fonds 8**
Choir	**Fonds 8**
Pedal	**8, 16**
	–Diaps. 16
	–Dulciana 16
	–Violone 16
	Claviers accouplés
	Tirasses
	Choir slightly open

Andantino serioso.

The manual changes correspond to those in France: Swell=Récit, Choir=Positif, etc.

Measure

25	r.h., b.2, **Great** (blue)
31	b.1, r.h. C♯ tied as common note to l.h., b.2 C♯
35	r.h. before b.2; l.h. before second eighth note:
	Gén. 2 (blue)
	+Lieblich Bourdon 16 (Choir)
	+Trumpet 8, Clarion 4 Swell à la main (red)
46–47	**mettez tous les fonds 16** (blue)
50	b.2, **Contra Viola Swell**
52	b.1, **+Violone 16 (Choir)**
54	b.1, **Gén. 3**
	+Echo Cornet, Nazard, Tierce (Choir) (blue)
	Tuba 8 (Choir) (red)
	+Double Diapason 16 Great
56	***pp***
56–60	**progressivement péd. Rouleau**
60	***ff***
64	b.3, **Force moyenne** (red)
99	b.1–4: tie mark over the upper left-hand part indicating legato chromatic line
113	b.3, *ff* (red)

117	b.3, **+Hautboy, 8, 4**
	<u>**sans anches G**</u>[.O.] (blue)
141	b.2, **moins fort** (red)
165	b.3, *ff* (red)
167	b.1, *f*, b.3 *ff* (red)
169	b.1, *f*, b.3 *ff* (red)
170	b.3, <u>**sans anches G**</u>[.O.], <u>**Péd., Pos.**</u> (blue)
181	**Rouleau** [*diminuendo* with the Crescendo Pedal to b.3] *pp*
182	**Péd. plus douce, Sans Tirasses**
183	<u>**+Octavin, Plein jeu**</u> (blue)
214	b.1, **Tirasse Swell**
230	b.3, **Tirasse P**[os] (blue)
231	Pédale, b.3, **Basse Hautbois**
254	fermata over Pédale F ♯, <u>**changez péd.;**</u> <u>**Tirasse R.**</u> (blue)
	sans anches R., [illegible] **à la main, ne laisser que la Trompette** (blue)
	à la main: Swell –Hautb., –Trumpet 8, Clarion 4 (red)
258	<u>**Préparez au Positif: Cor-de- nuit, Fl. harm.**</u>
	blue comma at end of measure indicating a break
259	blue comma at end of measure indicating a break
260	*Molto lento:* in margin, after the double bar: <u>**découplez tous les claviers; au R. la Flûte + la Tromp.**</u> (blue)

Andante.

Registration (blue):

r.h.	**R. Clar**[inette] **solo**
l.h.	**Pos. Bourdon, Fl. Harm.**
	Péd. S/basse 16, Bourd. 8 (or Péd. 8, 16 doux)

Registration (black):

Attention: Solo. Découplez les claviers.

Gén. ④:

r.h.	**Solo Clar**[inet].
l.h.	**Swell Rohr Gedeckt 8**
	Ped. Subbass 16 (sans Tirasses)
15	b.2, **+Geigen (Swell)**
17	b.1, **–Geigen (Swell)**
23	b.1, **+Geigen (Swell)**

27 b.1, **–Geigen (Swell)**
42 in margin, after the double bar: erased and very faint.
    What is legible conforms to Franck's registration for
    the next movement.

Allegro.

Registration for BBC, London, in black:

Ajust. ②:

Gt. Closed; Gt. Enclosed

Solo – Ch. Positif

par main: Tirasse Solo

The Positif manual is directed to be played on the Solo.

Registration in red:

Solo – Ch. En bas jouer au Choir

Registration for a German organ in black:

**Solo: Zauber flûte 8, Concert flûte 8, Stopped flûte 4,
Flauto Piccolo, Oboë 8 Ped: Subass 16, Flûte 8**

Solo ② written in blue.
95 **Take off Choir stops.**
93 for m. 97: **Solo – Ch.** (red)
99 b.2, **Zauber fl., Concert fl.**

Andante.

Registration for England in black:

**Gen. ⑤. Choir: Dulciana 8, Violoncelle 8, Echo Flute 8, Ped.
Sub. 32, Sub. 16, Flute 8**

Andante begins on the Solo **sans Tirasses** with **Vox Angelica 8,
~~Voix Céleste 8~~** and **Viola da Gamba 8.** This was probably set
on **Solo Ajust. ③**

22 in margin, after double bar line: **Gr. Unenclosed.**

All°. non troppo e maestoso.

Combinaison Gén. 1

Claviers acc[ouplés]., Tirasses.
3 b.3, **–Ch. –Péd.**
17 **V[iolon]c[e]lle. 8, Fl[ûte]. Oct[aviante]. 4.,
    Péd. plus fort**
21 b.3, **+Basse 16** (blue); **(Solo – Choir)** (black)

23	**ne conservez que: R. Flûte, Hautb., Pos. Quintaton 16, Cor-de-nuit, Fl. harm.** (blue)
	jouer au Choir
25	**Pédale 16, 8 seule, Tirasse solo**
26	**Solo Combinaison ajust** ② **; jouer au Choir**
34	b.3, **Pédale douce**
36	b.3, **Subbass 16, Solo: sans Tirasse**
37	b.2, **Solo Comb ajust** ③ l.h. on Solo
38	r.h. on Solo
42	b.2, **Combinaison Gén** ① ©1
	b.3, **préparez anches R.** (blue)
	Péd. b.4 **Tirasse R.** (blue)
43	b.2 **(Choir)**
44	b.2, **anches R.** (blue)
	Péd. b.4 **Tirasse Pos.** (blue); **Tirasse Swell,** [hands play on] **(Great)**
44–46	**Péd. = Rouleau**
45	b.1, **(P.R.)** (blue)
	b.2, **anches Pos.** (blue)
	Péd., b.4 **Tirasse Choir**
46	Péd., b.4 **Tirasse G.** (blue) **Tirasse Great**
47	b.2, **anches G.** (blue)

Beaucoup plus largement que précédemment.

1	b.3 *ff* (red); **anches Péd.** (blue)
2	*ff* (blue)
31	**moins fort** (red)
60	**prepare Ch**[oir] **Tuba 8**
68	end of measure: **en bas Choir**
69	above staff: **plus fort** (red)
70	over staff: **Great** (blue)
84	refering to following measure, b.1, l.h.: **sempre Choir**
99	b.1, **Great** (black)
111	*fff* (red); **Chamade** (blue)

Prélude, Fugue et Variation

Prélude.

Registration, upper left of page (Red):
Pos. **Clarinette**
G. **Bourdon 8**
Péd. **S/B 16, 8**

Registration (Blue):
G.O. **Fonds 8 4 16**
R. **Hautb.**
Pos. **Bourdn. 8**
Péd. **16 p.**

Registration, top center of page (red):
R. **Gambe**
G.O. **Bourd. 8**
Péd. **S/Basse 16**

Registration at bottom center of page (blue):
R. **Hautb.**
G.-C. **Cor-de-nuit (accouplés)**
G. **Flûte harm.**
Péd. **s/b 16, B 8**
28   Pédale: b.1, **8p.** (blue)
39   Pédale: b.1, **Bourd. 8** (blue)
43   Pédale: [b.8] **ôtez 8p.** (blue)
50   in margin, after double bar: **enlever Clarinette;
     Hautb. R.; Tous les fonds 8 16 et 4;
     Claviers acc**[ouplés]. (red)

Lent.

Fonds 8, 4 (blue)
9   in margin, after double bar: **ôtez B. 16, Prestant
    G**[.O.]. (blue); circled: **4′** (black)

Allegretto ma non troppo.

Beginning: **accoupl. P. – R. (blue); enlevez** [remove] **4 et 16** (red)
Phrases: mm. 1–5; 6; 7–8; 12–13; 14.
34   b.2–3, *poco rit.*
35   b.2, Red circle within which is smaller blue circle with
     an intersecting horizontal blue line; plus sign (+)

276

after Pedal F♯, both indicating a side change for a recording session.

58 b.3, last eighth notes, alto and tenor taken in left hand
59 b.1, first eighth notes, alto and tenor taken in left hand
    b.1, second eighth note, alto E♯' taken by r.h., tenor C♯' taken with l. h.
77 b.1, above staff: **G[.O.]. 16 et Prestant** (blue)
    b.1, below l.h. staff: **remettez 16 4**
81 over bar with the 9/8 meter change: **4'** circled.

In margin: **découplez; enlevez** [take off] **fonds 8. 4.; ne conserver que le Bourdon 8 au G[.O.].; Pos: Clarinette**

Variation.
24 fingering: b.4: **4** [3-2-1] **3** [2-1]; b.7: **4**[-3-2-1] (black)
25 fingering: b. 1: **5** [4-3-2-1- -] (black)
36 Pédal: **Bourdon 8** (blue)
48 **ôtez anches III.** (blue)
49 Pédal: **Gambe** (blue)

After last measure: **3 faces** – obviously referring to "three sides"

Pastorale

Registration (all markings are in blue):

R.   **(sans Tromp**[ette.]**)**
Pos. **Quintaton** [16], **FH** [Flûte harmonique], **Quintaton, Cor-de-nuit**
Péd. Soubasse, Basse 8
G.[O.] B[ourdon] **16. FH** [Flûte harmonique]
5 **R.** added after P. indicating the Récit was to be coupled to the Positif (as Franck indicated.
   Pédal: Tirasse P. [Thus, both the Récit and Positif were coupled to the Pédale.
13 **Tirasse P.**

Quasi allegretto.
41 above staff: **Trompette R., (Viole de gambe), Clair**[ion]**. 4, Oct**[avin 2]
   Pédale: **Tirasse P.**

42   above l.h. staff: **Tromp. R.**
80   b.3, l.h., arrow before last eighth note E: **sans Clairon ni Octavin**
98   b.1, **ajoutez Octavin R.** after P. **R.**
109   arrow before last eighth note B: ôtez **Octavin R.**
      Blue circle within which is smaller red circle with an intersecting horizontal red line.
127   after P. **R.**
142   **ôtez Tr**[ompette]. **Cl**[airon]. **Oct**[avin]. **R.**
147   in margin before *Andantino:* **R. V. céleste, Gambe P. Quintaton, Cor-de-nuit Péd. [illegible] sans Tirasses découplez**
181   **G.[O.] B**[ourdon]. **8**
187   in margin, after double bar: **2 faces** [2 sides, referring to his recording].

Prière

No marks.

Final

All markings are in blue.

Pédale: before first note: *ff*

1   *ff*
28   above staff: **ôtez Basson 16**
120   b.3, **enlevez anches, mixtures, etc.**
121   b.1, **ôtez anches Péd.**
123   before b. 1, **diminuendo [mark]**
125   **ôtez Octavin R.; ôtez anches G.C.**
127   b.1, **ôtez Prestant 4**
157   **Tirasse R.**
163   **ôtez Tirasses**
185   b.1, l.h., second eighth note, D, **P**[ositif]; below staff: **Tirasses GPR**
199   b.2, **Tirasses**
215   between staves, after first beat: **Prestant**
226   l.h., before last note, F#: **Octavin**
237   b.4, **anches G.C.**

239 b.4, **anches Péd.**
307 fingering: r.h. – 4 -3 -2 -3 -4 -1 -2
308 fingering: r.h. **3 2 1 2 1** - - -
           l.h. - **2 3 4** - - 1 2
314 fingering: r.h. - **3 1 2 1 2 3 1**
315 fingering: r.h. **2 1 3 2 3 1** - -
           l.h. - 2 3 4 1 3 21
382 b.2, *fff*

Fantaisie in A

Registration: Same as Franck's but Tournemire qualifies *anches*
with **Mixt.**
III.   **Fonds 8. Hautb. (blue)**
       Tr. Clairon (red)
 II.   **Fonds 8 16 (blue)**
       (Mixt. Anches préparées) (red)
  I.   **Fonds 8. 16 (blue);**
       (Mixt. Anches prép.) (red)
P[éd]. **8 16** (blue)
       (Anches prép.) (red)

 1   **I. II. III.** (blue)
     Tirasses I. II. III. (blue)
27   red square around registration
42   b.3, red square around registration
59   alto part is played in the right hand, keeping the re-
     peated thirds in the left.
62   over b. 3, **–anches III.** (red)
63   above b. 1, **–Gambe III.** (blue)
     ôtez anches R. is circled in red
     blue arrow to l.h.: **–16 I. II.; Montres 8,**
       Gambe 8 I. II. (blue)
66   fingering, b.3, l.h.: **3**
                         5
71   fingering, b.3, l.h.: **3**
                        4–5
73   b.3, l.h. G-natural is tied to b.1 of m. 74.
87   between manual staves: **+Gambe III.** (blue)

96   above b.1: **–Hautb. III.** (blue)

102 Registration circled in blue and **et Céleste** added after
      Voix humaine (blue)

      Pédale registration underlined (black)

123 ~~*ôtez anches R.*~~ heavily crossed out in red.

      b. 1, between staves: **III.**

127 Pédale: ôtez Tirasses

140 b.3, **(conservez Céleste)** added after *ôtez Voix humaine*

143 b.1, **ôtez Céleste**

148 b.3, ~~*mettez Tromp. R.*~~ (crossed out in blue); **III./II.** (blue)

150 breath mark before b. 3; b.3 **+Tromp. Cl. III.** (red)

      b.3, r.h. thumb glissando from A to G#⁩ in m. 151 and
        from G#⁩ to A in m. 151 and back to G#⁩, m. 152, b.1

151 Pédale: **Tirasse III.** (blue)

154 arrow on first r.h. note: **Fl. 4 III.** (blue)

156 **+Oct**[avin] **2 III.** (blue) (boxed in red)

158 Pédale: **+Tir. III.**

162 between staves: **+16. I. II.** (blue)

      Pédale: **Tir. I. mettez les Tirasses** (blue)

165 crossed out *ff* (black)

175 crossed out *ff* (black)

178 **–anches III.**

      between staves: **–16 I. II.**

180 **–Octavin III.**

182 ~~*ôtez anches R.*~~ [red]

188 **attention** (red)

189 ~~*G.O.*~~ crossed out (black) and **I. II. III.** written (black);
      mettez les Tirasses circled in blue; *mettez anches R.* and
      remettez tous les . . . circled in red

191 **+Flûte 4** and **+Prestant II.** (blue)

192 b.1 arrow to b. 1: **+Prestant I.**, + **Flûte 4**, **+tous les
      fonds 8 à agitato** [blue]

194 *anches P.* circled in red with arrow to first soprano
      note. Pédale: **+16 I. II.** (blue)

196 *anches G.O.* and *anches Péd.* circled in red. Red arrow
      pointing to first soprano note, indicating the anches
      are to be added there.

      Below pedal staff: **attention** (blue) [note to stop-puller,
      Pierre] **Moreau (Bombarde)** (red)

198   above *Très largement* à **agitato**

214   above staff: **–anches péd. I. II.** (red)

       Below staves: **B̲ B̲**: **–les Prestant, –les Flûtes 4** (blue)

218   l.h. all thumb glissando to m. 19, b. 1

221   *ôtez anches G.O. et P.* circled in red

       lift indicated by a diagonal black line before m. 222, b.1

226   C drawn (in black) around left hand part, perhaps indi-
       cating all to be taken by l.h.

230   **–16. I. II.** (blue) **ôtez anches R.** and *ôtez quelques* circled
       in red.

       Below l.h. staff: **–Montres, Gambes I.**[and] **II.,**
       –Gambes III. (blue)

239   b.3, l.h. fingering: **3**
                                       4–5

241   b.3, l.h. fingering: **4**
                                       5

243   b.3, l.h. fingering: **3**
                                       4–5

250   b.3, l.h., last sixteenth note, G♯: **2–1**

253   b.3, l.h., last sixteenth note, G♮: **2–3**

254   b.1, l.h., low B crossed out and replaced by a quarter
       rest. B half-note written on b. 2 and tied to next
       measure.

261   b.2, **B.B.**

263   **–Flûte 4 III.** (blue)

275   ~~*ôtez la Flûte du P*~~ and **Bourdon Solo II.** added (black)

Cantabile

Registration at left (red):

   III.   **Trompette Solo**

   II.   **Bourdon 8**

    I.   **Fonds 8 Péd. Contreb. 16, Flûte 8**

           Tir. II.

Registration at right (blue):

  G.O. **Montre 8, Bourd. 8, Gambe 8**

  Pos.   **Fluit 8**

            Hautbois

  Récit. Trompette Solo, Bourdon 8

Péd. Subbass 16, Gedekbass
(acc. G.O. au Rugp[positief])

Printed registration: *Claviers séparées* is underlined in blue.

Boite 3/4 ouverte

1   **+Tirasse G.O.**

mm. 6, 11, 25, 30   **+Tirasse**

mm. 3, 8, 13, 27, 32   **–Tirasse**

43   r.h. **acc**[ouplés]. **Récit/Positif** (blue)
    l.h. **G.O. - Rugp.** (blue)

50   b.2, **–III./II.** (blue)

51   b.1, **I. –Montre** (red)
    +T[irasse], **+B**[ourdon] (red)

52   **Tirasses G.O., Pos.** (blue)

62   b.2, treble clef's F♯^{i} (fingered with a **2**) is bracketed (in black) to be played with the l.h. D♯ (**4**) and l.h. C♯ (**5**)

65   **sans acc**[oupler]. **Pos./Récit**; between staves: **découplez**; Pédale: **sans Tirasses** (blue)

67   b.3, **Péd. –Bourd. 16** (red)

76   **–Hautbois, +Éoline,** _____ (black)

78   b.1, above staff: **Récit –Tromp., +Hautbois**; between staves: **Rugp.**; above Pedal staff: **au Rgp. (–Spitsfluit, +Bourd. 8** (blue)

82   b.4, **Péd. –8** (blue and red)

86   b.2, above staff: **Récit –Hautb., +Éoline, Céleste;** (blue); **–Gedeckt** (black)

Pièce héroïque

Registration (blue):

  III. Fonds. 8 –Anches
  II. Fonds 8 (Anches et mixt. préparées)
  I. Fonds 8 et 16 (Jeux d'anches et mixt. préparées)
  Péd. 16 8 (Anches préparées)
       Tirasses

Registration (red):
- **R.**   **Fl., Gambe, Hautb. et tous les 8. Trompette. Acc**[ouplé R.P.]
- **Pos.** **Flûte 8, Bourd., Kérau**[lophone]**., Diapason**
- **G.O.** **Fonds 8 16**
- **Péd.** **16 8**

      Anches prép. G. et Péd.

   47   second sixteenth-note: **ôtez Diapason** (red)

(red):
-   78   b.3, **–Tr**[ompette]**. R**[écit].
-   80   above staff: **découplez**

      G. Flûte, Gambe et Bourdon, 8 ôtez le reste

      R. Hautb. et Flûte

      <u>**Enlevez Tirasses**</u>

(blue):

      = acc. III., Hautb. solo

      = au II. Bourdon

(black):
- **G.O.** **Flûte 8 seule, –Montre**
- **Récit.** **+Trompette, –Basson**
- **Pos.** **+16**
- 107   b.1, above the staff: **Mettez tous les fonds G.O., acc**[ouplés] **et Tirasses** (red)

      above Pédale staff: **au II., + Fonds 8. 4.** (blue)
- 109   b.1. **–Trompette R.**
- 111   **Tous les fonds R.** (red)
- 112–13 **Pos: Diapason** (red)
- 113   **+anches III.** (blue)
- 121   b.1, above staff: **+16 II.** (blue)
- 125   b.1, **+anches II.** (blue)

      above Pédale: **anches G.** (red)
- 127   **ôtez anches G.** (red)
- 129   **–anches II., –Bourdon 16 II.** (blue)
- 139   **+Diapas**[on] (red)
- 145   above staff: **anches G.** (red)

      +16 au II., +anches I. (blue)
- 147   above staff: **Octavin** (black)

150 second half of b.1, **Pos. Quinte, Doublette** (red)
179 between staves: **Basson 16** (red)
179 above Pédale: *fff*

Choral I in E

  3 r.h., b.1, alto E: number 3, perhaps referring to the measure number.
 46 before b. 3: double bar with fermata above and below (black)
147 Pédale, b.3, **Tirasse G.** (black)

Choral II in B Minor

Registration (red)

Préparés:
  R.   **P[lein]. jeu, Tromp., Clairon, F.H., Gambe.**
  P.   **Prinzipal, Cor-de-nuit, Hautb.**
G[O.].   **Fl. H., Montre 8, B[ourdon] 8, Salic[ional], B[ourdon] 16**
  Péd.   **Tous les fonds Clav[iers]. acc[ouplées]., Tir. Gr.[O.]**
   1 **Les III. Tirasses** (black)
 41 **+anches Swell (Cornopean 8, Clarion 4)** (red)
    III. +4
    Solo, Swell, Great (black)
 49 b.1, **+Tuba** (red)
    +Tirasses et flûtes 4, Solo, Great (black)
 57 **Prestant, Mixt. Pos.** (black)
    +Trumpet, –Clarion (red)
 59 l.h., b.1, natural sign written before the G.
 64 b.3, blue diagonal line above staff indicating a lift
 65 Péd. **ôtez anches G.** (red)
 69 **–anches III.** (red)
 72 before b.3, **ôtez anches R.** (red)
 80 b.2, **–appel anches III., –anches 4** (red)
 83 before b.3, vertical black line indicating a break
 89 second sixteenth of b. 1, **P. boîte fermé**
 90 **–Tirasse Great** (black)
105 b.3, **–anches, enlevez Fl. 4 and Piccolo 2** (red)

108   b.3, **–Mixt. II.** (red)
109   **Péd. –Tirasses** (black)
112   **Swell Salicional and Vox angelica** (black)
114   b.1, vertical black line indicating a lift before second
        sixteenth note (black)
        ôtez P[éd.] C[ontre] **basse et les Tirasses** (red)
115   **Préparez +Montre, Bourdon I.** (black)
126   big blue fermata over double barline
148   *1° Tempo ma un poco meno lento*
        Péd. –Fond 8 16 4, –les Tirasses, I. tacet +appel Péd.
        (red)
162   Pédale: **(Trompette)** (red)
169   **Péd. +Fonds 16 8 et Tir. II.** (red)
170   b.2, **Péd. –Trompette** (blue)
177   **–Tirasse II.** (blue)
179   b.3, **rall.** (black)
180   b.1, **–acc**[ouplement]**, anches II.** (black)
        b.1, second eighth, **R.** (black)
188   b.1, **acc**[ouplés] **II./I.** (red)
204   **–Quint, Doublette, Plein jeu au II.** (red)
210   after double bar: **Sw. +Mixture** (blue)
211   **+16 II; Tirasse I.** (red)
        +16 au II. (black)
215   b.1, **Great +16 Open Diapason** (black)
218   b.3, **Great +2** (black)
224   b.3, **+anches II.** (red) [obviously referring to m. 226]
226   **–Tir. I., –Clairon, Trompette 8** (red)
230   b.1, **I. +Trompette et Clair., Plein jeu et Doublette**
        (blue); **Great anches** (red)
233   b.1, **(Great +Twelfth and Fifteenth)** (black)
234   **(I. –Montre 16), +Tir. I.** (red)
241   *Ôtez anches G.O.* and *Ôtez anches Pos.* in following
        measure are circled in red.
247   **(Péd. +anches 8 16)** (blue)
258   b.1, **I. +Bombarde** (blue)
        b.1, Pédale: second eighth note, **+appel. Péd., +Tir.**
        III. (red)
266   b.1, Pédale: **+Bombarde** (blue)
271   **II. –Prest., –Flûte 4** (black)

272   b.1, Pédale: **–Tirasses I. II.** (black)
      b.2, **III. –Mixture, anches.** (blue)
      b.2, **–Montre, –Gambe au II., découplez** (black)
273   b.1, r.h. **–Flûte harm**[onique] **au II** (black)
      Pédale: **–Tirasse III.** (black); **–Flûte 4** (blue)
      b.2, **–16 au II.** (black)
274   b.1, Pédale: **32′, Bourdon 16 seulement** (black)
275   b.1, **au II. +Salicional, +Gambe** (black)
285   b.1, Pédale: **ôtez 8 et 16** (blue)
      b.1, arrow to second eighth note indicating: **Choir** (black)

Choral III in A Minor

Registration on opposite page (blue):
  R.   **Fl. 4, Gambe 8, Fl. Trav. Diapason, Hautb. Trompette, Sopr. Plein jeu, Octavin**
  P.   **Fl. 4, Cor-de-nuit, Salicional, Principal 8**
G.[O.]   **Prestant, Bourd**[on] **8, Fl. H. 8, Gambe, Montre, Trompette, Clairon**
  Péd.   **S**[ous]**Basse 16, Bourdon 8, Pédale: F**[lûte]
      Claviers accouplés; Tirasse G.[O.]

All notations are in blue unless otherwise indicated.

Note at upper left of page: **Inauguration Recital: Tir. I. et II. seule**

Registration for Flor Peeters's Studio Organ
  II.   **Rohrfluit 8, Spitsgambe 8, Blokfluit 4, Nasard**
  I.   **Prestant 8, Bourdon 8, Prinzipal Chantant** [Zingend Principaal] **4, Cymbal**
Péd. 16 8 Tirasses

Next to printed registration Tournemire has erased **Mixt. Anches** (red)
  6   **G**[O.] **+Oct. grave, +Bourdon 16)**
  8   b.1, **–Oct. graves; II. I. –16**
 15   **+Oct. grave, +16**
 20   **–Oct. grave, –16**
 23   **+Oct. grave, +16**

+Oct. gr. I., 8 4 Péd. (red)

26 b.1, **ôtez anches G.**[O.]

27 b.1, **–Nasard, –Principal 4**

30 before b.3: double bar drawn in with fermatas above
    and below (red)
    b.3, **II. –Octaves graves**

32 **(découplez)**

33 **II. –16**

48 b.1, below staff: **Pos: ôtez Salicional, Principal**
    middle of bar: **I. +Zingend 4**

49 b.3, above staff: **16 G.O.**

53 **+Oct. graves, anches, copula R.**
    +16 II. (black)

54 b.3, **Tirasse P.**

56 b.3, **II.**

79 below staff; **ôtez 16 au II.**

79 at end of measure is a blue circle surrounding a red
    circle with a red horizontal and vertical line drawn
    through it, indicating a record side change.

80 **I.** [to be played on the Grand-Orgue rather than the
    Positif]
    II. –16 O. graves, –Montre

90 b.3, **Péd. –4**

91 b.1, **Octaves graves, II. –Prestant**

92 **préparé Tromp. Solo** (black)

93 **au R. ne laiser que le Hautbois**
    Pos. Cor-de-nuit solo
    Péd. la Tirasse du Pos.

96 **–Oct. graves**
    III. Trompette solo (red)

97 after measure in margin: **au II. C** [illegible] **au Solo;**
    au I. Bourdon 8 seul

117 b.1, after first beat a red circle with a blue circle inside
     with a blue horizontal and vertical line drawn
     through it, indicating a record side change.

119 b.2, **III. Trompette, Clairon; II. Quinte; I. Plein jeu,**
     Bombarde

120 b.4, before last eighth note: **II. +Montre**

127   second sixteenth note: **Diapason R.**

128   b.3, **I. +16,**

       Pédale:+P[os.] + II.

131   b.2, second eighth, soprano A♭':

       +Principal Chantant 4

134   b.3, **attention, Raymond** [Petit]**!** (red)

136   **anches du R.**

       +Woudfluit 2, Péd. F[luit]

137   b.3, **−Tirasses, les anches G**[O.]**, sans Bass**[on] **16**

139   b.1, **Pos. anches**

142   **+Chalumeau, Zwitserse Pijp 2, Péd. 4**

146   **Tirasse II;** at end of measure: **sans Pl**[ein]**. jeu ni Oct.**

       enlevez tous les mixtures ne conservez que les 8 et 4

171   **+Nasard, Terts, +Octave grave; +Tir. I. II.**

172   **+Cymbel**

173   b.1, **Tirasses I. et II.** [sic]

       b.3, **+flûtes 8 pieds, +Chalumeau 16, +Octavin R.**

177   b.3, **+anches Péd.**

183   b.3, **Oct. aig.** (red)

185   b.3, **Oct. aig.** (red)

190   b.1, **+8 Péd.** *ff*

       b.3, **+Bomb.** (red)

199   **+Oct. gr.** (red)

Glossary

Accouplement du R. au P.
Récit coupled to the Positif at unison pitch.

Accouplement du R. au P. Tirasse du P.
On Cavaillé-Coll organs (and all mechanical-action organs) if the Récit is coupled to the Positif and the Positif is coupled to the Pédale, the Récit is automatically coupled to the Pédale—and its keys visibly move. On organs whose couplers do not mechanically move, it is necessary to couple the Récit to the Pédale in addition to the Positif to Pédale.

Accouplez le R. au P.
Couple the Récit to the Positif.

Ajoutez la Trompette du R.
Add the Récit Trompette. In order for the Trompette pipes to speak, air must be admitted to their windchest. This is done by depressing the *Anches Récit* pédale de combinaison. If the Trompette is to be added by hand, the Anches Récit must be down; if it is to be added by foot, the stop knob must be drawn.

Ajoutez les jeux d'anches du R. et les fonds de 16 pieds.
Depress the *Anches Récit* pédale de combinaison. All previously prepared stops controlled by this ventil would sound. At Sainte-Clotilde these would have been:

        4 Flûte octaviante

        2 Octavin

        8 Trompette harmonique

        4 Clairon

Add the manual 16′ flue stops. At Sainte-Clotilde these would have been:

Grand-Orgue	Positif
16 Montre	16 Bourdon
16 Bourdon	

Ajoutez un jeu de 8 ou de 4 pieds à la Pédale
Prélude, m. 39, *Fugue et Variation*, m. 37
    Add an 8′ or 4′ stop to the Pédale. To add an 8′ stop Franck could have coupled either the Positif or Grand-Orgue to the Pédale. To add a 4′ stop he could have begun with the Grand-Orgue coupled to the Pédale (with or without the Pédale 8′ Flûte) and had the Grand-Orgue 4′ Octave drawn. Depressing the *Anches Grand-Orgue* would have caused the 4′ to play in the Pédale. The left hand, playing on the Positif, would not have been affected.

Ajoutez successivement les jeux d'anches à chaque clavier de façon à arriver graduellement au Grand-Chœur.
    Add successively the anches ventils of each manual and Pédale in such a way as gradually to obtain full organ. This was done in order from right to left: Récit, Positif, Grand-Orgue, and Pédale.

Animez - -
Livlier, more excitedly.

Animez beaucoup.
Animatedly, very lively.

Avec une certaine liberté de mesure.
With some (undefinable, yet understood) rhythmic freedom.

Beaucoup plus largement qu'à la page 3.
Grand Chœur, Grande Pièce symphonique
    Much slower than the *Allegro non troppo e maestoso* at the bottom of page 3. Note that page 3 is in 2/4 and the *Grand Chœur* is in 4/4.

Bourdons de 32, 16, 8.
The only 32′ stop on the Sainte-Clotilde organ was a Quintaton; on other organs it might be labeled Soubasse or Bourdon.

Cantando.
Broad, singing line.

Chanté.
To the fore; to be brought out.

Claviers accouplés.

All manuals coupled together at unison pitch. At Sainte-Clotilde there were only two manual couplers: *Récit au Positif* and *Positif au Grand-Orgue.*

Claviers séparés.

Uncouple all the manuals from each other.

En élargissant un peu.

A slight *rallentando* . . . broaden . . . stretch the tempo.

Express.

Expressively.

Fonds de 8 pieds.

All 8′ flue stops except celestes. On the organ of Sainte-Clotilde this equalled 12 eight-foot stops.

(Péd.) Fonds de 8 et 16 pieds.

Flue stops of 16′ and 8′ pitch. The Sainte-Clotilde organ had only one rank of open flue pipes at each pitch.

(R.) Fonds et jeux d'Anches.

All stops of the Récit except the Voix céleste and the Voix humaine.

(R., P., G.O.) Fonds et Anches de 4. 8. et 16 pieds sans Prestant.
Final

Only the foundation stops and anches of 4′, 8′, and 16′—without the 4′ Prestant. Since the 4′ Prestant of the Positif and Grand-Orgue at Sainte-Clotilde was not on the Anches ventil, it would not have been silenced when the anches were taken off and the organ reduced to 8′ stops.

Flûte de 8 pieds.

8′ Flûte harmonique only. The only other "flûte" was a Bourdon (stopped flute).

Jeux d'anches préparés.

The stops on the Anches windchest could be drawn but would remain silent until wind was admitted to the chest by means of a pédale de combinaison.

Jeux doux.
Choral III in A Minor, m. 97

Soft stops. The Pédale is reduced to 16′ and 8′ stops only, without the Tirasses (pedal couplers).

Mettez les tirasses du P. et du G.O.
Final
　　　With the Récit uncoupled from the Positif, the melody is heard in the Pédale played on all flue stops.

Mettez le 32 pied.
Draw the 32′ pedal flue stop.

Molto slargando.
Gradually become much slower.

Moins douce.
Less softly...a little louder: add another stop or a coupler.

Ôtez graduellement les jeux d'anches aux Péd., au G.O., et au P.
Final, m. 126
　　　Gradually take off the Anches of all divisions except the Récit.

Ôtez le Clairon du R.
Allegro, Grande Pièce symphonique, m. 98
　　　Take off the Récit 4′ Clairon (by pédale de combinaison) because later the 8′ Trompette is to be added with it.

Ôtez anches du R.
Release the *Anches Récit*, thereby silencing any stops on that chest.

Ôtez les 16 p[ieds] et quelques 8 p. au P.
Take off the 16′ stop (Bourdon) and some of the 8′ stops of the Positif.

Ôtez tous les jeux d'anches excepté ceux de R.
Release the Anches ventils of all manuals and the Pédale, leaving only those of the Récit. This was done from left to right: Pédale, Grand-Orgue, and Positif.

Péd: des 8ves graves à tous les claviers.
Depress the sub-octave coupler pédales de combinaisons of all manuals.

Retenez.
Ritardando, delaying the time gradually.

Séparez le R. du P.
Uncouple the Récit from the Positif.

Séparez les claviers.
Uncouple all the manuals from each other and from the Pédale.

Supprimez graduellement quelques jeux au P.
Prière, last 9 measures
Since the unenclosed Positif accompanies a melody that gradually diminuendos, some of the five stops have to be taken off: at least the Montre, Flûte harmonique, and Viole de gambe.

Tirasses.
Pedal couplers; from the verb, *tirer*, to pull, because they pull down the manual keys. When no manuals are specified, all are coupled to the Pédale.

Tirasse du G.O.
Couple the Grand-Orgue to the Pédale.

Toujours avec une certaine liberté de mesure.
Prière, m. 132
With some rhythmic freedom until further indication to the contrary, i.e., *Très mesuré*.

Toujours G.O.
Continue playing on the Grand-Orgue. This precautionary notice is used when one hand is to go to another manual but the other hand is to remain on the manual (in this instance, the Grand-Orgue) on which it has been playing.

Très-expressif et très-soutenu.
Very expressive and sustained.

Très lié.
Very legato.

Très long.
Very long. Obviously, held longer than it would be with just the accompanying fermata.

Très mesuré.
In strict tempo.

Voix humaine.
Even though not indicated, the Tremulant should be drawn with the Voix humaine.

Selected Bibliography

Additions to Bibliography published in *Toward an Authentic Interpretation of the Organ Works of César Franck*

Albrecht, Hans. "César Franck, Ch. M. Widor und A. Guilmant als Orgellehrer," *Musik und Gottesdienst*, June, August, and October 1975.

Archibold, Lawrence, "'We Have No Idea of the Liberty with which Franck Played His Own Pieces:' Early French Recordings of César Franck's A-Minor Chorale [*sic*] and the Question of Authenticity," *The Organist as Scholar: Essays in Memory of Russell Saunders*, ed. Kerala J. Snyder. Stuyvesant, New York: Pendragon Press, 1994, 83–116. An excellent essay that is flawed by the author's having based many of his conclusions on the erroneous date of "c. 1933" for Marcel Dupré's Decca recordings of the *Trois Chorals* made at St. Mark's Church, North Audley Street, London. In fact, the recordings were made in 1948.

Bartelink, B. "L'Organiste," *Gregoriusblad*, September 1990. Address: Gregoriusblad, Drift 23, NL–3512 BR Utrecht.

Barth, Oskar A. "Zum Verständnis der Trois Chorals von César Franck," *Ars Organi*, September 1990, pp. 128–33.

Burg, Josef. "Schüler erleben ihren Orgellehrer César Franck," *Ars Organi*, September 1990, pp. 115–123.

Busch, Hermann Josef. "César Franck und der Gregorianische Choral," *Ars Organi*, September 1990, pp. 124–28.

————. "Von César Franck zu Jean Langlais," *Musica sacra*, No. 3, 1987.

[Cavaillé-Coll, Aristide.] *Orgues d'Église et de Salon*. Exposition Universelle de Paris, 1878: Classe 13—Instruments de Musique. Paris: Privately printed, 1878. Contains the specification of an orgue de salon exhibited in the Galerie des Instruments de Musique in the Palais du Champ-de-Mars and the "Composition des Jeux" of his organ in the Grande Salle des Fêtes, Palais du Trocadéro.

Craighead, David; Antone Godding, "A Comparison of the 1959 [1956] Durand and Kalmus editions of Franck's organ works with the original printing," *The American Organist*, April 1985, 56–58. The corrections collated in this article are found at the end of each chapter in the present book.

Davaille, Michel. "L'Harmonium de César Franck," *FFAO—L'Association des Amis de l'Orgue de Jehan Alain*, Numéro 15, 1990.

Dinneweth, Paul. "Het orgel von César Franck," *A.D.E.M.*, No. 3, July–September 1990.

Dubbeldam, Jet. "La tradition du Troisième Choral de César Franck," *Het Orgel*, July–August 1988.

Dufourcq, Norbert. "Prier à l'orgue en France: Essai sur la *Prière* de César Franck." *César Franck*, Cahiers et Mémoires, No. 44. Paris: *L'Orgue*, October–December 1990, pp. 81–90.

Dunham, Rowland W. "From Yesterday No. 2: Franck, Libert, Widor," *The American Organist*, December 1954, pp. 402–3.

Eck, Ton van. "César Franck speelt...César Franck," *Gregoriusblad*, No. 3, September 1990, pp. 241–59; No. 4, December 1990.

_____ . "Die Orgel von Ste. Clotilde in Paris," *Ars Organi*, September 1990, pp. 134–49.

_____ . "L'Orgue de Sainte-Clotilde et l'art de la registration chez César Franck," *César Franck*, Cahiers et Mémoires, No. 44. Paris: *L'Orgue*, October–December 1990, pp. 81–90.

Eschbach, Jesse E. "Paris, Bibliothèque Nationale, MS 8707: A New Source for Franck's Registrational Practices and Its Implications for the Published Registrations of His Organ Works," *French Organ Music from the Revolution to Franck and Widor*. Rochester, N.Y.: University of Rochester Press, 1995, pp. 103-117.

Fanning, Emory. "Chorals II and III: Two Franck Autographs," *The American Organist*, December 1990, pp. 112–14.

_____ . "A propos des manuscrits des Deuxième et Troisième Chorals," *César Franck*, Cahiers et Mémoires, No. 44. Paris: *L'Orgue*, October–December 1990, pp. 65–72. A French translation of the above article that appeared previously in *The American Organist*.

Fauquet, Joël-Marie. "L'Orgue de Ducroquet et la 'Fantaisie de Saint-Eustache' (1854)," *César Franck*, Cahiers et Mémoires, No. 44. Paris: *L'Orgue*, October–December 1990, pp. 73–80.

Franck, César. "Avertissement," *Chant Grégorien, restauré par le R.P. Lambillotte; accompagnement d'orgue par César Franck*. Paris: Leclére, 1858.

Godding, Antone; David Craighead, "A Comparison of the 1959 [1956] Durand and Kalmus editions of Franck's organ works with the original printing," *The American Organist*, April 1985, pp. 56–58. The corrections collated in this article are found at the end of each chapter in the present book

Harwood, Ronald. *César and Augusta*. London: Secker & Warburg, 1979; Boston: Little, Brown and Company. A well researched, beautifully written, and deeply moving historical novel detailing Franck's intimate relationship with Augusta Holmès.

Hastings, Karen. "From Manuscript to Publication: Implications in Performance Practice of the First Choral of Franck," Stanford University Doctoral Paper, June 1987. Reprinted in *French Organ Music from the Revolution to Franck and Widor*. Rochester, N.Y.: University of Rochester Press, 1995, pp. 119-139.

_____ . "Le Premier Choral: Du manuscrit à l'édition princeps," *César Franck*, Cahiers et Mémoires, No. 44. Paris: *L'Orgue*, October–December 1990, pp. 47–64. A condensation in of the author's "From Manuscript to Publication."

_____ . "New Franck Fingerings Brought to Light," *The American Organist*, December 1990, pp. 92–101.

Jacquet-Langlais, Marie-Louise. "Les Six Pièces," *César Franck*, Cahiers et Mémoires, No. 44. Paris: *L'Orgue*, October–December 1990, pp. 4–25.

_____ . "Les Six Pièces," *César Franck*, Cahiers et Mémoires, No. 44. Paris: *L'Orgue*, 1990, pp. 4-25. Translated as "The Organ Works of Franck: A Survey of Editorial and Performance Problems," and reprinted in *French Organ Music from the Revolution to Franck and Widor*. Rochester, N.Y.: University of Rochester Press, 1995, pp. 143-188.

_____ . *L'Œuvre d'orgue de César Franck et ses mystères*. Texte de l'exposé présenté dans le cadre de la III. *Internationale Orgeltagung*, Winterthur/Suisse, September 23–28, 1990.

Jespers, J. "Aspects liturgiques de son œuvre d'Orgue," *Gregoriusblad*, September 1990.

Klotz, Hans. "Romantische Registrierkunst—César Franck an der Cavaillé-Coll-Orgel," *Musik und Kirche*, Heft 5, 1975.

Langlais, Jean. "Propos sur le Style de César Franck," *Jeunesse et Orgue*, No. 37, Automne 1978, pp. 6–7.

Latry, Olivier. "A Masterclass on César Franck with Olivier Latry," *The Sydney Organ Journal*, June–July 1994, pp. 17–25. A transcript of a tape recorded masterclass held on April 15, 1994 at the Sydney (Australia) Conservatorium of Music, translated by Pastór de Lasala; revised and edited by Ralph Lane. *Choral II in B Minor* is discussed extensively.

Leupold, Wayne. "The Organ Manuscripts of César Franck," *The American Organist*, December 1990, pp. 109–11.

Lueders, Kurt. "Approaching Franck's Organ Works From Within: Considerations on Interpretation," *The American Organist*, December 1990, pp. 102–08.

Lueders, Kurt; Ton van Eck. "Franck, Cavaillé-Coll, and the Organ of Sainte-Clotilde," *The American Organist*, December 1990, pp. 115–19.

Manz, Andri. "Prélude, Fugue und Variationen über César Franck: Einige Gedanken anldsslich seines 100 Todesjahres," *Musik und Gottesdienst*, No. 6, October 1990, pp. 285–310.

Pieters, F. "Het leven van César Franck," *De Orgelvriend*, No. 10, October 1990.

Roth, Daniel. "Some Thoughts on the Interpretation of the Organ Works of Franck, on His Organ, and on the Lemmens Tradition," *French Organ Music from the Revolution to Franck and Widor*. Rochester, N.Y.: University of Rochester Press, 1995, pp. 189-198.

Sabatier, François. *César Franck et l'Orgue*. Paris: Presses Universitaires de France, 1982.

——. "Les Trois Pièces du Trocadéro (1878): Un manuscrit rivilateur," *César Franck*, Cahiers et Mémoires, No. 44. Paris: *L'Orgue*, October–December 1990, pp. 26–34. An article based on the series that had appeared in *The American Organist*, July, August, and September 1990.

Sanger, George. "Chromaticism in the Solo Keyboard Works of Franck and Fauré," Ph.D. dissertation, University of Pittsburgh, 1976. UM No. GAX77–03035.

Seipt, Angelus. "César Francks Symphonische Dichlungen," Ph.D. dissertation, Köln, 1980.

Smith, Rollin. *Toward an Authentic Interpretation of the Organ Works of César Franck*. New York: Pendragon Press, 1983.

Smith, Rollin. "The Organ of the Trocadéro and Its Players," *French Organ Music from the Revolution to Franck and Widor.* Rochester, N.Y.: University of Rochester Press, 1995, pp. 275-308.

Valkestijn, J. "Franck's Vocal and Liturgical Works," *Gregoriusblad,* September 1990.

Verkade, Gary. "César Franck: *Grande Pièce symphonique*: Some Aspects of Form," *The Diapason,* January 1993, pp. 11–14.

Viret, Jacques. "César Franck vu par ses élèves," *La Tribune de l'Orgue,* June 1988.

Voeffray, Edmond. "Des tirasses de Franck, spécialement en ce qui concerne leurs cascades," *La Tribune de l'orgue,* June 1995, pp. 8-11.

Wegener, Bernd. "César Francks Harmonik," Ph.D. dissertation, Köln, 1976.

Winn, Edith Lynwood. "Memories of César Franck," *The American Organist,* July 1927, pp. 170-71. A fictionalized tale of the author's meeting an aged student of Franck in the rue Molière. The particulars are based on Gabriel Pierné's memoir.

Index

Boldface indicates illustrations.

Hautbois, its place in the *Fonds de 8,* 65
Haydn, Franz Joseph
  O salutaris, 24
  Sancta Maria, 21
Heller, Stephen, 9
Herz, Henri, 2
Hexameron, 2
Hill, Norman & Beard organ, Queen's Hall, London, 105
Hobbs, Allen, 182, 264, 269
Holmès, Augusta, **208,** 209-11, 231, 249
  Noël, 254*n*
Hugo, Victor, 26
Hummel, Johann Nepomuk, *Concerto in B Minor,* 3

Il est né le divin enfant, 23
d'Indy, Vincent, 1, 4, 9, 29, 31, 33, 41, 51, 103, 161, 181, 185, 209
  on the *Cantabile,* 183-84
  on the *Final,* 161

Jean Langlais Collection, Duquesne University, 263
Jeux d'anches, their function, 64-65, 67

Kalmus edition, 56
Kauntzinger edition, 57
Küthen, Abbé W., on motive of the *Grande Pièce symphonique,* 85

Labunsky, Ann, 269
Lambillotte, Louis, 16
  his *Chant Grégorien,* 137
Langlais, Jean, 40, 58-59, 66*n,* 87, 93, 111, 134*n,* 146, 153, 159, 160, 181, 197, 201, 228, 232, 235*n,* 250-51, 254, 260

Lebel, Louis, 40
Latry, Olivier, 231
Lebègue, Nicolas, 75
Leborne, Simon, 3, 4

Lefébure-Wély, Louis-James-Alfred, 20-23, 135, **152,** 165
  dedicatee of the *Final,* 151-53
Legato, 59
Légion d'Honneur, 41
Lehman, Robert, 212
Lekeu, Guillaume, 209
Lemmens, Jacques-Nicolas, 12, 16, 133, 81
  École d'Orgue, 97*n*
  Méthode d'Orgue, 133
Lenoir, Alfred, 34, 51
Leopold I, King of Belgium, 2
Litaize, Gaston, 40
Liège Conservatoire, 2
Liszt, Franz, 2, 3, 9
  Fantasy and Fugue on the Chorale "Ad nos, ad salutarem undam," 34, 80, 165
  on the *Six Pièces,* 161
London.
  Broadcasting House of the BBC, 264
  Organ Music Society, 264
  Queen's Hall organ, Dupré's recording of, 105
  Saint Alban's Church, Holborne, 264
Loisel, _____, his *Seven Last Words,* 24
Loret, Clément, 27
Loret, Hippolyte, his organs, 25
Louis XVI, King of France, 11

Madeleine, La, 28, 31, 45, 153, 165
Mahaut, Albert, 41, 133, 134*n,* 211, 231
  on the *Cantabile,* 183

About the Author

ROLLIN SMITH is the author of *Toward an Authentic Interpretation of the Organ Works of César Franck, Saint-Saëns and the Organ, The Organist's Book of Days, The Reynolda House Aeolian Organ, The Aeolian Pipe Organ and Its Music,* numerous essays on organ performance, and the editor of a distinguished collection of music editions. As a concert organist he has played throughout the United States, appeared at National Conventions of the American Guild of Organists, the Organ Historical Society, the American Liszt Society, and made twenty-five organ recordings. He studied in Paris with Jean Langlais and holds a Doctor of Musical Arts degree from the Juilliard School.